PROTESTANT
WORSHIP

PROTESTANT WORSHIP

A Multisensory Introduction
for Students & Practitioners

O. Wesley Allen Jr.

Abingdon Press™
Nashville

PROTESTANT WORSHIP:

A MULTISENSORY INTRODUCTION FOR STUDENTS AND PRACTITIONERS

Copyright© 2019 by Abingdon Press

All rights reserved.

Library of Congress Cataloging-in-Publication Data has been requested.

ISBN: 9781501842658

19 20 21 22 23 24 25 26 27 28—10 9 8 7 6 5 4 3 2 1
MANUFACTURED IN THE UNITED STATES OF AMERICA

In a Christian service of marriage,
Bonnie Cook and I promised
to join with each other
from that time onward,
to share all that is to come,
to give and to receive,
to speak and to listen,
to inspire and to respond,
and in all our life together
to be loyal to one another
with our whole being
as long as we both shall live.

Bonnie,
on this twenty-third anniversary
of that wedding,
I love you more than ever,
make the same commitment to you
I did in our youth,
and dedicate this book to you.
With all my heart,
Wes
August 12, 2018

CONTENTS

Contents

ACKNOWLEDGMENTS

This textbook has been in the making for a number of years, and it is better for the number of people who have been hospitable, supportive, and have given feedback. Many of the strengths of the book are due to their input, but any shortcomings of the book are mine.

This book began as classes at Lexington Theological Seminary. I have tried to take elements of the online pedagogy I learned in teaching those courses and apply them to the experience of liturgical history, theology, and practice I hope readers could have. I am thankful for the LTS students who served as the original testing and refining ground for this content.

The book has come to completion while I am teaching at Perkins School of Theology at Southern Methodist University. I am especially grateful to Bill Lawrence, dean emeritus, Craig Hill, dean, and Evelyn Parker, associate dean, for the support they have given and interest they showed in the innovative side of this project. Also, Alyce McKenzie and Mark Stamm, my colleagues in the arena of homiletics and liturgics have been supportive of me pursuing this project even though either one of them could have done a better job with it. Moreover the support from the Lois Craddock Perkins fund and a grant from the Hardt Practical Theology Endowment contributed significantly to the technological elements of the work.

Too many read small segments of the book to list here, although I am grateful for them all. Three Rons, however, read the initial text extensively and gave me ecumenical feedback: Ron Allen, from the perspective of the Christian Church, Disciples of Christ; Ron Lucky from the perspective of the Evangelical Lutheran Church of America; and Ron Byars from the perspective of the Presbyterian Church, USA, and from his years of experience teaching and writing in the arena of liturgical studies.

Natalya Cherry served as my research assistant through the last half of the process of developing this work. She was more than an "assistant," though: she was a great conversation partner. Readers will especially find her hand at work in the videos found in the chapters dealing with baptism and Table. You will find several of these videos at **www.abingdonpress.com/protestantworship**.

Speaking of those videos, the churches in the Dallas metropolitan area that invited us in to record sacraments, ordinances, and hymns and take pictures of their worship spaces epitomize Christian hospitality. They allowed us to interpret their worship and work in order to contribute to any training of future pastors and worship leaders that this project might represent. I am grateful for their ministry and their willingness to share it in this format.

I also owe a debt to Steven Linebaugh. I orginally hired him for his graphic design abilities (his work is seen throughout the book!) but he became my Adobe guru, helping me with all kinds of software issues that an amateur like me could not figure out on my own.

Finally, a word of appreciation for Abingdon Press. Authors often feel the need (and should) thank their publishers for the work they have done to help a book come out in print. But the amount of time and energy the people at Abingdon have put into bringing out the experimental form of this book—an interactive eTextbook, and indeed their willingness to take a risk on that format when it is far from being a standard in the classroom deserves high praise. My name may be the one on the cover, but because of the digital and experimental nature the fingerprints of Connie Stella (senior acquisitions editor), Christy Lynch (production manager), Jeffrey Moore (production design manager), and Paul Frankyn (associate publisher for Bibles, leadership, and theology) are all over the work. I cannot adequately express how grateful I am for the chance they gave me.

INSTRUCTIONS

Welcome to the first multimedia book on Worship. The book is available in two forms, ebook and print. The ebook is filled not only with text, it includes pictures, audio files, videos, and interactive elements. The print book includes a few of the visual elements, and you can access many of the others online at **www.abingdon press.com/protestantworship**.

Unless otherwise noted translations of liturgical texts quoted in the book are in the public domain and can be found online. There are, for many of the texts, more translations available in print form. The use of the public domain translations is not meant to commend the quality of the translations but the ease at which readers can access the full resource online. For readers pursuing more in-depth research on a text, it is suggested that they find more critical, recent translations to use.

THE UNIVERSE OF CHRISTIAN WORSHIP

It is no easy task mastering the wide range of topics, practices, skills, and disciplines involved in studying and leading Protestant worship. Start with all the different elements that can be involved in a single worship service: prayer, proclamation, dance, drama, baptism, Eucharist, scripture, theology, ethics, ritual, congregational singing, instrumental music, praise, lament, petition, offering, pastoral care, commissioning, blessing, PowerPoint presentations, video clips, responsive readings. . . . Add to this list the wide variety of academic disciplines that are employed in the study of worship: theology, Church history, biblical interpretation, anthropology, sociology, psychology, ritual studies, homiletics, ecumenism, interpretation of liturgical texts, aesthetics, technological studies, cultural studies, communication theory. . . . Now finally mix in the fact that worship takes place in a Church that is a blended and often dysfunctional family of many different theologies, histories, practices, cultures, divisions, unions. . . . How is one even to *begin* learning all that is needed to plan and lead congregational worship faithfully and effectively?

This book offers such a beginning. As a *basic* introduction (an intended tautology), it deals with the full spectrum of elements related to the Sunday assembly (and a few beyond) but is selective about its approach to these various elements, leaving deeper investigation and analysis for more focused studies. The book is analogous to an introduction to physics, in which the whole of the universe—its expanse, history, laws, and current state, as well as the methods of inquiry and resulting theories—must be explored in a single textbook to be used in a single semester course. Indeed, the study of physics serves as a playful metaphor for organizing our work in this book. After all, Christian worship names a universe of meaning that spans the whole of human existence, and indeed of creation, and interprets that universe of meaning for the congregation through the lens of the Christian story and its sacred texts and traditions.

Applied loosely, the metaphor of physics organizes our study of the basics of Christian worship. We start with the **Big Bang**, which in physics refers to a theory for how the universe began and why it continues to expand. For Christian liturgy, a core theology of worship and an overview of the historical development of Christian worship mark our point of origin.

Having introduced the issue of history, we move to **Time** and examine the Christian emphasis on Sunday as the Lord's Day, the structuring of the hour of worship, and the liturgical calendar. Along with time, **Space** defines the boundaries of the universe. In the study of Christian worship, space concerns us in terms of the physical structures of worship as well as the symbolism, furniture, and art that fill that space.

Matter is the physical substance of the universe. The physical matter of worship consists of water, bread, and wine. In this section, we deal with the rituals of baptism and Communion. While we tend to think of the universe in terms of matter, however, everything is actually composed of **Energy**. As a metaphor for elements of worship, energy identifies the category of enacted worship. In this section, we study the spoken, sung, and embodied elements of participation in worship.

All of the above topics deal primarily with the regular, weekly worship of Christian congregations. But as the primary ritualizers of the community of faith, pastors also spend significant time shaping and officiating at occasional services, especially weddings and funerals. Given the social and psychological dynamics surrounding these pastoral rites, this section of the book is appropriately labeled **Chaos Theory**.

Due to the wide range of liturgical topics with which we deal in the book, no single method of presentation will work for every chapter. Nevertheless, a general approach will shape our discussion. When appropriate, we will begin with a review of the **historical** development of the practice or issue at hand. These reviews will follow basic historical divisions introduced in the Big Bang section. The history of liturgical developments stretches from ancient Jewish and Greco-Roman precedents for Church practice, through the early church, medieval Christianity, and the Protestant Reformation(s), to twentieth-century liturgical renewals.

The historical review will invite a discussion of different **theological** perspectives on the practice or issue being examined. Teasing these out often requires an examination of historical and liturgical **texts**. Texts of services broadly include both the rites and ceremonial of worship. *Rite* is a technical term in liturgical studies referring to the actual words spoken or sung during worship. *Ceremonial* refers to the actions performed during worship. Such ceremonial is at times prescribed in the *rubrics* of a liturgical text—directions, traditionally printed in red (from the Latin *rubica* for red), for appropriate actions that accompany words.

Finally, the historical, theological, and textual discussions will provide a foundation for **practical** application to planning and leading worship today. This practical aspect will include descriptive elements along with some prescriptive suggestions. While the ecumenical nature of this introduction requires us to keep such prescriptions broad, we will try to attend to different styles of worship—for example, traditional and praise services—throughout the book.

Worship constitutes the central task of the Church, the activity from which all other ecclesial activities proceed as the community of faith goes about the work of participating in the *missio Dei*, the mission of God. Pastors, worship leaders, and congregations need a broad overview of the wide variety of purposes, functions, and elements of Protestant worship to help them worship in truth and spirit (John 4:23-24) so that they can in turn faithfully engage in all forms of ministry and service to God and neighbor.

Thus worship theology and practices should not be taken lightly. A traditional Latin saying, **Lex orandi, lex credendi**, is translated "The law of prayer [is] the law of faith." Sometimes the saying is expanded to include **lex vivendi**—"The law of prayer is the law of faith and the law of life." What this saying means is that the way congregations worship translates into the theology, practices, and ethics of individuals and the community as a whole. Intentional worship that grows out of a healthy appreciation and critique of tradition, paired with a desire to offer praise to God and speak to the needs of worshipers in a manner appropriate to the congregation's contemporary context, is central to the Church's mission in forming disciples of Christ and impacting the world.

This process has both positive and negative consequences. "Good" worship leads to "good" faith, and "bad" worship leads to "bad" faith. The terms *good* and *bad* are left ambiguous here on purpose, because different theological orientations and liturgical traditions will fill them with meaning in different ways. The point, however, is clear. Worship informs the theological worldviews and lives of worshipers. When worship is done well, the effect can be transformative. When worship is done poorly, the effect can be detrimental. Worship planners and leaders have immense responsibility. May this basic introductory text help set them traveling down the path of fulfilling that responsibility faithfully and effectively.

PART ONE

THE BIG BANG

The Big Bang is a metaphor for the point of origin, some thirteen or fourteen billion years ago, when the universe was extremely dense and hot and rapidly began to expand and cool, resulting in the continual expansion of the universe as we know it in its current state. Before we can begin to study the various elements that comprise Protestant worship today, we need a sense of the origins and the ongoing evolution/expansion of Christian liturgical patterns and practices across the ages and the globe. But before we even begin such a historical review, we must define some core terms and concepts that will shape our conversation. We must first answer the question, What is Protestant worship?

RITUAL AND WORSHIP

To define the subject of our study, that is, Mainline Protestant worship, we must place it in a context of related terms. The terms can be illustrated with concentric circles. The concepts in the outer circles name categories inclusive of the smaller ones inside them. We start with the broadest term and work down to the narrowest one.

RITUAL

In common parlance, **ritual** is often used with a negative connotation in juxta-position to "true" worship, as if formal ritual means simply running through a script

1

and related actions in a rote fashion without meaning. When used as a technical term, however, ritual encompasses all worship, regardless of its level of formality.

While it is easy to characterize worship as ritual, it can be difficult to determine more broadly what counts as ritual and what does not. Scholars in the field of ritual studies nuance their definitions of ritual in different ways. They disagree about what characteristics differentiate rituals from habits or customs. For the purpose of studying the particular rituals involved in Mainline Protestant worship, however, we need not get involved in this debate. The following definition will suffice for our introductory purposes:

> **Rituals** are *the patterned, symbolic enactment of a community's historically rooted identity and values.*

Let us consider this definition piece by piece.

Community. In colloquial speech, we often speak of personal rituals. "My morning ritual" involves showering, shaving, dressing, eating breakfast, and brushing my teeth. But in technical terms such a personal patterned behavior is better labeled as a habit. We appropriately speak of individuals performing a ritual alone only when they have learned a ritual through their participation in a community that uses that ritual to enact its shared identity and values. For something to fit our technical definition of ritual, then, it must be practiced by a community that uses the ritual as part of its *shared* process of making meaning.

A community is any group of people in a relationship, from two to two billion. Types of communities include friends, lovers, families, clubs, schools, sports teams, nations, societies, subcultures, and religions. The Latin root of the word community is *communis,* meaning "common." Thus a community is any group of human beings who share something in common, something that binds them together. Such commonality can range from the love shared by a couple or faith in a shared value system to something as widespread and surface-level as a shared geographical location. That which members have in common can be expressed in many ways, one of which is ritual.

To flip this assertion over, we can say that *every* community in relationship for any extended period of time is ritualistic. The group, consciously or unconsciously, develops recurring patterns of speech, vocabulary, gestures, and actions that express and interpret the community's identity and values.

Historically Rooted Identity and Values. This identity and these values have their origins in the community's past—in the historical events, stories, traditions, and/or texts of early manifestations of the community that are considered in some way authoritative for the contemporary community. These authorities may well be studied and reinterpreted by each generation for each age, but rarely are they completely abandoned as long as the community exists and its core identity remains intact. New layers of identity and values may be added but in a way consistent with, perhaps even implied by, the original authorities.

Thus rituals, especially those central to a community's self-understanding, are generally conservative in nature. They can involve outdated, even antiquated, actions and language. New meanings may be associated with such language and actions, but a community maintains these archaisms out of a sense of continuity across time, especially in terms of a connection with the founders of the community.

Enactment. A community enacts its shared values and identity in its rituals. This assertion does not mean that the community must *re*-enact an event or story from the founding community in its rituals. A ritual need not be a theatrical play in which the participants take on roles from the authoritative story to which the ritual points and from which it comes. For example, the ritual of singing "The Star Spangled Banner" at various public events originated in and refers to a military event in early American history but is a far cry from the reenactments of significant US battles that occur on the anniversary of and at the site of those battles. Instead, the national anthem enacts dedication to values of freedom, military strength, and courage as a key element of national identity.

The power by which rituals enact meaning can be better seen through the lens of **speech act theory**, first proffered by J. L. Austin in his 1962 book, *How to Do Things with Words*. Austin noted that we generally think of language as referential—we speak words and sentences that *refer* to things, actions, events, and ideas beyond the utterance itself. When I say, "The couple walked down the aisle," I am speaking referentially. The word *couple* refers to the physical reality of two people who exist beyond my having named them. The word *walked* refers to a specific behavior that occurred apart from my having described it. And *down the aisle* refers to a specific setting that exists beyond my having spoken it.

Austin points out, however, that some language *acts* instead of refers. Sometimes speech is self-contained in the sense that *saying it is doing it*. A person getting married saying to her partner, "I promise," is not referring to a promise external to the speech; the speech *is* the act of making the promise. In other words, while some language refers, other utterances perform something. Thus when we say that rituals enact meaning, we mean that they do not simply refer to meaning external to the ritual, they also "perform" meaning within the community. Rituals do not only refer to the values and identity from a community's past; they make meaning of and for the community in the present.

Symbolic. The claim that rituals enact instead of simply refer to communities' identities and values must be tempered by the recognition that rituals rarely have a practical purpose in terms of achieving something directly related to the actions being performed (e.g., one does not place one's hand over the heart during the Pledge of Allegiance to warm the chest; nor does one participate in the Eucharist to satisfy physical hunger). Unlike habits, which often simply accomplish tasks (such as a person always eating the food on his or her plate in a certain order), or customs, which govern etiquette of interaction between people in a group (such as shaking hands or bowing as part of a greeting), rituals express, interpret, and make meaning for and by a community. The actions and words of communal rituals symbolically point beyond themselves to and participate in the community's key values, including elements of its sense of identity and purpose. (We will discuss symbols in greater depth in the chapter on sacraments/ordinances.)

Patterned. As noted above, enactment, like acting in non-ritualistic settings, usually implies both speech and physical action. We speak the Pledge of Allegiance, but we stand and place our hand over our heart to do so. We usually script and choreograph, at least to some degree, the enactment of ritual. In other words, ritualistic behavior and speech is patterned. We perform a ritual in the same or similar way, time after time, following at least somewhat of a consistent ordering of speech and action, to reinforce its importance and meaning.

In addition to speech and action, the aspect of pattern includes *timing*. Communities often enact their rituals on some schedule that expresses their values and sense of identity in relation to elements found in their early authorities. Families gather each evening for dinner with the table set in a particular way, family members sit in particular seats, and someone says grace using particular phrasing. Kiwanis meets on the third Monday of every month with name tags, a meal, reports by officers, and a guest speaker. Independence Day is celebrated on the Fourth of July in relation to the signing of the Declaration of Independence with time away from work, barbeque, patriotic concerts filling the television channels, and the sights, smells, and sounds of battle filling the air in the form of fireworks.

So while the word *ritual* might be used differently in various settings and the technical definition nuanced in different ways by different scholars, for the sake of serving as an entry into the study of Mainline Protestant worship, our working definition of ritual throughout this book will be the patterned, symbolic enactment of a community's historically rooted identity and values. If any of the elements of this definition do not apply to an action or speech, it may best be labeled something other than ritual.

WORSHIP AS RITUAL

Put simply, **worship** is religious ritual. The etymological root of worship is **worth + ship**. To worship something is to declare it, attend to it, and serve it as worthy of a community's strongest devotion. Of course, we can and do count many things in our individual and corporate lives as worthy of our devotion: family, morals, career, nation, education, money, political affiliations, friends, tradition, home. Consciously or unconsciously, we place these different devotions in hierarchy. We are not devoted to them equally—for example, most people place loyalty to family above loyalty to friends.

Religions, by definition, focus on what they claim is or should be the community's primary or ultimate value. To worship anything lower than that which is ultimate constitutes idolatry.

4

Worship, then, is

> patterned ritual performed by a *religious* community to enact symbolically its historically rooted identity and values *as derived from and as an expression of its ultimate devotion.*

If we keep moving to the smaller circles of our earlier diagram, we can focus our definition with even more specificity. We move from religion in general to the Christian religion specifically. If worship is religious ritual, then **Christian worship** is

> patterned ritual *through which the Church* enacts its historically rooted theological identity and values as derived from and as an expression of its ultimate devotion *to God-in-Christ.*

Whatever language we use to describe "Christian worship" must be applicable to the wide variety of Eastern Orthodox, Roman Catholic, and Protestant traditions. The definition includes those patterns and symbols used by all, involves the lowest common denominators of identity and values that stretch across the whole of the historic and global Church, and must be theologically rooted in the scripture and tradition embraced by all worshiping communities. In other words, when we speak of Christian worship, we must speak in broad terms that avoid specificity related to any one branch of Christianity over against another.

To narrow our focus to a more manageable one, we can say that **Protestant worship** is

> patterned ritual *though which Protestant churches* enact their theological identity and values as derived from and as an expression of their devotion to God-in-Christ *as interpreted by, informed by, and evolving from the sixteenth-century Protestant Reformation(s).*

To speak of Protestant worship, one must speak in terms of common denominators shared across the wide variety of denominations and nondenominational congregations that are heirs to the Reformation(s). (We will use *Reformation(s)* in this textbook to acknowledge, on the one hand, that a plurality of movements and reformers existed that should not be reduced to a single understanding of Protestantism and, on the other hand, that in the midst of these differences, common themes bound, and continue to bind, the movements together theologically and liturgically.)

Of course, a lot of time has passed since the sixteenth century, and the different traditions that have evolved from the Reformation(s) can look quite different. The well-known motto of the sixteenth-century Reformation(s), *Ecclesia Reformata, Semper Reformanda* ("the Church reformed, always reforming"), all but dictated that this must be the case. As individuals and communities continued (and still continue) reforming the Church, worship in different denominations, traditions, and congregations has been re-formed by very different theologies into very different styles and practices. Thus to speak of Protestant worship, one must still speak in broad terms, which can result in ambiguity.

We can narrow significantly, however, by focusing on **Mainline Protestant worship**, that is, worship in the *historic, established Protestant denominations*. A definition of Mainline worship generally conforms to that of Protestant worship but excludes fundamentalist, evangelical, independent/nondenominational, and Pentecostal worship. This distinction is not intended to claim that Mainline, evangelical, independent/nondenominational, and Pentecostal traditions do not share theological, historical, or liturgical connections with Mainline denominations. Nor is it to assert that there are no fundamentalist, evangelical, or Pentecostal individuals or communities in Mainline denominations and their worship services. Numerous historic and cultural reasons could be given for distinguishing Mainline traditions from these other movements, but those reasons do not concern us here. Our concern here is purely liturgical. Mainline churches in the latter third of the twentieth century converged around ecumenically shared liturgical theologies and practices. (We will discuss the process by which this convergence occurred in the next chapter.) This convergence does not erase differences, indeed some significant differences, in the ways these different communions worship and think about worship, but it does bring them close enough together to be able to discuss the Mainline group with a significant level of specificity.

We could, of course, move to even greater levels of specificity. For instance, **denominational worship** amongst the Mainline churches is the

> patterned ritual though which *a particular Mainline denomination* enacts its theological identity and values as derived from and as an expression of its devotion to God-in-Christ, interpreted and informed *by a particular lineage of the Protestant Reformation(s)*.

Presbyterian congregations, for example, share worship practices and theology not found in United Methodist, Lutheran, Episcopalian, or United Church of Christ traditions.

Denominations, however, are not monolithic. Individual congregations with different histories, situated in particular geographical and cultural locales, positioned in different places on the theological spectrum, and so on, worship in different ways. Variations in worship practices within a denomination often express difference more in terms of degree than substance, but these can still be important differences. Thus **congregational worship** in Mainline Protestant circles can be defined with the greatest degree of specificity as

> patterned ritual *though which a particular congregation* enacts its theological identity and values as derived from and as an expression of its devotion to God-in-Christ, interpreted and informed by a particular denomination of the Protestant Reformation(s).

No textbook can adequately account for all the possible differences among all the different levels of Christian worship. To deal with the widest circle of Christian worship leaves too broad a spectrum to be helpful to those readers in the Mainline traditions who are beginning to study worship. A focus on "Christian worship" would necessitate the inclusion of Roman Catholic and Eastern Orthodox worship theologies and practices, which would mean our work would need to be either much longer or more watered down. While Mainline Protestants can (and should) learn a great deal from these traditions—and indeed we will at times draw on ancient and medieval liturgical theologies and practices to provide a historical backdrop for Protestant theologies and practices—such an approach offers too broad of a focus for a basic introduction. The same situation exists, albeit to a lesser degree, if we try to address all Protestant worship and include fundamentalist, evangelical, independent/nondenominational, and Pentecostal traditions.

Dealing with the smaller circles of denominational or congregational approaches to worship, on the other hand, provides too narrow of a focus—comparison and contrast with traditions that do not venture too far away from one's own can be an extremely useful exercise. Protestant worship planners and leaders in any individual tradition (as well as those in nondenominational churches) can better accomplish their work when they have some sense of what they share with other traditions and what is unique to their own denomination. Thus, this introductory text will focus on the level of "Mainline Protestant worship." Still, a caveat is needed: this level of focus will require generalizations about worship that readers may find at times to be imprecise or even incorrect in relation to worship they experience in their own denomination or congregation. Thus readers will need to be ready to nuance the discussion at times in relation to their particular liturgical contexts.

A PRACTICAL THEOLOGY OF PROTESTANT WORSHIP

We immediately come upon just such a situation requiring nuance of the reader when we turn from broad definitions of worship as ritual to the attempt to develop a theology of Christian or even Mainline Protestant worship. Not only do different liturgical practices across Protestantism shape worship in significant ways, but so do different ecclesiologies, Christologies, and soteriologies. For example, a Presbyterian congregation with evangelical leanings understands what happens in worship (and especially in preaching) differently than the way a progressive Episcopal congregation understands what happens in worship (and especially the sacraments). For the purpose of this basic introduction, therefore, let us propose a **practical theological model** for examining what happens in worship rather than a liturgical theology rooted in a particular theological understanding of the nature of God and of God's providential and redeeming care for and through the Church.

In the nineteenth century, **Søren Kierkegaard** suggested that most Christians view worship in the same way they experience the theater. (See Søren Kierkegaard, *Purity of Heart Is to Will One Thing*, trans. Douglas V. Steere [New York: Harper and Row, 1948].) A play involves three main groups of participants: the actors on stage, the audience in the seats, and the prompters who feed lines to the actors from offstage. Worshipers, Kierkegaard argues, usually view God as the prompter—the one who feeds lines to those up front in the chancel, the stage. The choir, the liturgist, and, of course, the preacher serve as actors who perform for the congregation sitting in the pews as an attentive audience.

Kierkegaard severely critiques this view. We should not turn worship into a place we come to "get" something from God, the preacher, or the gathered community (be it entertainment or something more admirable such as inspiration, guidance, comfort, fellowship, or so on). In modern terms, we would call this view a consumeristic approach to worship.

Instead, says Kierkegaard, we should come to worship to "give" something to God—our corporate praise and adoration. He illustrates this claim by turning the image of worship as a play on its head. Worship, he says, can be appropriately compared to a play, but only if the roles differ from normal expectations. In a proper understanding of worship, the people up in the chancel leading worship simply serve as prompters. They feed lines to the real actors, the congregation. The congregation performs the worship for the real audience, God.

This understanding offers a clear improvement over a consumeristic approach. Kierkegaard, however, overcorrects. While we should come to worship primarily to offer God our praise and prayers, other parts of the worship service, such as the reading of scripture and the proclamation of the sermon, are clearly directed to the congregation. Worshipers' expectations would be too low if they did not come to worship hoping to encounter the Divine, to experience a sense of transcendence, to stand in awe of the Holy. We offer God praise, and in the same hour of worship, God's presence, good news, and grace are offered to us. Thus, give-and-take communication—that is, **conversation**—offers a better metaphor for worship than a theatrical performance. Let us explore this metaphor of conversation for worship in depth and use am evolving diagram to help us.

WORSHIP AS RITUALIZED CONVERSATION

The give-and-take conversation between God and those assembled in the nave does not represent the whole of the conversation that takes place in worship. Other voices are present as well. But the voices of God and the congregation are the most prominent ones, so we begin with them.

God is represented in our diagram using the larger and bolder font and is placed at the top of the image because, theologically speaking, God is the initiator of all divine-human encounters. God spoke first by calling creation into being. Every human expression to God since has been response. God makes Godself known to us. God engages us in relationship. God became incarnate in Christ and sustains us through the Spirit. The transcendent God becomes immanent in creating, sustaining, and redeeming the world (and the Church).

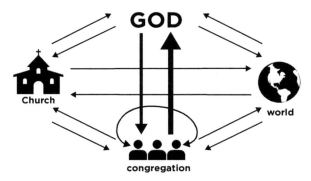

The core liturgical structure of word followed by table, proclamation followed by response (see the section of chapter 4 entitled "Sunday Morning Ordo"), acknowledges God's initiative in worship. God offers us grace and we respond with thanksgiving and praise; Christ calls us to follow and we become disciples—not the other way around. We do not initiate the conversation that occurs in worship any more than we baptize ourselves into the faith. In worship, God's self-revelatory voice is and should be the most prominent. God's initiation of the conversation is evident in the simple fact that the longest amount of time given to any liturgical act in worship is usually assigned to the proclamation portion of the service, which symbolically ritualizes God's voice more prominently than any other element. In no other part of the service do those in the pews remain in a receptive mode for nearly as long as they do during the reading of scripture and the offering of the sermon. But the voice of God is, of course, not limited to those moments in worship. God's voice is represented as calling us into worship and sending us forth from it. At times hymns are worded as if God is speaking to those gathered. And, most importantly, in sacramental traditions that view God as the primary actor/speaker in baptism and Eucharist, God-in-Christ speaks as loudly and directly as during the sermon, though the mode of revelation is admittedly quite different.

God offers the worshiping community Godself and the **congregation** responds. While response is secondary in terms of theological order, as Kierkegaard has reminded us, the worship service is primarily a ritualized occasion in which the people gather to make an offering of their common devotion and thanksgiving to the self-revealing God. The whole of the liturgy is constructed as a response to the God who has initiated a conversation with us. It is no coincidence that since the time of Augustine, we have labeled the worship experience a "service" that we offer to God—in fact, a German word for worship is *Gottesdienst*, God-service. The very purpose of worship is to respond dutifully to God's creative, redeeming, and sustaining care. We pray an invocation not because we think God will not show up in worship unless we do so or because we experience God primarily as absent (although we certainly know times when we experience God as silent). We invoke God's presence at the opening of worship precisely as a response to having experienced God as always and everywhere present with us (Emmanuel). We confess our sins not because we are trying to convince God to forgive us; but in response to having experienced God's grace, we recognize and are compelled to name our own sinfulness. We offer our petitions and supplications not in attempts to persuade God to care about the suffering and evil that infests our world, but in response to having experienced God as concerned about those very things. In other words, the whole of worship is response to God's prevenient (coming before) grace (including those elements in which God is the designated speaker).

In any given Christian worship service, the congregation responds to the particular element(s) of the good news proclaimed within the liturgy on this particular occasion (because no single worship service can include the entirety of God's good news). More broadly speaking, however, the whole of the service (indeed the pattern and practice of gathering for worship repeatedly) is a response to the whole of God's good news—that which is named in this particular service; that which has been proclaimed, experienced and known on other occasions; and that of which we have yet to learn. Many traditions recite an ancient creed in worship for this very reason—it names the breadth of Christian faith over against the narrow focus of the particular themes and texts for the given day. Thus, while our diagram appropriately places God at the top with a larger font, the arrow flowing from the congregation to God is paradoxically larger than the arrow flowing from God to the congregation. Faithful response of the sacred community is not an afterthought—it is the very goal of Christian worship.

Worship is **liturgy**, after all. We have thrown this word around here and there already in this chapter but should clarify its meaning and significance. In common parlance, people often use the word liturgy to refer to the kind of worship offered in "high" churches (in other words, formal forms of worship found in churches such as those in the Anglican tradition). In this sense, liturgy refers to the written words in bulletins and worship books prescribed by the denomination for congregational use.

The Greek root for liturgy, though, is *leitourgia*, which comes from *laos* (people) + *ergon* (work). Liturgy as a synonym for Christian worship means the "work of the people" offered to God. Therefore, liturgy more broadly and properly refers to *all* of the words and actions used in *any* Christian worship service, regardless of style. Every church, from a Roman Catholic to a Church of Christ congregation, is liturgical in this sense. And claiming our worship as liturgy calls us to plan and participate in worship in such a way that all the people gathered are invited, allowed, even expected, to respond to and perform for God.

This liturgical work of the people, obviously, requires that there be "a people." As noted earlier, communities—not individuals—perform rituals. Forming a community in conversation constitutes a key aspect of liturgy, so the diagram includes a loop around congregation. In a very real sense in worship, anytime the congregation speaks (say, in prayer) or anyone from the congregation speaks to the congregation (say, in a sermon), the congregation speaks to itself, growing as a people. While the congregation's voice is most evident in those elements of worship that are direct speech oriented toward God (e.g., acts of praise and prayer), the congregation speaks to itself most obviously in moments such as the sharing of announcements or prayer concerns or in the passing of the peace.

The congregation, whether speaking to God or itself, does not speak *ex nihilo* (Latin, "out of nothing"). Concepts, forms, and expressions of our contemporary faith-talk—of our proclamation, adoration, petition, and sharing—have been shaped by the historic Church and continue to be shaped by the global Church. The individual congregation is but a single, local expression of the one, holy, apostolic, and universal **Church**. (Although stylistic practices vary, in this theological model of worship we capitalize Church to indicate the historic, global Church over against the local congregation so as to clearly distinguish the two voices in the liturgical conversation.) Every time a congregation gathers to worship, it does so as a participatory expression of the communion of saints. While congregations enjoy much room for creativity in worship, they speak in line with or over against the way the Church has spoken liturgically and theologically for two millennia. The Sunday morning worship service, in other words, stands as a single moment in an ancient and ongoing (even eschatological) liturgical conversation that is an expression of the communion of saints across all times and places.

The broader expressions of the voice of the Church that joins in the local liturgical conversation should be those of the universal, historic Church, of the specific denominational tradition of the congregation, and of the various expressions of the global Church today. Worship planners should be intentional about allowing all these dialects to be heard regularly in the liturgy.

The Church's voice speaks most prominently in liturgical elements that come from tradition, such as creeds and older hymns/global music. But biblical readings, sacraments/ordinances, traditional prayers, and even liturgical structures also offer moments when the communion of saints speaks symbolically within a specific gathering of the faithful. At times, the voice of the Church resonates with the congregation's as it speaks prayerfully, and sometimes it resonates with God's as God reaches out to the congregation. This last note serves as a reminder that preachers especially have the responsibility to allow the historic Church to speak in sermons by referring to and interpreting figures and doctrines from the Church's history that inform the Church's theology.

Just as the congregation does not speak *ex nihilo*, so neither does it speak in a vacuum. The Church may strive not to be "of" the **world**, but it is certainly "in" it. For the liturgical conversation to be as full as it can and should be, the voice of the broader world needs to be heard regularly in congregational worship. When the needs of the world are voiced in worship, the congregation's liturgical offering to God involves a commitment to bring justice, charity, service, and social transformation to society. When the strides made in human understanding in fields such as science and history are spoken of, the congregation's faith is given the chance to remain faithful and relevant to contemporary worldviews.

Moreover, the congregation's liturgy must be contextual to be relevant. Worship planners can consider local, national, and global issues, values, knowledge, and cultures in shaping the prayers of and proclamation for the congregation. Only then does liturgical faith-talk exhibit the recognition that, as creator, God cares for all of creation, and all of creation is a gift to worship. To ignore the voice of the world in worship is paramount to distorting the character of God, diminishing the *missio Dei* (the mission of God) in which the Church participates, and ignoring the importance of the achievements of human reason and culture for the life of the Church.

The voice of the world speaks most prominently in the liturgical elements that allow for variation from week to week. While some congregational songs certainly call the congregation to engage in the world in broad fashion, the sermon marks the place where the world calls the congregation most directly to its work outside the walls of the church building and the place where contemporary knowledge and experience informs the congregation theologically. On the other hand, the congregation expresses its concern and care for the world most explicitly in prayer, where the congregation lifts up specific contemporary issues to God in the form of petitions. The climactic moment of the world being given voice, however, comes in the Sending Forth with the commissioning of the congregation to leave worship and return to their lives and work in the world. Worship has not been an escape from the world but a liturgical conversation with it and a preparation for living the Christian life in it.

An imprecise but perhaps helpful way to think about these different voices speaking in worship is to consider them in relation to the classical description of the **five primary functions of the Church**. While these terms typically relate more to the whole of congregational life, they are all found in worship as well. The voice of God speaks to the congregation, the wider Church, and the world in **kerygma**, the Greek word meaning "proclamation." The voice of the congregation speaks to God, the wider Church, and the world in **leitourgia**. As noted earlier, this Greek word forms the root of *liturgy* and refers to "the work of the people." Of course, in worship the congregation speaks to itself and builds community, so its voice also functions as **koinonia**, the Greek word for "fellowship." The voice of the wider, historic, and global Church speaks to the congregation, God, and the world in **didache**, the Greek word for "teaching." And, finally, the voice of the world speaks to the congregation, God, and the wider Church, calling those gathered in worship to **diakonia**, the Greek word for "service."

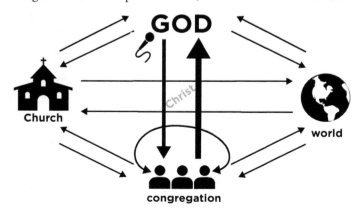

Another helpful way to think about the different roles of these voices in the liturgical conversation to each of the four conversation partners in worship is to see the conversation as mediated by **Jesus Christ**. The cruciform nature of the diagram visually suggests this mediation by Christ, which can be named differently in relation to each of the four conversation partners in the worship model. The person and work of Christ is the central revelation of *God*. The *congregation* gathers and prays in "the name of Christ." The *Church* universal constitutes the body of Christ. And finally, Christ was born, ministered, died, and was raised "once for all," that is, for the redemption of the *world* (and not just for the Church). (Some traditions might name the mediating role more in relation to the Holy Spirit than Christ, but the basic theological approach remains the same.)

PLANNING AND LEADING THE LITURGICAL CONVERSATION

In Kierkegaard's metaphor of worship as a theatrical performance, those standing in the chancel serve as prompters, feeding the congregation (i.e., the actors) their lines as they perform for their audience, God. Instead of a prompter, our conversational model holds one who leads worship to be more like a person who moves around in a dialogue group, asking someone a question, holding the microphone while the person speaks to the others in the group, and then moving on to the next speaker. In other words, if Christ is the *mediator* of the liturgical conversation between the four voices in the diagram, then the worship planners, musicians, liturgists, and preachers serve as its **moderators**. Worship planners and leaders, to a great extent, decide who will speak, when they will speak, and what they will say.

Naming this fact explicitly makes clear that the nature of the liturgical conversation is not as simple a matter as the diagram and our discussion thus far would lead us to believe. As helpful as heuristic models may be in grasping and managing complex dynamics such as those involved in Christian worship, they are also reductionistic. They are limited in their ability to name that complexity fully. In true conversation, participants act both as speakers and as listeners. There is a reciprocal, spontaneous give-and-take that distinguishes conversation from the monological and scripted qualities of various elements of Mainline Protestant worship.

To moderate an extemporaneous conversation is to have considerable power. The moderator may be the one who sets the agenda and gathers the participants in the first place. She can allow the conversation to move in certain directions and keep it from going in others. She can give some participants the opportunity to speak unhindered and cut off the speech of others. By her tone and mannerisms, she can give credence to some ideas and be dismissive of others in ways other participants in the conversation cannot. And the moderator of the liturgical conversation possesses a level of power even more significant than this. Add to gathering the participants, setting the agenda, and lifting up certain voices over against others the fact that worship leaders script the conversation (to a great extent) in advance and represent the different participants in the actual enactment of the scripted conversation. Let's consider the moderation of each liturgical conversation partner in turn.

In worship, worship leaders speak on behalf of *God*. They decide what God would say to these people on this particular liturgical occasion. While they may do so as thoughtfully, pastorally, and faithfully as their abilities allow, this means that usually the senior pastor (or primary preacher or presider at the sacraments in a congregation) represents God to the community in a way others in the community are not seen as doing. In a postmodern world that views authority from on high with significant suspicion, such localization of God's metaphorical voice is practically and theologically problematic. It should not be the minister who serves as God's mouthpiece but the community as a whole. The multitude of people and situations in the congregation through which God can be heard (e.g., music, art, church school, committee meetings, social justice action, works of charity, and fellowship meals) needs to be valued over against the Reformers' use of "Word of God" to refer to Christ, scripture, and preaching. To reserve solely for the ordained preacher the right and responsibility to speak for God distorts a biblical view of the body of Christ as a community composed of persons called to the ministry of the baptized and endowed with a plethora of spiritual gifts that are to be used for building up the Church and for ministry to the world (1 Cor 12). This applies not only broadly to the mission of the Church but specifically to the work of worship (1 Cor 14:26). Even a pastor ordained to word and sacrament should not be seen as holding a monopoly on God's voice in the congregation even while standing in the pulpit or lectern, or at the table or the font. To represent the fullness of what God might have to say to a congregation, multiple representatives need to be not simply allowed but encouraged and equipped for various modes of proclamation in the liturgical life of a congregation.

A similar situation exists for the voice of the *congregation*. In many Mainline worship cultures, the congregation speaks more often in unison than do individual members of the gathering speak their own thoughts and name their own emotions or concerns. A liturgist usually represents the congregation in offering to God a prayer in a single voice; or when the congregation does speak in unison, worship planners have composed or chosen the words that those in the pew speak or sing. They decide what the congregation should say to God on this particular occasion—what adoration should sound like and what petitions should be offered on this day. While liturgists do these tasks as thoughtfully, pastorally, and faithfully as their abilities allow, this means that these representatives and worship planners (again, often senior ministers or ministerial staff) have significant power and authority in defining a congregation's voice and experience in worship. Care must be taken to expand the congregational voices that plan and speak publicly in worship. Making time in worship for the sharing of joys and concerns before a pastoral prayer or, better, using the form of a bidding prayer, invites multiple voices to participate in a unified expression of adoration and petition. Moreover, using worship planning teams/committees composed of a group diverse in terms of age, gender, education, economic status, race, ethnicity, political orientation, sexual orientation, relationship status, and so on and so forth will lead to unison liturgical actions better representing the spectrum of perspectives in the community.

The historic voice of the *Church* can be overbearing in congregations where nothing new ever seems to be uttered, as if contemporary situations do not call for the reconsideration of historical elements and expressions of the Christian faith. Conversely, the voice of the Church can be ignored when the hubris of the contemporary in congregations deems the past (except perhaps for the past found in the biblical canon or in that particular congregation) irrelevant for contemporary faith.

Worship planners and preachers need to work to bring the voice of tradition into worship in a balanced manner—celebrating the congregation's inheritance and the faith passed down to contemporary communities while theologically critiquing elements of hegemony in the Church's history. Worship leaders decide what the Church should say on this particular occasion—what theological and ritual elements from the universal Church warrant account in this local congregation and which ones are to be criticized, ignored or discarded. While they do this as thoughtfully, pastorally, and faithfully as their abilities allow, this again means that these representatives of the Church (often senior ministers or ministerial staff) have significant power and authority in defining the congregation's experience of the communion of saints and of the historic Christian faith. Even though the clergy will often be the only ones in most congregations who have the education that allows them to draw on the theology and practices of the historical and global Church in a sophisticated way, it is inappropriate in a postmodern age for these clergy to allow the Church to speak only in ways that agree with their theology. The body of Christ that stretches over two thousand years and reaches across the globe is not a monolithic institution and should not be represented as such. Clergy can present a myriad of traditional and historical issues, persons, doctrines, events, and movements from Sunday to Sunday, year to year, in the liturgical life of the congregation. They can also model critical engagement with those voices and empower the congregation to reflect on their existent significance.

Finally, the voice of the *world* speaks in worship. While the world is heard occasionally in hymns and traditional readings, it primarily speaks in the sermon and in the prayers of the people. The worship leaders for the day decide whether and, if so, what social concerns of the world are to be lifted up on a given Sunday. They decide whose experiences in the world deserve to be named as valid and whose are ignored. They decide what aspects of secular, human reason are brought into liturgical expressions of the Christian faith and which ones are silenced. While they do so thoughtfully, pastorally, and faithfully, this means the worship leaders not only control speech "inside" the faith (i.e., the voices of God, the Church, and the local congregation), they also have power over defining the community's experience and liturgical encounter with the contemporary context in which they worship. This is inappropriate given that worship leaders have no leg up in their knowledge of the world over the people in the pews. Ordained clergy may legitimately claim to have higher levels of insight into scripture and tradition given their specialized training,

15

but they have no monopoly whatsoever on reason that comes from the world or on experience of/in the world. Indeed, their narrow training may put them at a disadvantage in these areas. Means must be developed whereby those in the pew can bring their knowledge and experience of the world into the planning and enactment of the liturgy. But even the knowledge and experience of the whole of a congregation is limited. Worship leaders, preachers, and planning teams must intentionally seek out underrepresented knowledge and experience of the world that need to be voiced in the liturgical conversation, especially in congregations composed primarily of those privileged in terms of economic status, political power, access to education, gender, sexual orientation, age, and abilities.

CONCLUSION

In this chapter, we have set forth the beginning point of our basic introduction, the start of the Big Bang, if you will. Rituals are the patterned enactment of a community's historically-rooted identity and values. Ritually speaking, then, Protestant worship is religious ritual through which Protestant congregations enact their theological identity and values as derived from and as an expression of their ultimate devotion to God-in-Christ as interpreted, informed by, and evolving from the sixteenth-century Reformation(s) and their various denominational heirs. Theologically speaking, worship is a sacred, ritualized conversation between God, the gathered congregation, the historical and global Church, and the world—a conversation mediated by Christ and moderated by the worship leaders.

We will return to the concept of ritual and the practical theological model of worship-as-conversation over and over again in the following chapters. But perhaps it is important to name what is at stake in getting a sound theological foundation in place for designing and leading Protestant worship. As noted in the introduction, a Latin saying often used in liturgical theology is ***Lex orandi, lex credendi, lex vivendi***, "The law of prayer [is] the law of faith [and] the law of life." Worship leaders need to shape the best liturgical conversation possible every time the sacred assembly gathers for worship in order to fund this process. Intentional worship that grows out of a healthy appreciation and critique of tradition, paired with a desire to offer praise to God and speak to the needs of worshipers in a manner appropriate to the congregation's contemporary context, is central to the Church's mission in forming disciples of Christ and impacting the world.

PROTESTANT WORSHIP AND THE COMMUNION OF SAINTS

The "Big Bang" is a metaphor for the universe's beginning. The smallest, densest, hottest concentration of matter and energy "exploded," rapidly expanding and cooling over thirteen billion years ago. While more intense in the beginning, that expansion of the universe continues today. We understand the current state and shape of the universe and its potential futures better by understanding its history, even if that historical picture at times appears less clear than we would like.

Similarly, we cannot understand, design, and lead Mainline Protestant worship appropriately today without at least a basic understanding of the beginnings and evolution of liturgical practices and theology. As we stated in the last chapter, our denominations and congregations do not worship today *ex nihilo*. Almost everything we do in worship has a precedent that extends further back in Church history than we often recognize on Sunday morning. Many of those things have roots in the rapid development of Christian worship practices at the beginning of the Church, but many others developed more slowly over the two thousand years the Church has been at worship.

Congregational worship, then, provides one of the most obvious witnesses to the **communion of saints** found in the Christian faith. The local congregation at worship represents but one manifestation of the body of Christ that includes all of those who have gone before us and passed down the faith and ways of worship to us.

To be sure, however, worship structures, practices, and theology have not been static over the two millennia of the Church. Just as the universe has evolved greatly since the Big Bang, so have our worship practices evolved significantly and moved in diverse directions. Just as many current worship practices have old, even ancient, antecedents, so, too, other worship practices developed *over against* older practices that were reformed, revised, or rejected. In today's ecclesial culture, we hear much talk about "**worship wars**" and renewing worship. In truth, this dynamic is nothing new. The whole of liturgical history can, in some ways, be seen as the continual striving of

17

the Church to renew its worship in order to grow in faithfulness to the God we worship and in our witness to the Christ event that shapes our worship. In other words, in every moment of the Church, those studying, designing, leading, and reforming worship have tried to create a sacred conversation between God, the congregation, the historic and global Church, and the world that is mediated by Christ and is true to the origins and core of the faith while also being fitting for the sociohistorical moment in which the Church found itself. Thus, at different times, the Church has renewed, rejected, or reclaimed older practices and theologies of worship as well as created new ones that grew out of the older ones.

Remember that we noted in the last chapter, however, that **ritual**—the patterned, symbolic enactment of a community's historically rooted values and identity—is conservative in nature and usually evolves slowly. To change ritual is to change (even if only slightly) the values and identity of the community and thus to alter its relation to its historical roots. This characteristic of ritual draws our attention to several things concerning Christian liturgy. First, it provides an important warning that in reforming liturgy we should be careful not to move so quickly that we might throw out the baptism with the bath water, so to speak. The overwhelming commitment in our culture to the new, to immediate gratification, to contemporaneity and extemporaneity, can result in losing some of the gifts our past has to offer us.

Second, the slow evolution of ritual pushes us to recognize that while liturgy usually changes slowly, it does (and must) change. Too strong of a commitment to past worship theologies, styles, structures, language, or actions can become idolatrous. "That's the way we have always done it" never provides a sufficient liturgical rationale all by itself. We must hold the traditions that formed our practices and beliefs in tension with our contemporary needs and worldviews that call for change.

Third, the fact that ritual evolves slowly also alerts us to the fact that with most liturgical shifts there will be tension between some who think the change is wrong and others who are impatient with the slowness of change. The evolution of liturgical practices is a history of worship wars, where some saw change as necessary for the Church to be faithful in new contexts and others saw change as unfaithful to the purposes of worshiping God-in-Christ as revealed in the past. Change is inevitable, but not all change is appropriate. These struggles can be divisive, but they can also be gifts of times for discerning whether we simply want the change for the sake of change or we believe the liturgical shift provides an appropriate way of offering God evermore faithful **worth+ship**.

Finally, the recognition that ritual evolves slowly (for the most part) also serves as a warning for readers working through this chapter and seeking to make sense of historical references throughout this textbook. In order to cover such a huge span of complicated liturgical developments, the historical schema used here significantly oversimplifies the background of liturgical practices, theologies, and processes by which liturgical shifts occurred. It is also selective in terms of discussing elements of the ecclesial family tree that lead specifically to the North American context of Mainline Protestant worship. The romp through two thousand years of liturgical evolutions and revolutions in this chapter will be revisited a number of times later in the book in relation to narrower topics. Even such expansion, however, is limited. As a basic introduction, this textbook provides a broad historical framework that gives students a starting point but ultimately leaves them unsatisfied with that starting point, thus inviting them to pursue more nuanced and critical liturgical studies.

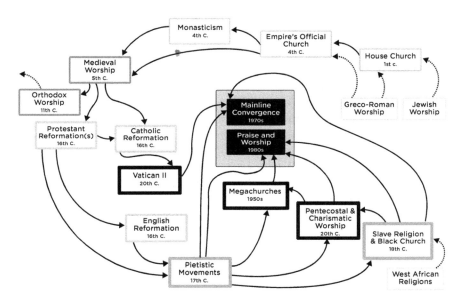

The diagram seen here will serve to guide our historical overview. (The chronological flow is pictured as beginning near the top right hand side of the graphic and moving counter clockwise in a swirl that eventually lands in the center.) The history of liturgical developments extends from Jewish and Hellenistic worship that influenced the origins of Christian worship through the early Church and medieval Church periods to the Reformation(s) and subsequent liturgical developments, all of which feed into the current state of North American Mainline Protestant worship that involves both the liturgical convergence growing out of the renewal of traditional liturgical forms and the praise and worship movement that grew out of more recent liturgical developments.

The dates listed with each entry in the chart indicate the century in which the era or movement began. Some were confined to the time period listed and others extended well beyond. The discussion that follows will unpack those entries in more nuanced detail. The arrows do not indicate a strict genealogy, so to speak. Instead, they represent a variety of influences and developments. Thus, the chart displays both entries branching out in different directions and entries with multiple sources leading into them. It is important to remember that there were many other theological, social, and political reasons and elements related to these developments, but in this work we are attending only to the liturgical relationships.

JEWISH AND GRECO-ROMAN WORSHIP

The earliest Christians—like Jesus and the disciples before them—were Hellenistic Jews. By at least the time that the Jewish Christian Paul was a missionary in the middle of the first century, Gentiles were being included in the Church. It is not surprising, then, that almost all of the early practices related to Christian worship (and indeed many practices that continue to be central to Christian worship today, such as the liturgical use of scripture, proclamation and instruction, baptism and table fellowship) evolved from Jewish and Greco-Roman worship practices.

First, the **Jewish background**. The Hebrew Bible, which served as the scripture for the earliest Christians, is filled with descriptions of worship practices that spanned different periods of Israel's history, and the Psalms especially provide actual prayers and songs used in worship. In truth, however, we know very little about the actual worship practices of Jews at the time of the beginning of the Church. Therefore, we can only talk in broad strokes.

The **Jerusalem temple** stood at the center of Jewish religious, cultural, and political life until 70 CE when the Roman army destroyed it in response to the Jewish Revolt. Temple worship focused on the sacrificial cult. Priests made sacrifices of vegetation and animals on behalf of laity for all kinds of reasons, from thanksgiving for a good harvest to repentance of sin. Many of these sacrifices were connected with the annual cycle of special holy days in which Jews, both in Judea and from the **Diaspora**, made pilgrimage to Jerusalem. It is little wonder that sacrificial language has played such an important role in the Church's theological and liturgical interpretation of the Christ event.

Weekly synagogue worship and related devotional practices in homes were even more influential on the early church. Although its early history is pretty cloudy, the synagogue may have originated in the wake of the destruction of Solomon's temple (587 BCE) and the Babylonian Exile (597–538 BCE). It was during this period as well that much of the Hebrew canon was written, redacted, and compiled, resulting in Israel evolving into a people of the book, with communal worship focusing, to a great degree, on the reading and interpretation of texts.

From the time the temple was rebuilt in Jerusalem following the exile (517 BCE) until the point at which the Roman army destroyed it in 70 CE (i.e., the period of Second Temple Judaism, which includes the beginnings of the Church), local synagogue worship continued alongside centralized temple worship. Significant diversity existed among synagogues, including worship practices, in different geographical locales (especially differences between Judean and diasporic synagogues). Moreover, many of our sources concerning early synagogue worship come from after the fall of the Jerusalem temple, at which point the role and practices of the synagogue shifted significantly. Still, the sources describe common elements in enough detail to make some general claims.

While the Jerusalem temple served as the national place to which Jews came for special occasions in their lives and for annual holy days (if they were able, economicaly and geographically speaking), the synagogue served as the place where the local community gathered weekly as part of their Sabbath observance. While temple worship focused on the offering of sacrifices and thus required the service of priests, synagogue worship focused on the reading and study of Torah and the Prophets, led by rabbis. While the temple as a holy site was set apart from the ordinary lives of Jews, the lines between community worship in the synagogue and worship in the home, especially when the family gathered around the table, was intimately related. The Jewish study of scripture and sharing of meals with devotional content were important forebears of Christian worship focused around word and table.

The **Greco-Roman background** of Christian worship is less obvious and less central to our introductory study, but needs to be acknowledged. Diverse religions existed in the ancient Mediterranean world and with this pluralism came a great deal of syncretism of worldviews and worship practices. As with Second Temple Jews, Gentiles of the day observed religious rituals related to meals and ceremonial baths that influenced sacramental theology and practices of the early church. Sacrifices played a role in most religious traditions, thus reinforcing Jewish sacrificial language in shaping Christian liturgical language and concepts. As Christianity moved into later centuries and evolved into the official religion of the Roman Empire (see below), the Church assimilated Greco-Roman worship practices and dates (e.g., taking over the winter solstice festival for the date of Christmas) and combined these with liturgical dates and practices related to Jewish calendar (e.g., Easter from Passover and Pentecost from *Shavuot*). Perhaps the most enduring elements of Greco-Roman ritual practice still to be found in the Church today, however, are those related to ancient weddings (see the discussion in the chapter on the history and theology of weddings).

THE HOUSE CHURCH

In the **New Testament**, we only have snippets that describe or refer to the earliest Christian worship practices, and the best interpretation of these snippets is not always clear. Moreover, we know that from the earliest period of the Church through the eleventh century, there was a great diversity of worship practices. Still, some things are fairly evident. After Jesus's crucifixion and resurrection, Christians in and around Jerusalem continued worshiping in the synagogue and temple. Before much time at all passed, however, they supplemented Sabbath worship with worship on the **Lord's Day** (i.e., Sunday, that is, the day of resurrection). As a young Jewish sect, they worshiped in the home of a Christian, usually one with economic means to sponsor the community. Presumably, Christian worship at this point closely resembled Jewish worship, but it also began to evolve quickly.

Since Gentiles also observed devotional practices in the home, the house church was a natural location for them when Christian communities came to include them along with Jewish Christians. As the Church became more Gentile, much Jewish influence remained but the emphases evolved. Worship shifted from Sabbath to Sunday instead of the Church observing both. Worship continued to involve the study of scripture, prayer, and table fellowship, but new hermeneutics (methods of interpretation) emerged in service of biblical interpretation and proclamation, and the Table took on new meaning as it referenced the death and resurrection of Christ. Worship continued to be held in the home of a wealthy patron, but a private location became a necessity as Christians began to experience various forms of social ostracism and at times political and even violent persecution. Eventually, dwellings were redesigned specifically as worship buildings, with separate spaces provided for a service of the word, for the Meal, and for baptism.

OFFICIAL RELIGION OF THE EMPIRE

Once Emperor **Constantine** legalized Christianity with the **Edict of Milan** in 313, and certainly after **Theodosius I** (371–395) passed a series of laws leading to the prohibition and persecution of non-Christian religions, making Christianity the official religion of the Roman Empire, the Church gained significant power and influence in society. It shifted from being a somewhat secretive movement or countercultural community to a public institution with power. With this shift came significant changes in worship.

The most obvious change was that since Christian communities no longer had to hide, finally had governmental support, and were allowed to own property, they could now build public buildings for worship. One of the main forms these buildings took was simply an adaptation of a common architectural pattern used in Roman architecture for public buildings—the **basilica**. This structure still continues to influence church architecture today.

A second liturgical development that resulted from the Church becoming institutional is that some liturgical language and patterns began to be formalized, as represented, for instance, by the influential **Apostolic Tradition**. The process of standardizing liturgies and practices would be a slow, millennium-long process, but without governmental support, practices could have well remained distinct from house church to house church, or at least city to city. With a stronger institutional identity, a stronger hierarchy in the Church developed that allowed for the standardization of liturgical rites in wider and wider geographical regions. As part of this formalization of the liturgy, worship leaders began wearing liturgical garb—for example, different types of **albs**—that created an atmosphere of dignity and splendor. These vestments were adaptations of clothing from the Roman hierarchy—that is, no longer the same clothing of the common people.

A third lasting liturgical development resulting from Christianity's becoming a government recognized and sponsored institution is that the language of worship in the West shifted from Greek to **Latin**, the common language of the Roman Empire. In fact, the use of Latin would continue in the Church's worship (and persists to this day in some Roman Catholic gatherings) for over a thousand years after Latin ceased to be a spoken language.

MONASTICISM

Individual monasticism (*monasticism* comes from the Greek word *monazein*, which means "to live alone"), in which individual Christians fled to the Egyptian desert to lead a life of asceticism and contemplative prayer isolated from the concerns of cultural existence, began in the mid to late third century. Likewise, **communal monasticism**, in which small communities of men or women who lived apart from culture but together in work, service, prayer, and worship, originated in the early fourth century. Yet only after Christianity became recognized and then legal in the late fourth and early fifth centuries did monasticism become significantly appealing to Christians who thought that accommodation to the Empire was an unfaithful way of being Christian.

Ironically, those monastic communities, originally formed with the intention of withdrawing from the world, developed practices that would later become widely influential in the Church's worship, especially medieval worship. As part of their attempt to fulfill Paul's instruction to pray without ceasing (1 Thess 5:17), the monks, following the Jewish practice of praying at certain hours of the day, divided the day into hours of prayer.

Particular liturgical structures were specified for each hour of prayer. **The Daily Office**, or **Liturgy of the Hours**, as this practice came to be called, included praying the entire Psalter (book of Psalms) every week. While singing and chanting had already been used in Sunday worship, **plain chant**—a style of singing a single melody line in unison without accompaniment—developed for singing the Psalms in these settings as well as singing other parts of the liturgy.

MEDIEVAL WORSHIP

Medieval worship is difficult to synthesize in a basic introduction. After all, the period as a whole comprises about half of the history of the Church. In the middle of this era (1054), the **Great Schism** between the East and the West occurred, with the Eastern Orthodox and Roman Catholic Churches parting ways. For our purposes, we need not attend to the worship theology and practices in the Orthodox Church because it has had little direct influence on the evolution of Protestant worship. (It is worth noting, however, that in the ecumenism of the late twentieth century and following, there have been conversations among Orthodox, Roman Catholic, and Protestant liturgical scholars, with Orthodox scholarship having significant influence, especially on eucharistic liturgies.)

Medieval worship in the West comprised a complex mix of liturgical conservatism and innovation. Latin remained the language of worship after the fall of the Roman Empire even though laity no longer spoke it. Similarly, as clothing styles changed among the populace, clergy continued wearing versions of the clerical garb of the late Roman Empire. These **vestments**, in turn, evolved in ways that represented particular clerical offices and liturgical functions.

As a result of such trends, a wider and wider separation grew between the clergy and the laity, and nowhere was this distinction more evident than in worship. For laity, worship became less participatory than in earlier days. They stood in the **nave** (i.e., the area where pews are placed to day) watching the clergy up in the **sanctuary** (i.e., the chancel area) perform worship in a language they did not speak and dressed in a way that set them apart. In other words, priests offered the Mass, sacrificing Christ in the Eucharist on behalf of the people, usually without the people actually receiving in the Eucharist.

Chant continued to play a significant role in medieval liturgy, although the persistent use of Latin and increasingly elaborate melodies discouraged the congregation from singing, thus restricting participation, for all intents and purposes, to the clergy. The medieval period saw great movement in terms of standardization of the liturgy so that the same language and patterns were used across Europe, with the **Roman Rite** taking precedence over all other regional liturgical traditions by the eleventh or twelfth century, which included the standardization of chant melodies.

A radical innovation in worship music occurred, however, when **pipe organs** began to be built in churches. The addition of instrumental music to worship would change the character of Christian worship forever. Around this same time, music annotation was developed so that melodies no longer had to be memorized to be used in worship. This meant that the standardized tunes of chant could give way to more complicated and diverse music in weekly worship. Indeed, these innovations meant that, among other things, **polyphony** (musical textures consisting of two or more simultaneous melodies) was now possible. The further development and standardization of tonality would eventually lead to the displacement of unison singing as the dominant practice for congregational song and give rise to the practice of singing in **harmony** (musical textures consisting of simultaneous pitches or chords supporting a main melody).

One of the most significant liturgical developments of the medieval era took place in the arena of sacramental theology and practice. Much of sacramental and ritual evolution in the Church occurred organically without significant theological exposition. For instance, after Christianity became the official religion of the Roman Empire, baptism of adult converts was rarely needed, so infant baptism became the standard practice of the Church. Not until the medieval period, however, did theological justification of this practice in relation to the doctrine of original sin fully develop. Such reflection on the essential characteristics of sacraments further led to defining and interpreting specific practices of the Church as its **seven sacraments**—baptism, Eucharist, confirmation, confession, marriage, ordination, and extreme unction (anointing of the sick, which is part of but not limited to what is commonly called "Last Rites"). These theological developments also led to changes in the way these sacraments were administered, which can be seen, for instance, in the practice of laity only receiving the host (i.e., the bread) at the Eucharist, while the clergy received both the bread and the wine.

THE PROTESTANT REFORMATION(S)

During the period of the medieval Church, numerous attempts at theological, hermeneutical, practical, and liturgical reforms arose and failed. By the sixteenth century, though, the social, economic, and political situation had changed in ways such that groups could successfully pull away from the Roman Catholic Church in various parts of Europe. This period is commonly referred to as the Protestant Reformation due to significant common, overlapping themes and practices across these groups as well as significant influence flowing across different regions. The diversity of the reforming efforts, however, along with the resulting plurality of Protestant denominations that grew out of these efforts, signal that we should really consider the sixteenth century as a time of multiple interconnected yet distinct reformations with a range of interconnected yet distinct shifts in liturgical theology and practice. In this chapter, we will primarily name common themes across these different reformations, but in later chapters on narrower topics, we will need to distinguish between different liturgical theologies and practices. Thus we will refer to this period as that of the Protestant Reformation(s).

Movement away from elements of Roman Catholic theology as well as interpretations and uses of scripture resulted in significant, even radical, liturgical changes. Indeed, such dramatic (and rapid) liturgical changes had not been experienced in the Church in over a thousand years. This period was one of rare ritual evolution hastened by the social, political, and intellectual earthquake (occasioned in part by the invention of the printing press) occurring in Europe following the **Renaissance** and heading into the **Enlightenment**.

Protestant worship began to use the **vernacular** of the congregation instead of Latin, making it more participatory for the laity than one in which they watched clergy performing acts of worship on their behalf. With this move, worship became more of an aural experience emphasizing the reading and interpreting of scripture, than a visual one focusing on the Eucharist.

Beyond this shift, Protestant liturgical developments moved in similar directions but did not take the same path. Take **worship music** for example. While most Protestant groups left chanting in Latin behind, Martin Luther embraced a wide range of worship music, Ulrich Zwingli rejected almost all worship music as distracting from the word of God, and John Calvin allowed only the singing of the Psalms.

Similarly, common movement toward recognizing only **two sacraments**—baptism and Eucharist—occurred across Protestant lines, but the interpretation and practice of these two ritual actions ranged significantly in different Protestant factions. Those who continued to practice infant baptism did so by drawing on particular theological and scriptural rationales, while others rejected the practice on other scriptural bases. With respect to the Table, different reformers held very different theological positions regarding the real presence of Christ in the bread and wine specifically or in the practice more generally. And with the great weight placed on the proclamation of the word of God as center of worship, some Protestant movements relegated the Eucharist to an occasional rather than weekly observance.

THE CATHOLIC REFORMATION

The Catholic Reformation has often been called the "Counter Reformation" by Protestants who view it primarily as a response to and rejection of the Protestant Reformation(s). While the Catholic Church of the sixteenth century did indeed reject and react against the Protestant Reformation(s), this view is too limiting and biased with respect to what occurred in the Roman Catholic Church at this time, and thus the better label is the **Catholic Reformation**.

This reform took place through the twenty-five sessions of the **Council of Trent** stretching from 1545 to 1563. In addition to major theological stances taken by the Council, significant liturgical developments also occurred. The Council affirmed Catholic liturgical and sacramental theology of the day and tightened liturgical practices significantly, finally doing away with regional variations in worship.

Developments from this Council are called "Tridentine," and, thus, the standardized liturgy that came out of the Council is called "the Tridentine Mass." The name is somewhat misleading, however, in that the **Tridentine Missal** (worship book, or etymologically, the book of the Mass) was not a book of new liturgical forms but a narrowing of acceptable older liturgical language. The liturgy continued to be spoken in Latin in all geographical areas of the Church, but all churches now used the same prayers and standard elements of worship, namely, those that had been used in the Roman Rite during the medieval period. The Council also standardized an annual **liturgical calendar** and set of **lectionary readings**. These readings usually consisted of an Epistle and Gospel lesson. Moreover, worship music was simplified. Polyphony had come to dominate Church music, leading to the concern that the words could not be understood or at times even heard. Therefore, the Council set forth strict guidelines for music intended for use in worship in an attempt to ensure that the text could always be understood.

Tridentine decisions continued to define Catholic worship for four hundred years until the 1960s (see below in this chapter on the **Second Vatican Council**).

THE ENGLISH REFORMATION

In England, reformation took a unique and pendular path during the Tudor dynasty. **Henry VIII** (reigned 1509–47), who had been a defender of the faith, broke from the Roman Catholic Church when the pope refused to grant him an annulment so that he could take a new wife with hopes of siring a male heir for the throne. While the Church of England broke with the Roman Church around the same time as the Protestant reformers on the continent, the Church of England at this point was quite

Catholic in tone, theology, and liturgical practice and, in fact, remained much more so than other Protestant movements/traditions/churches.

When young **Edward VI** (r. 1547–53) was on the throne, the church moved in a much more Protestant, specifically Calvinist (Reformed), direction. During this period, **Thomas Cranmer**, who had already been Archbishop of Canterbury under Henry VIII, made significant changes in liturgy and wrote the first (1549) and second (1552) editions of the *Book of Common Prayer*, which have had enormous influence on liturgical language in Protestant traditions (especially English-speaking traditions) far beyond the boundaries of Anglicanism.

When Edward died without a male heir, his older half-sister, **Mary I** (r. 1553–58), reinstituted Catholicism with a vengeance. She executed nearly three hundred dissenters, thus causing her to be dubbed "Bloody Mary."

When Mary, in turn, died without a male heir, her younger half-sister, **Elizabeth I** (r. 1558–1603), ascended to the throne. Under her longer, more stable reign, the government sought to reconcile religious divisions in the land. While the theological and liturgical pendulum continued to swing to and fro in the Church of England for some time after this, the "**Elizabethan Religious Settlement**" marks the beginning of Anglicanism as we know it today.

In terms of the liturgical theology and practices that developed and evolved from Cranmer's leadership and that were reestablished under Elizabeth's reign, Anglicanism has sought to embody a ***via media***, or "middle way," marked by compromise between Catholic and Reformed Protestant ways of worshiping. A prime example can be found in the sacraments: the Church of England continued to count all seven sacraments of Catholicism as valid sacraments, but distinguished between baptism and Eucharist as the **two major sacraments** and the others—confirmation, confession, marriage, ordination, and holy unction (anointing of the sick)—as the **five minor sacraments** since they are not "sacraments of the Gospel" and thus not deemed necessary for salvation.

Of course, not all in Britain thought the reforms of the Church of England went far enough in the direction of Calvinism. These groups came to be called pejoratively **Puritans**, with some Puritans remaining in the Church of England working for reform and others becoming separatists. The separatists, especially, argued that the monarch should not be the head of the church and that worship should be regulated by scripture alone instead of by the *Book of Common Prayer*. This liturgical theology led to simplicity in worship in terms of language, vestments, music (including organs), and space. Many Puritan families would eventually migrate to the New World for both religious and economic reasons, and they would have a profound impact on cultural and religious life in North America.

PIETISTIC MOVEMENTS

After Protestantism settled in throughout Europe, became mainstream in culture, and made its way to North America, some felt it had lost its power. One response was the development of pietistic movements. *Pietism* can be used as a technical label for a specific Lutheran reform movement of the seventeenth and eighteenth centuries started by Philipp Jakob Spener (1635–1705), but we use it here more broadly to refer to movements in the Church that emphasized experiential and practical aspects of Christian faith and practice including (in different ways and to different degrees) as wide a range as Moravians, Baptists, Anabaptists, Methodists, Presbyterians, and Disciples. Such pietistic movements were evangelical in nature and spread across Europe and North America as exemplified in the **First Great Awakening** (mid-eighteenth century) and especially the **Second Great Awakening** (early-nineteenth century). These movements were both heirs of the Enlightenment in terms of the rise of individualism, and they struggled with the Enlightenment in terms of reason displacing revelation as the primary mode of determining truth. In terms of worship, leaders of these movements focused on creating personal/individual and often emotionally charged experiences of salvation or of an assurance of salvation in or through the worship event, especially the sermon.

Whereas Protestant singing in earlier days had focused mainly on singing scriptures, especially the Psalms, hymns were now written that named contemporary doctrine and experience. Eventually, **gospel hymns** of the nineteenth century would move toward expressing that experience more and more in terms of individualistic devotion.

The **revivalists** in these pietistic movements often moved worship outside of church buildings. Much of America was a frontier, and Christianity adapted as a **frontier religion**. Revivalist worship took place in homes, places of business, saloons, and camp meetings. An evangelical orientation toward the repentance and conversion of all sinners (including those who were raised Christian but never experienced "new birth") dominated preaching so that invitations and altar calls after the sermon became the main purpose of the whole worship service. At times and in some strands of this pietistic movement, the emotions in these services would rise to the level of ecstatic expression, including rolling on the ground and speaking in tongues.

These pietistic movements fed into the historic Protestant denominations that came to be considered the **Mainline churches**, but in them the pietistic emphasis on personal experience of salvation was domesticated, combined with, and/or subordinated to other emphases. In evangelical denominations and independent congregations, this emphasis continues to play a more central role, although the degree of emotional expression has also been domesticated, albeit to a lesser degree, in these traditions as well.

SLAVE RELIGION AND THE BLACK CHURCH

West Africans were forcibly brought to North America and enslaved (from the sixteenth to the nineteenth century, some twelve million Africans were shipped to America as slaves via the **Middle Passage**). Many were forced by their masters to convert to Christianity, take Christian names, and worship like their masters. They sang hymns from England and heard white preachers proclaim forgiveness of their sins and cite Paul in exhorting them to be obedient to their masters in order to get into heaven.

But slaves did not simply adopt Christianity as it was forced upon them. Slave communities adapted white Christianity to fit their concerns and needs and, in the process, claimed Christianity for themselves. They "stole away" to worship in secret to what was called a **"hush harbor"** (sometimes, "brush arbor"), away from the over-sight of their white masters. This secret worship has come to be called the **"invisible institution"** and represents a radical reform of the Christian worship that was oppressively forced upon them. Because of the secretive nature of this worship and because masters rarely allowed slaves to learn to read and write, we have little record of the practices of the invisible institution; but we are able, thanks to oral tradition, to name some characteristics of the worship practices of slaves.

Slave worship creatively combined elements and practices from the mainstream Protestantism of the slave masters, the pietistic/evangelical movements that had sought to save the souls of the slaves, and the diverse West African religions passed down orally from generation to generation of slaves. This last element is especially noteworthy. Given that Christianity itself had dominated Western culture since the late fourth century, not since the early church adopted ancient Jewish and Greco-Roman worship practices had other religions had such a strong influence on Christian worship. West African religions were diverse and should not be reduced to simplistic beliefs or practices. Nevertheless, it can be argued that the use of drums in traditional religions informed slaves' use of their hands and feet to beat out rhythms and to dance in worship, the use of call and response as a traditional form of singing continued as a practice of congregational song, the image and storytelling techniques of the **griots**—West African historians, storytellers, poets, and/or musicians—influenced the slave preacher's style (and perhaps content), and those rituals from homelands in Africa that involved ecstatic spiritual experiences informed ecstatic practices in Christian worship such as the **"ring shout."**

English hymns that taught traditional Christian doctrine were supplemented with **spirituals** that expressed to God a wide range of emotions from praise to anguish. In addition to an emphasis on the individual forgiveness of sins and over against calls to obey the master, slave preachers spoke of the God who delivered the Israelite slaves from Egypt as the one who would come to liberate them as well. Preaching took on a narrative and musical quality not found in white preaching, and the work of the people involved the use of call and response and of the whole body in movement during singing.

"The Black Church" is a misnomer because it implies a unity when it is the case that African American communities of faith after the Civil War varied significantly in terms of denomination, theology, polity, worldview, and approach to worship. Yet, many scholars continue to find it a helpful term in order to recognize that the oppressive heritage of slavery and the liberating practices of slave worship have shaped African American congregations in general and worship in particular in

29

some common ways. Worship in African American congregations in the post-Civil War and Jim Crow eras continued to be influenced by the worship practices of the invisible institution. Other influences, such as African Americans' striving to rise up in society and churches' becoming more institutionally oriented, tempered the influence of traditional worship, especially in African American congregations that were part of larger, predominantly white denominations. At times, the singing of spirituals and expressiveness in music and preaching were frowned upon and worship became more formal. During the Civil Rights Movement, however, some African American communities found empowerment in reclaiming their unique heritage over against trying to assimilate into white culture.

Through this process, the influence of the heritage of slave religion and the voices and practices in the contemporary Black Church began to be embraced in the late twentieth century by predominantly white Mainline churches as well. For example, most denominational hymnals these days include examples of spirituals from the era of slavery and **Black Gospel hymns** from the twentieth century. African American approaches to preaching also have come to be appreciated, studied, and adapted by white preachers.

PENTECOSTAL AND CHARISMATIC WORSHIP

While the pietistic movements named above continue to inform strains of theology and liturgical practice in what came to be called "Mainline" Protestantism, emotional expression in worship was significantly domesticated in white Protestant congregations in the twentieth century. The frontier camp meetings of the nineteenth century had given way to established, institutionalized, middle-class congregations and denominations. But emotional emphases from elements of the pietistic movements and from African American worship resurged in a new way in the **Pentecostal movement** that erupted on the American scene at the beginning of the twentieth century. Twentieth-century Pentecostalism, foreshadowed by evangelists in the late nineteenth century, has its roots in nineteenth-century Wesleyan Holiness movements and some parallels in Europe in the early twentieth century. Most scholars and historians, however, mark the preaching of William J. Seymour that sparked the three-year-long **Azusa Street Revival** in Los Angeles, California, beginning in 1906, as the beginning of twentieth-century Pentecostal movements.

Worship at the revival was racially integrated in a way few other examples of Christian worship were in that day. It focused on a personal experience of salvation manifested in **gifts of the Holy Spirit**. In addition to baptism with water, it was stressed that people also need to experience the **baptism of the Spirit**. The emphasis on the freedom of the Holy Spirit to move and speak as it chooses meant that worship valued spontaneity in following the leading of the Spirit and had much more informality and less structure than Mainline or evangelical worship. Following the lead of the Spirit meant that any worshiper could be "slain in the Spirit" and thus led at any time to pray, sing, dance, run the aisles, offer testimony, or (especially) speak in tongues.

As Pentecostal movements established congregations, many moved toward more set structures of worship with clear, established lines of worship leadership. While these patterns resembled those found in other Protestant worship traditions, Pentecostal worship always protected room for a higher level of spontaneity and individual experience and expression of the presence of the Holy Spirit.

In the 1960s, elements of Pentecostal beliefs and worship practices began to gain a foothold in Roman Catholic and Mainline Protestant denominations and eventually in some evangelical congregations. These groups within established theological and worship traditions comprise the **Charismatic Movement**. Charismatics emphasize baptism of the Holy Spirit and ecstatic worship experiences, although they tend to emphasize speaking in tongues less than Pentecostals. Also, instead of requiring an unstructured liturgy given over to the leading of the Spirit, Charismatics have usually found ways to incorporate spontaneous expression into the inherited structures of their liturgies (e.g., times of simultaneous, extemporaneous prayer set within the service).

Even in places where Charismatic worship failed to take hold or where full-blown Charismatic worship was temporary, the movement had an impact on Mainline Protestant worship. The inclusion of individual, external expressions of emotion and spiritual experiences found its way back, in the late twentieth century, into the Protestant streams that had distanced themselves from their pietistic, evangelical, and/or revivalists roots in the nineteenth century. These expressions can be verbal (e.g., saying "Amen" during a choral anthem or sermon) or physical (e.g., raising hands during prayer or praise songs).

MEGACHURCH WORSHIP

Megachurches are usually defined as Protestant congregations that have more than two thousand attendees in worship on a weekly basis. While there have occasionally been such large congregations in the history of the Church, this phenomenon really started in the 1950s and began to proliferate in the 1970s. These churches are largely evangelical, an orientation that led to the liturgical innovation of the **seeker service**. Seeker services aim at attracting and converting newcomers to the Christian faith. In order to attract nonmembers to worship in a welcoming manner, seeker services often avoid traditional theological vocabulary, remove many of the traditional elements of worship (e.g., communal prayer, the Eucharist), and adapt contemporary forms of entertainment for evangelistic and liturgical purposes (e.g., popular music styles and videos).

Due to the numerical success of megachurches, many Mainline congregations have sought to borrow and adapt megachurch methods for their own settings. While such congregations are more likely to maintain historical liturgical traditions, they will change their service or start a new one to attract seekers with the assumption that the style and practices in the service must be accessible to those unfamiliar with Christian faith or worship. In some ways, this approach intentionally puts the seeker back into Kierkegaard's theater-church (as described in the previous chapter). Seekers are allowed, even encouraged, to come to worship to be entertained passively *so that* at some point they will participate more actively in worship (doing the work of the people) and claim the faith and worship as their own.

SECOND VATICAN COUNCIL

As charismatic and megachurch worship was finding its beginnings, a radically different direction in the evolution of Christian worship was occurring in the Roman Catholic Church. Growing out of some nineteenth-century scholarly attempts to recover medieval practices, such as Gregorian chant, Catholic (and Protestant) liturgical historical scholarship in the early twentieth century gained great momentum. Eventually, this **Liturgical Movement** was able to reach even further back than medieval practices due to newly discovery patristic texts, the **Didache** (a late first-century document that includes instructions for baptism and the Eucharist) and **The Apostolic Tradition** (a late fourth-century church order, traditionally but incorrectly attributed to Hippolytus of Rome, that contains liturgies for baptism, the Eucharist, and ordination). *The Apostolic Tradition* was especially influential in liturgical scholarship and worship renewal.

The Liturgical Movement played a key role in the liturgical reformation that would become part of the Second Vatican Council, which extended from 1962 to 1965. Vatican II dealt with the Roman Catholic Church's relation to modernity and advanced major shifts in theological and biblical studies. But no shifts were greater than those in the arena of worship, which changed liturgical practices ratified at the Council of Trent four hundred years earlier.

The **Constitution on the Sacred Liturgy** was approved in 1963. It sought greater lay participation in worship. To achieve this end, the entirety of the Mass could now be celebrated in the vernacular of the congregation rather than in Latin. Music could reflect the culture of the congregation. The altar was pulled out from the back wall so that the priest could stand behind it, no longer having his back to the congregation during the Eucharist. With laity now symbolically gathered around the table *with* the priest, they were allowed to receive both the bread and the wine instead of the bread only.

The Council also placed much stronger emphasis on reading and interpreting scripture in worship. Much of pre-Vatican II preaching in the Roman Catholic Church was doctrinal in nature. In 1969, the ***Ordo Lectionum Missae*** was published to help achieve this aim. It provided a new **lectionary** with an Old Testament, Psalter, Epistle, and Gospel reading (lection) for every Sunday related to the liturgical calendar. To ensure congregations were exposed to more of the biblical canon, a three-year cycle was established for the lectionary instead of simply an annual cycle. This change led to a revitalization of Catholic preaching, as exemplified in the influential document, *Fulfilled in Your Hearing: The Homily in the Sunday Assembly*, produced by the United States Conference of Catholic Bishops.

MAINLINE CONVERGENCE

Vatican II was also concerned about divisions in the Christian Church and invited a large number of ecumenical observers to the Council. In terms of liturgy, Mainline Protestant scholars had also been influenced by the Liturgical Movement, and especially by the discovery of *The Apostolic Tradition*.

A number of reforms from Vatican II had a major impact on Mainline Protestant worship. First and foremost was the liturgical year and a new lectionary. North American Mainline denominations began reclaiming traditions in relation to the **liturgical calendar** and in the 1970s experimented with forms of the liturgical calendar and a three-year lectionary they adapted to fit with their particular denominational emphases. In 1983, the **Consultation on Common Texts** created an ecumenical version of the Roman Catholic Lectionary called the Common Lectionary. After the first three-year cycle was complete, input from scholars, pastors, congregations, and denominations resulted in the **Revised Common Lectionary** (RCL), published in 1994. Today, this lectionary is the dominant lectionary used in Protestant churches that follow the liturgical year and has been adopted as well by those higher liturgical traditions in Protestantism (e.g., the Episcopal and Lutheran Churches) that have long had their own lectionaries.

Alongside this development, there was also ecumenical movement in sacramental theology and practice. In 1982, the **World Council of Churches** published the Lima Document, more commonly known as "**Baptism, Eucharist and Ministry**" (BEM). This document was incredibly influential in shaping conversations about the interpretation of and what happens in the administration of baptism, Eucharist, and ordination. While denominational interpretations of the sacraments remain divergent in some significant ways, practices have become quite similar across most Mainline denominational lines. Settings of **The Great Thanksgiving** prayed at the Table and liturgies used at baptism have begun to converge in most Mainline churches, showing obvious attempts to return to and adapt liturgies from *The Apostolic Tradition* as influenced by BEM and Vatican II.

The liturgical convergence in Mainline traditions is difficult to exaggerate. Laity who are unaware of nuances of denominational history and theology can move between congregations of different Mainline denominations feeling quite at home in worship. They find similar liturgical calendars, common scripture readings, a broadly familiar **ordo** (Gathering, Proclamation, Response/Table, and Sending Forth), and similar sacramental practices across denominational lines. While the ecumenical movements of the twentieth century did not bring about a union of denominations in the way many had hoped, they did bring Protestant worship much closer together.

PRAISE AND WORSHIP

Whereas the liturgical reforms of Vatican II and the ecumenical movement were renewing traditional Mainline worship, influences from the likes of African American, Charismatic, and megachurch worship signaled the need for historic denominations to regain an emotional, experiential element to worship, paving the way for Praise and Worship.

The desire for emotively expressive worship came along at a time when **Contemporary Christian Music** was finding its way into churches as well. In the late 1960s, the **Jesus Movement** in California began to spawn music with devotional lyrics that sounded more like folk/rock music than traditional Christian hymnody. In the 1970s, the Contemporary Christian Music industry grew outside the Church. Evangelical music publishers and performers created music for public consumption in the form of Christian radio stations, concerts, and recordings.

This phenomenon continued to grow, and by the late 1970s and early 1980s, the music started to move into evangelical worship, in part as a response to the desire to create worship with the emotional, experiential quality missing from traditional worship. While the music is called "contemporary" because it uses styles and instrumentation found in contemporary secular music, the theology of the music is often more traditionally evangelical than the theology espoused in more traditional forms of worship represented in the Mainline Protestant convergence. Thus, "**praise music**" is a better label than "contemporary music." Instead of a congregation singing hymns in harmony led by an organ and choir, a "worship leader" (in this sense, a title referring to one who leads singing as opposed to any participant in leading liturgy as a worship leader) and praise band lead the congregation in unison singing.

In the praise and worship movement, proponents argue for distinguishing between "praise" and "worship" as very different liturgical actions with different purposes. We are to praise God before we pray to God. Therefore, (although conceived of differently by different congregations) a series of praise songs are used at the beginning of the service to prepare the congregation for "worship" (i.e., the time in which prayer is offered and scripture is read and preached).

As the movement made its way into Mainline congregations, the distinction between praise and worship diminished over time. The fourfold ordo (Gathering, Proclamation, Response/Table, Sending Forth) merged in various ways with the twofold movement from opening praise music to worship.

Along with utilizing modern styles of music, praise and worship often includes other modern forms of communication, such as varied uses of **technology**, especially video and computer images projected on a screen. The style of worship in these settings is usually less formal than that found in traditional worship. Many congregations originally embraced this form of worship as a way of evangelizing younger people who were not attracted to Church because it seemed outdated. Using contemporary forms of music and technology conveyed that the gospel is relevant to contemporary life.

The incorporation of this approach to worship in Mainline congregations has had a positive impact, but it has not been without significant tensions. Praise music has a strong evangelical bent to it that is not always fitting for some Mainline theological traditions. Moreover, worship spaces built decades earlier do not easily accommodate a praise band or the equipment needed for projection technologies. Often congregations will have separate traditional and praise and worship services, in a sense creating a divided congregation, often along generational lines. With varied degrees of success and failure, some congregations have tried **blended services** that incorporate traditional hymnody and praise music, informal and formal elements, and traditional liturgical communication and projected images.

CONCLUSION

Knowing where a liturgical practice or theological perspective on worship originated, why it was important, how it has evolved, and how it is practiced today is important for effective worship planning and leadership. Too often, clergy, worship committees, worship teams, and congregations have discussions and make decisions concerning worship practices that focus on what individuals like (i.e., matters of taste) without being informed by our history. While liturgical history should not be an anchor that weighs down the Church "reformed and always reforming," neither should we change worship simply to change worship. Knowing whence we have come will always help us better discern where we ought to go.

The Mainline Protestant church is at an intriguing moment in terms of the future of worship. In what ways will worship that is informed by the liturgical renewal consensus evolve next? In what ways will praise and worship evolve next? Will one win out over the other? Will they converge in practice and theology or move apart? Worship leaders need to be courageous, leading congregations into new and relevant ways of offering God adoration and experiencing the good news of Jesus Christ. But they also need to help congregations cherish their histories and the ways in which their worship is an expression of the communion of saints, a manifestation of two thousand years of the worshiping community of faith. The ship must continue to sail, but to journey without an anchor is foolish, since one can never know for certain where future storms will arise. Our brief survey of liturgical history reminds us that ritual evolves slowly but also that it evolves *constantly*. While the Church needs to be innovative in terms of its liturgical theology and practice, rarely must we rush impatiently into the next phase of evolution, and never without significant reflection on how the next phase grows out of what Christians have valued and practiced before.

PART TWO
TIME

Time is the measurement by which we name the sequence, duration, and intervals between different events. It is a key concept in physics. In the seventeenth century, the great physicist Isaac Newton argued that time was an essential, absolute, and unchanging dimension of the universe. It was not until three centuries later that Albert Einstein changed our view of time with his theory of relativity, which claims that rates of time are dependent on relative motion.

In contrast to physics, philosophy and theology often speak of time as a social construct. Different cultures define and interpret the span, significance, and experience of temporal periods in different ways. Measuring time, then, is not a neutral activity. To mark time in certain ways over against other ways is to assign meaning. Ritual, therefore, as the patterned, symbolic enactment of a community's historically rooted identity and values, involves time in relation to the *patterned* aspect of its function.

Students and leaders of Christian worship need to recognize that the contemporary church is heir to such a cultural and ritualistic construct of time. Many worship practices are defined in terms of a Christian theology of time. Observance of Sunday as the primary day of worship, the structure and flow of the "hour" of worship, and the evolution of the liturgical calendar are all expressions of the Church's theology of time. In this section of our introduction, then, we examine the core temporal patterns of Christian worship.

THE LORD'S DAY

We take time for granted in the normal course of our lives. We simply assume our clocks and calendars are "correct." We assume a constant of the earth rotating on its axis, the moon revolving around the earth, and the earth revolving around the sun. But as simple a recognition as the fact that, when a woman in Newport, Rhode Island, checks her alarm clock in the dark at the same time that a man in Newport, Oregon, checks his wristwatch in daylight, they find measurements that are three hours apart, shows that we humans designate time in relation to our *experience* of the world as much as in mathematical determinations. What constitutes "early morning" is different for a farmer than for someone who works the night shift at a factory. Our calendars say a new day begins at midnight, but if we are awake at 1:00 a.m., we commonly experience it as part of the same night we were having at 11:59 p.m., with a new day beginning after we go to sleep and wake up again.

Our experience of time is not simply a matter of choice. We have inherited cultural interpretations of the significance of seconds, minutes, hours, days, weeks, months, and years—interpretations that have changed throughout history. This is as true in the Church's marking of time as it is in everyday secular life. At the center of Christian time is Sunday, the Lord's Day. But there is a history behind the significance the Church places on this day.

CYCLICAL TIME VERSUS LINEAR TIME

We experience time in relation to change. All living things move through birth, growth, maturation, death, and decay. Nothing changes (for good or ill) without time passing. So any process implies the passage of time. Thus we experience time as though it is part or even constitutive of nature itself.

How we measure and name natural changes, however, is not natural at all. Throughout the course of human history, conscious and unconscious decisions have been made about measuring and interpreting the passage of time. "**Someone**" decided to call the rising and setting of the sun a "day" and divide the combined periods of light and darkness into twenty-four hours, each hour into sixty minutes, and each minute into sixty seconds, instead of breaking the day into ten hours, each with ten minutes, each with ten seconds. Someone decided that the cycle of the phases of the moon would be a time segment called a "month." And so on and so forth.

Of course, these "someones" did not start off with a common understanding of Greenwich Mean Time. In different places, periods, and cultures throughout human history, time has been viewed and measured differently. For example, many ancient cultures viewed time as **cyclical**, based on the repetition of the seasons of the year. This view of time repeating itself makes sense, given that human sustenance and the experience of the production of food is dependent on the cycle of climatic seasons.

This cyclical patterning of time, in turn, funded socioreligious beliefs and practices. Myths of dying and rising gods were related to the cycle of winter giving way to spring over and over and over again, to the planting, growing, harvesting, and dying of plants over and over and over again. Creation was viewed as recurring (at least metaphorically) over and over again. An ancient symbol for this view of time is the ouroboros, a snake or lizard eating its own tail. Especially important to recognize is that in this worldview, revelation of divine activity and purposes occurs primarily in and through the processes of **nature**. We know the divine through the cycles of nature and the natural laws that control them.

In contrast to the cyclical view of time, other ancient cultures interpreted time as moving in a **linear** fashion. In this worldview, the cycle of days, months, seasons, and years is still experienced as part of the natural order of the world, but the cycles are not ultimately seen as determinative of human experience of existence. Time is considered to be unrepeatable. Existence is defined by past, present, and future. Creation started time and all of time moves toward a possible (or intended) end.

Judaism and its descendent, Christianity, hold this linear view of time. "Let there be light" is the beginning of time. Even though the poetic creation story in Genesis 1 is told using the repeated refrain, "There was evening and there was morning . . ." creation is presented as a singular event. Creation has its beginning in God's purposes and moves toward its end in God's purposes (the Greek word *telos* means "end" not only in the sense of "cessation" but also in the sense of "goal"). An ancient symbol for this linear view of time is the Alpha and Omega, the first and last letters of the Greek alphabet, God (or Christ) as the Beginning and End.

The understanding of revelation of divine activity and purposes in this linear view of time is radically different than that in cyclical time. Revelation occurs primarily in and through the events of **history** instead of nature. God created nature but is not bound within it or subject to it. God's primary arena of activity is within the linear movement of human (and cosmic) history. God is known as the God of Abraham, Isaac, and Jacob. God liberated the Israelite slaves from Egypt. God sent prophets to pronounce God's intentions in relation to sociopolitical events. God gave Jesus Christ to die as a ransom for the ungodly at the "right time" (Rom 5:6; 1 Tim 2:5-6). This is why Christian theologians can speak of the "Christ event" as the center of history— not as a literal, temporal description about how long human history has lasted or will last, but as a theological center through which we measure and understand all that has occurred and will occur in linear history in relation to the birth, ministry, death, resurrection, and exaltation of Jesus Christ. This perspective is where the calendar designations BC ("Before Christ") and AD ("*Anno Domini*," Latin for "in the year of the Lord") came from. (It should be noted that since not all who measure time in a linear fashion share this theological view of the Christ event, most scholarship today uses the designations BCE ["Before the Common Era"] and CE ["Common Era"].)

LINEAR TIME AND CYCLICAL PATTERNS OF WORSHIP

What are the implications of this linear view of experiencing and measuring time (and thus of interpreting history) for the Christian understanding and practices of worship? The linear movement of time is often referred to using the Greek word **chronos**, which is the root of the English word "chronology." *Chronos* is what we study in history; it is what we measure with clocks, or as they were once called, "chronometers." Christians assume *chronos* is the regular, linear passage of time in which they and God live and act.

On the other hand, the Church worships cyclically. We worship each week on Sunday. Each year we work through the same cycle of liturgical seasons—Advent, Christmas, Epiphany, Lent, Easter, Pentecost, Ordinary Time. This creates quite a paradox: even though our community's foundational identity and values are narrated in terms of God's activity in linear time, our ritualized, patterned enactment of this linear narrative occurs in a cyclical fashion.

This paradoxical worship practice can be related to yet a third (not yet introduced) understanding of time. The Greek word used to name this understanding of time is **kairos**. While in ancient Greek, *kairos* is often simply used as a synonym for *chronos* (e.g., "At that time Jesus" did such and such, in Matt 11:25; 12:1), the term can also mean "opportune time" or the "right time" (as in 1 Tim 2:6 and Rom 5:6 cited above). Contemporary Christian theology often uses *kairos* in this way. In this sense, *kairos* is neither cyclical nor linear. It is a moment in *chronos* when the extraordinary is possible or happens. It is a juncture in time that can change the course of linear history—an individual's or community's history. *Kairos* is God's eternal time breaking into *chronos*. It is ahistorical, opportune, existential, even eschatological time.

Worship is one arena—arguably the primary arena but not the only one—where the Church opens itself to *kairos*. In worship's cyclical ritual patterns, Christians celebrate and experience God's eternal time (*kairos*) as liturgical speech and actions and enact different elements of God's providential and salvific role in history (*chronos*), especially in (but not limited to) the Christ event. Put differently, worship planners and leaders strive to develop cyclical patterns of worship (Sunday after Sunday, year after year) in which Christians come to know the gifts of *kairos* that have been revealed throughout *chronos* in their own particular historical moment.

FROM SABBATH TO SUNDAY

The central worship practice related to this construct of time is that of worshiping weekly on **Sunday**. This practice is the first, although not by any means the only, answer to the question, "When should the Church worship?"

As we have noted, the Church inherited its core construct of time from Judaism. Of course, heirs are free to do with their inheritance as they please. When we compare Christian and Jewish practices related to time, we should not be surprised to find similarities that reflect this inheritance, along with differences that signal ways the Church has moved away from its honored ancestor.

From Judaism, the Church inherited the measurement of the week, with the week ending on the day of rest. (The "weekend" in the Western calendar and secular practice evolved from this marking of time.) Central to Jewish identity and values is the observance of the Sabbath. This practice is named repeatedly in the Hebrew Bible, but most explicitly in the creation story of Genesis 1:1–2:4. God creates the world in six days and rests on the seventh:

> Thus the heavens and the earth were finished, and all their multitude. And on the seventh day God finished the work that he had done, and he rested on the seventh day from all the work that he had done. So God blessed the seventh day and hallowed it, because on it God rested from all the work that he had done in creation. (2:1-3)

Jews honor the Sabbath as a holy day of rest and worship.

The ancient Israelite understanding of time had the day beginning at sundown. As with the week, this construct is also codified in the creation story with the refrain, "And there was evening and there was morning, the _____ day" (Gen 1:5, 8, 13, 19, 23, 31). Even though most Jews today experience their lives in relation to the Western understanding of the day as beginning at midnight (or actually at sunrise), they still observe the Sabbath as beginning at sundown on Friday and ending at sundown on Saturday.

The earliest Christians were Jews. They continued worshiping in the synagogue and the temple, and continued observing the Sabbath. That they struggled with the meaning of Sabbath observance as part of their new faith as early as the second generation of the Church is seen in the Sabbath controversies in the Gospels, written in last third of the first century (e.g., Mark 2:23–3:6). Very early on, however, they added worship practices to their corporate life that were unique to their Jewish sect. These practices reflected elements of their understanding of the world as Jews, but they were interpreted anew in light of their belief that Jesus was the Messiah and that his death and resurrection marked an eschatological turning of the ages.

As Christianity became Gentile, synagogue and temple worship were abandoned, and Jewish influence diminished, these new practices continued. Central to this evolution is the shift from worshiping on the Sabbath (the last day of the week) to worshiping on Sunday (the first day of the week). Originally Christians worshiped on Sunday as a supplement to their Sabbath worship. Eventually observance of **the Lord's Day** replaced Sabbath observance.

The rationale for this shift is based on the fact that for the Church, the Christ event as the center of time (as the *kairos* of all *kairoi*) becomes the primary narrative for interpreting time over against the story in Genesis 1. Put differently, redemption replaces creation as the central category for prescribing time theologically and liturgically. Instead of celebrating the day of rest, then, the Church celebrates the day of resurrection. Moreover, because the resurrection was discovered at dawn (and because Christians often had to meet in secret at dawn and saw the day as beginning at sunrise), the Church transitioned over time to measure days as beginning in the morning instead of at sundown. (There are two important exceptions to this transition. Worship on Christmas Eve and in the Easter Vigil continue to mark evening as the beginning of a new day and liturgical season.) The primary time of worship shifted from Friday evening to Sunday morning.

We find this movement from Sabbath to Sunday already being named in first-century documents. The earliest is in 1 Corinthians, written in the range of 53–55 CE. In his closing greeting, Paul instructs the house churches of Corinth to save money for a collection for the Jerusalem church so they do not have to scramble and collect money when he comes for a visit. In his instruction, we see that the Apostle simply assumes the Corinthian Christians gather weekly on Sunday:

> *On the first day of every week*, each of you is to put aside and save whatever you earn, so that collections need not be taken when I come. (16:2)

Nearly the same phrasing appears later in Acts (probably written in the last decade of the first century). Luke assumes that the church gathers on Sundays when he tells the story of Paul's healing Eutychus, who fell out of the window after listening to Paul preach all day (20:7-12). Not only does Luke assume the Church worships on Sunday but that this worship specifically involves the Table:

> On the first day of the week, when we met to break bread, Paul . . . continued speaking until midnight. (20:7)

These examples from the New Testament seem to show that the authors simply took for granted the practice of worshiping on the first day of the week. This should not lead us to think, however, that the transition from Sabbath to Sunday was one without any resistance. In the early post-New Testament Church, the practice of worshiping on Sunday is still being defended in *The Epistle of Barnabas* (written in the late first century or early second century). The author attempts to reconcile the shift with creation-based rationale for Sabbath worship by referring to the day of resurrection as the **eighth day of creation**, completing God's creative purposes for the world in the eschatological, redemptive work of Christ:

> The present sabbaths are not acceptable to me, but that which I have made, in which I will give rest to all things and make the beginning of an eighth day, that is the beginning of another world. Wherefore we also celebrate with gladness the eighth

day in which Jesus also rose from the dead, and was made manifest, and ascended into heaven. (15.8-9)

Similarly **Justin Martyr**, in the mid-second century, argues in his *First Apology* for Sunday as the day of Christian worship on the basis that it was the **first day of creation** and the **day of resurrection**:

> Sunday is the day on which we all hold our common assembly, because it is the first day on which God, having wrought a change in the darkness and matter, made the world; and Jesus Christ our Saviour on the same day rose from the dead. (67)

This Christian interpretation of Sunday comes full circle once Constantine legalizes Christianity. By this point Sunday is becoming "the Christian Sabbath," and exceptions to the enforced practice of resting on this day must be made for those whose work requires their attention on Sundays, as seen in this imperial decree:

> All judges, city-people and craftsmen *shall rest on the venerable day of the Sun*. But countrymen may without hindrance attend to agriculture, since it often happens that this is the most suitable day for sowing grain or planting vines, so that the opportunity afforded by divine providence may not be lost, for the right season is of short duration. (Found in Joseph Cullen Ayer, *A Source Book for Ancient Church History* [New York: Charles Scribner's Sons, 1913], 284–85; emphasis added.)

IMPLICATIONS FOR WORSHIP PRACTICES TODAY

For most of the history of the Church, the centrality and significance of Sunday for communal worship and for the lives of individual Christians could simply be assumed. In Western Christendom, the secular and religious calendars were one. But in our pluralistic, post-Christian age of the twenty-first century, this assumption is no longer the case. Secular life on Sunday no longer stops to make room for worship in the Church. Businesses are open on Sunday, baseball and soccer league games are held at 11:00 on Sunday morning, and media outlets publish and broadcast more loudly on the television and internet on Sundays than preachers can speak or gospel choirs and praise bands can sing. All these sorts of cultural phenomena challenge the significance and practicality of worshiping on Sunday.

Moreover, we live in an age of convenience with few time limitations to commercial endeavors or the sharing of information. Churches have to offer worship in the marketplace of twenty-four hour drive-through windows and the constant and near-omnipresent availability of the internet.

Given the lack of importance North American culture gives to Sunday as the Christian day of worship and the commercialistic desire to get what we want when we want it, some congregations are abandoning Sunday morning as the central time for worship. They experiment with other schedules for worship, especially looking for "convenient" times that might better attract busy newcomers, including even asynchronous online worship.

Of course, churches have always worshiped at times other than Sunday morning, but those other times were supplements to Sunday morning, not alternatives. The question with which some congregations and worship planners must struggle today is whether Sunday, as the Lord's Day, as the day of resurrection and the "eighth day" of creation, should still be observed as ritually *essential* for, or at least constitutive of, the Church's core historically rooted identity and values. What is gained and what is lost when Sunday is theologically and ritually de-emphasized?

In the early Church, when Christian worship on Sunday supplemented synagogue worship on the Sabbath, Sunday was not viewed as a "Christian Sabbath," as a day of rest. The Church gathered for worship on a work day, in a countercultural manner, at inconvenient times. This shows how important gathering on Sunday was to their central identity and values, historically rooted in the idea that the community was a manifestation of Christ's resurrection. With even the eventual understanding of Sunday as "Christian Sabbath" fading away along with Christian culture, should the Church re-emphasize this ancient practice and identity marker or find new times to gather for worship in accordance with new cultural patterns? In other words, how should the Church weigh accommodation to contemporary culture for the hope of holding on to or gaining more members over against claiming a countercultural identity derived from scripture and tradition?

SUNDAY MORNING ORDO

In the previous chapter, we noted that the Church paradoxically worships in cyclical patterns (such as the annual liturgical calendar) as an expression of our understanding that God, the Alpha and Omega, has revealed Godself, especially in the story of Israel and in the Christ event, throughout the course of linear history. Central to this cyclical patterning of Christian ritual is Sunday, the Lord's Day. The day of resurrection lies at the core of the whole construct of time that plays a role in the temporal expressions of the Church's faith, practice, and identity. It is on this day, more than any other (but not to the exclusion of others) that the Church opens itself to *kairos* in the midst of *chronos*—that is, God's eternal, ahistorical, opportune, existential, eschatological time breaking into the regular, linear, historical passage of time.

In this chapter, we move to another temporal patterning of Christian worship: the way the time during which the Church gathers to worship is structured. This patterning is characteristic of worship on the Lord's Day, but is not limited to it. Our topic is the ordo of Mainline worship.

Ordo, from the Latin meaning "order," is a term used in liturgical discussions to name the core Christian pattern of worship. The ordo can properly refer to the whole, regular pattern of worship, including, for instance, the emphasis on Sunday as the Lord's Day (discussed in the previous chapter) and the liturgical calendar (to be discussed in the next chapter). In this book, though, we use it in the more limited sense of the *order* of the liturgy, the core pattern of the single worship service and the rationale behind and significance the Church gives to that pattern. Our concern is not to prescribe the order of all liturgical actions in Mainline worship, as if there should be no room for variation from congregation to congregation, denomination to denomination, or even from season to season or Sunday to Sunday within a congregation. Instead, we will examine *underlying* structures shared by most Mainline Protestant traditions that not only allow for but invite variation.

The relationship between form and flexibility of worship is defined differently in different Mainline denominations. "Higher" liturgical traditions have service books that are authoritative and prescriptive for congregations. Two examples are:

Episcopal Church USA's *Book of Common Prayer* (1979, online)

Evangelical Lutheran Church of America's *Evangelical Lutheran Worship* (2006)

"Lower" liturgical traditions, by contrast, have service books that serve as denominational resources for pastors and worship planners:

African Methodist Episcopal Church, *AMEC Book of Worship* (1984)

African Methodist Episcopal Church Zion, *The African Methodist Episcopal Church Zion Book of Worship*

The Christian Church (Disciples of Christ), *Chalice Worship*

Christian Methodist Episcopal Church, *Book of Ritual*, new and rev.

Presbyterian Church (USA), *Book of Common Worship*

Reformed Church in America, *Liturgy of the RCA*

United Church of Canada, *Celebrate God's Presence*

United Church of Christ, *Book of Worship: United Church of Christ*

United Methodist Church, *The United Methodist Book of Worship*

Praise and worship services within Mainline churches move even further along the scale of flexibility, rarely drawing on service books at all. The "order of worship"—that is, the sequence of all liturgical actions and speech in a single service—across all these different traditions and styles of worship can vary greatly. Nevertheless, across these differences, Christian worship shares (or should share?) a core underlying ordo that has been brought to the surface in more and more explicit ways in the last half century, becoming a key element of the Protestant convergence.

The difference and relationship between an "order of worship" of a particular service and the "ordo of Christian worship" more broadly can be thought of using the analogy of the difference between story and plot. If someone is asked to summarize the **story** of a movie that is a romantic comedy, she or he will tell what happened in the order the events happened, something like:

Winifred and Jackson met on a cruise. They fell in love, but when the cruise was over Winifred went back home to New York and Jackson returned to Sacramento.

48

Winifred decided she couldn't live without Jackson, so she hopped a plane to California to surprise him, but he wasn't there. He had moved away without any forwarding address. She thought the whole relationship had been a lie and returned home, sobbing all the way. But when she arrived at her brownstone, he was sitting on her stoop. He had come to find her, but thought he had missed her forever, and he was crying. They embraced, and the crying ceased, until the audience saw Winifred crying again, this time tears of joy at her wedding on a cruise ship.

If someone is asked, however, to analyze the **plot** of the same movie, he or she would not just tell what happened but describe the relationship of the various movements of the story in terms of its underlying structure. Indeed, the person might note that the plot is standard (even clichéd) romantic comedy that is often expressed formulaically as

- girl gets boy;
- girl loses boy;
- girl finds boy;
- girl and boy live happily ever after.

These different movements can be labeled as the hook of the story, the conflict and rising action, the climax, and the resolution.

If worship, then, is described in terms of a story, one can say, "First the organist played a prelude by Bach; then a liturgist led a call to worship followed by an invocation; then the congregation stood to sing the hymn, 'Holy, Holy, Holy'; and then . . ." Described in this way, the order of worship sounds more like a to-do list of barely related tasks. But if worship is described in terms of its plot, that is, in terms of underlying ordo, a structure is named in which the community of faith gathers, hears the word proclaimed, responds to the word (usually by sharing a meal), and is sent forth to continue serving God in the world as they have in this worship service. Various actions comprise each of these movements, but now we can see the way worship unfolds in a logical and meaningful four-part flow instead of as an itemized list.

The main purpose of this chapter is to explore each of these four movements in contemporary practice in some detail, but first we should back up and attend to the origin of this ordo.

HISTORY OF THE CHRISTIAN ORDO
Origins

Like so much of Christian worship, the ordo has at least part of its origin in Jewish worship. We start with worship in the synagogue and then turn to worship in the home.

As noted earlier, there was significant diversity among ancient synagogues, and we do not have extensive information concerning worship in the synagogue in the first century CE preceding the rise of the Church. But we can turn to a familiar source to get a picture of synagogue worship that is instructive—the scene in which Jesus returns to the synagogue in Nazareth in Luke 4:

> When he came to Nazareth, where he had been brought up, he went to the synagogue on the sabbath day, as was his custom. He stood up to read, and the scroll of the prophet Isaiah was given to him. He unrolled the scroll and found the place where it was written: "The Spirit of the Lord is upon me, because he has anointed me to bring good news to the poor. He has sent me to proclaim release to the captives and recovery of sight to the blind, to let the oppressed go free, to proclaim the year of the Lord's favor." And he rolled up the scroll, gave it back to the attendant, and sat down. The eyes of all in the synagogue were fixed on him. Then he began to say to them, "Today this Scripture has been fulfilled in your hearing."

Luke wrote in the late first century to a Christian audience that was likely primarily Gentile, and we cannot be certain how much knowledge he had of the specific details of synagogue ritual in Galilee from earlier in the century. Moreover, his purpose is not to describe synagogue worship in some historical fashion but to make a christological claim. Thus much of what Luke might have thought to occur in worship is not narrated. For example, a common name in Hellenistic literature for the synagogue in the diaspora was "place of prayer." Clearly, prayer was a part of synagogue worship although the New Testament only once explicitly mentions prayer in the synagogue (Matt 6:5) and formal prayers such as the **Amidah** had yet to be institutionalized. Still, the limited description the Gospel of Luke offers in this scene is enlightening.

First, as we noted in the previous chapter, synagogue worship occurred on the Sabbath (although worship may have occurred on other occasions as well, such as market day or holy days). The New Testament narratives make a point of presenting Jesus and the disciples as well as Paul as participating in Sabbath worship in the synagogue (in addition to the story under considerations, see Matt 12:9; Mark 1:21, 29; Luke 13:10; Acts 13:14; 17:1-2; 18:4.)

Second, Jesus stands up to read scripture and is given the scroll of Isaiah. Luke does not specify why the scroll from Isaiah is chosen. The author may simply assume Jesus has requested this scroll and chooses to read Isaiah 61:1-2a (with a line inserted from Isaiah 58:6). Another possibility is that Isaiah 61 was understood to be the prescribed reading for the day. We do know that in first-century Judaism it would have been common for there to be a reading from the Torah and from the Prophets (see Acts 13:15; 15:21; there is no evidence of regular readings from the Writings). We also know that in the later rabbinic period, there were set patterns for reading through the Torah (every year or every three to three and a half years in different geographical regions), and this may have been the case for reading through the Prophets as well. There is no direct concrete evidence of such a lectionary in the first-century synagogue, but some scholars conjecture that the later practice had precedents during the early first century and suggest that this text may assume such a practice.

Third, the reading was followed by an interpretation (v. 20). Because of his christological interest, Luke makes Jesus himself the interpretation and presents Jesus as giving perhaps the shortest sermon in the history of preaching. Still, the pattern is clear enough. At the center of synagogue worship, at least as portrayed in the New Testament (a perspective presumably reflecting and influential on Christian worship practice), is the reading and interpretation of scripture.

While no New Testament writing mentions it, we also know that (at least at later dates) communal meals were a part of synagogue life as well. These meals likely included New Moon gatherings and some festivals. Some scholars speculate that Sabbath meals may also have been practiced in some locations. Whatever the case, these meals seem to have been more focused on communal fellowship and less on worship.

Meals in the Jewish home on the Sabbath and on holy days, however, were considered part of the pattern of Jewish worship. Weekly Sabbath meals included a **blessing ritual** involving wine and bread that gave God thanks for creation, thanks for past salvation as manifested in the exodus, and petitions for present and future salvation in accordance with the past, especially in the form of the appearance of the messiah. At Passover meals, this pattern was expanded into a full **Seder** so that prayer along with the recitation of the story of the exodus was combined with symbolic food so that the distance between past and present salvation was collapsed.

Given this Jewish background, it is no wonder that the center of the Christian ordo would become **word and table**—the reading and interpretation of scripture followed by a meal with prayer and symbolic food. We know both liturgical actions were important in the church as early as the mid-fifties CE, when Paul wrote **1 Corinthians**. In this letter, Paul deals with various divisions in the house churches of Corinth. In chapter 8, he introduces a division around whether Christians can eat meat that has been offered to idols. As he warns against the potential participatory nature of such eating, he exemplifies his point by referring to the eucharistic practice of the church in chapter 10:16-17:

> The cup of blessing that we bless, is it not a sharing in the blood of Christ? The bread that we break, is it not a sharing in the body of Christ? Because there is one bread, we who are many are one body, for we all partake of the one bread.

He returns to this meal as a point of divisiveness itself in chapter 11:17-34, which is worthy of reading closely in its entirety:

> Now in the following instructions I do not commend you, because when you come together it is not for the better but for the worse. For, to begin with, when you come together as a church, I hear that there are divisions among you; and to some extent I believe it. Indeed, there have to be factions among you, for only so will it become clear who among you are genuine. When you come together, it is not really to eat the Lord's supper. For when the time comes to eat, each of you goes ahead with your own supper, and one goes hungry and another becomes drunk. What! Do you not have homes to eat and drink in? Or do you show contempt for the church of God and humiliate those who have nothing? What should I say to you? Should I commend you? In this matter I do not commend you!

51

> *For I received from the Lord what I also handed on to you, that the Lord Jesus on the night when he was betrayed took a loaf of bread, and when he had given thanks, he broke it and said, "This is my body that is for you. Do this in remembrance of me." In the same way he took the cup also, after supper, saying, "This cup is the new covenant in my blood. Do this, as often as you drink it, in remembrance of me." For as often as you eat this bread and drink the cup, you proclaim the Lord's death until he comes.* (Emphasis added.)

> Whoever, therefore, eats the bread or drinks the cup of the Lord in an unworthy manner will be answerable for the body and blood of the Lord. Examine yourselves, and only then eat of the bread and drink of the cup. For all who eat and drink without discerning the body, eat and drink judgment against themselves. For this reason many of you are weak and ill, and some have died. But if we judged ourselves, we would not be judged. But when we are judged by the Lord, we are disciplined so that we may not be condemned along with the world.

> So then, my brothers and sisters, when you come together to eat, wait for one another. If you are hungry, eat at home, so that when you come together, it will not be for your condemnation. About the other things I will give instructions when I come.

The fact that Paul cites liturgical tradition (vv. 23-26 [emphasized above] and possibly 10:16-17) shows that the practice of observing this symbolic meal is well-established by the beginnings of the Pauline mission. Moreover, the warning Paul evokes in relation to abuse of the meal (in the next to last paragraph above) shows how seriously he takes the ritual.

In chapter 12, Paul begins dealing with a new divisive issue in the Corinthian house churches—that of spiritual gifts, specifically the gift of speaking in tongues. For our purposes, we need not deal with the particulars of Paul's argument except to note that it involves worship, since glossolalia occurred during (and in Paul's mind potentially disrupted) worship. In chapter 14, Paul concerns himself with the question of *orderliness* in worship as part of his dealing with this issue. In verses 26-33, he writes,

> What should be done then, my friends? When you come together, each one has a hymn, a lesson, a revelation, a tongue, or an interpretation. Let all things be done for building up. If anyone speaks in a tongue, let there be only two or at most three, and each in turn; and let one interpret. But if there is no one to interpret, let them be silent in church and speak to themselves and to God. Let two or three prophets speak, and let the others weigh what is said. If a revelation is made to someone else sitting nearby, let the first person be silent. For you can all prophesy one by one, so that all may learn and all be encouraged. And the spirits of prophets are subject to the prophets, for God is a God not of disorder but of peace.

In this passage, Paul does not explicitly mention the reading and interpreting of scripture, but he is clearly concerned with the issue of **proclamation** (exemplified in the vocabulary of teaching, revelation, prophecy, and interpretation), the purpose of which is the building up of the community (see 14:3-19).

Thus we see, in a community of Gentile Christians only twenty or so years after the death of Jesus, an adaptation of Jewish worship practices that includes both proclamation and a symbolic meal. It is not clear, however, at this point in history (the mid-fifties CE) whether the two actions were part of the same liturgical event or not. Paul discusses them separately, and nowhere in his writings does he explain their liturgical relationship—similar to the fact that he never discusses the place baptism has in relation to weekly worship patterns. He need not deal with such matters explicitly because his readers would already know these patterns. For us two thousand years later, though, the relationship of word and table in Paul's churches remains ambiguous.

The combination of the two into a single liturgical event does clearly seem to be the case some thirty to forty-five years later when Luke writes **Acts**. Following the story of Pentecost, the narrator states that the newly baptized "devoted themselves to the apostles' teaching and fellowship, to the breaking of bread and the prayers" (2:41). In this line, the two actions of proclamation and meal are named together, implying a close connection. One could argue, of course, that they are not explicitly named as being in the same worship service. Later in Acts 20, however, Luke tells the story of Paul healing Eutychus in Troas:

> *On the first day of the week, when we met to break bread, Paul was holding a discussion with them*; since he intended to leave the next day, he continued speaking until midnight. There were many lamps in the room upstairs where we were meeting. A young man named Eutychus, who was sitting in the window, began to sink off into a deep sleep while Paul talked still longer. Overcome by sleep, he fell to the ground three floors below and was picked up dead. But Paul went down, and bending over him took him in his arms, and said, "Do not be alarmed, for his life is in him." Then Paul went upstairs, and *after he had broken bread and eaten, he continued to converse with them* until dawn; then he left. (vv. 7-11)

Luke's primary purpose in telling this story is to affirm Paul's ability to heal, but in the course of telling the story he reveals some of his assumptions about Christian worship. The opening line (v. 7) is especially revealing: worship occurs on the first day of the week (Sunday), which is the set day for breaking bread and proclamation. Moreover, in verse 11 (the last sentence of the passage), we get a glimpse of Luke's assumption concerning order: discussion leads to the meal (and then more discussion). Thus by the late first century, at least in Luke's ecclesial context, word and table are the core ordo of Christian worship.

The **Didache**, which was probably written in the late first century near the time or soon after Luke–Acts was composed (although some scholars argue for a much earlier date of composition), does not name this reality. Again, the structure of word and table may have been assumed, but chapter 14 only explicitly speaks of gathering on the Lord's Day for "the eucharist." (Older scholarship assumed the *Didache*'s reference in chapter 14 and description in chapters 9–10 of "eucharist" to refer to the Lord's Supper. Many scholars now argue that the *Didache* uses "eucharist" a to refer to a broader communal meal [such as an Agape Meal or symposium]. For an in-depth discussion of the different possibilities, see Kurt Niederwimmer, *The Didache*, Hermeneia [Minneapolis: Fortress, 1998], 139–68.)

By the mid-second century, however, the movement from word to table is certainly firmly established. **Justin Martyr**, in his *First Apology 67*, writes the following often quoted passage:

> And on the day called Sunday, all who live in cities or in the country gather together to one place, and the memoirs of the apostles or the writings of the prophets are read, as long as time permits; then, when the reader has ceased, the president verbally instructs, and exhorts to the imitation of these good things. Then we all rise together and pray, and, as we before said [when discussing the admittance of only the baptized to the meal], when our prayer is ended, bread and wine and water are brought, and the president in like manner offers prayers and thanksgivings, according to his ability, and the people assent, saying Amen.

By Justin's day, the reading of scripture (what we consider the Hebrew Bible or Old Testament, referred to in this excerpt as "the writings of the prophets") is supplemented by reading the "memoirs of the apostles" (a reference to writings that would become those in the New Testament). A sermon by an official presider follows. The congregation responds to the time of reading and teaching with prayer and the Eucharist (which also involves prayer, but this time led specifically by the presider).

To summarize the historical review thus far, word and table were essential to Christian worship as early as the mid-first century; and at least by the mid-second century (although probably much earlier), the movement from the former to the latter was the standard pattern for worship on the Lord's Day.

The fact that these two elements served as the core pattern of worship imply the remaining two elements of the ordo (Gathering and Sending Forth) even though they are not explicitly discussed in the early literature. Other liturgical actions, such as prayer and hymns, are mentioned but not always in ways that provide insight into the order of the actions. But what is clear is that the community had to gather to worship together and had to depart as worship concluded. While we might be tempted to dismiss these outer movements as insignificant compared to the central acts of proclamation and meal, we should recall that the Greek label for the church was *ekklesia*, those whom God calls (*kaleo*) out (*ek*). The very act of gathering for worship apart from the wider world symbolizes *ecclesi*ological sensitivity. And while the Church may be "in the world but not of it," worshipers always gather from the world and are always sent back into it. Word and table are central to Christian worship, but their meaning is contextualized by the body of Christ coming out from the world to hear and eat together and then returning to the world having been nourished by scripture and proclamation, along with bread and wine.

54

Revisions

While the performance and ordering of different liturgical actions varied considerably across the ancient world, the fourfold ordo, the underlying structure of worship, was established early and remains intact today.

There has, however, been one major and influential change to the ordo in much of Protestant Christianity. In the Middle Ages, laypeople did not receive the Eucharist regularly at the Mass. There was a piety of unworthiness that shaped this practice, and the doctrine of transubstantiation allowed them to believe that simply witnessing the host elevated (seeing Christ sacrificed) was a means of grace. So infrequent was lay reception of communion that the **Fourth Latern Council** instructed in 1215 that at least yearly communion (on Easter) was required to escape being barred from the church.

The Protestant Reformers of the sixteenth century rejected transubstantiation and the view that each celebration of the Mass was a sacrifice of Christ, stressing that all the baptized were eligible to receive communion when it was offered. Many of the churches and towns who were not in the habit of weekly communion, however, did not want it that often, even though some Reformers argued in favor of receiving it weekly. The piety of infrequent reception was bolstered by the Protestant emphasis on the word of God. Scripture reading and preaching were at the center of worship, instead of the pairing of word and table. Thus the ordo essentially evolved into **Gathering**, **Proclamation**, **Response** (in forms other than the Table), and **Sending Forth**.

This evolution of the underlying pattern of worship was reinforced by the fact that not every Protestant community of faith during and following the Reformation(s) had ordained clergy present at every service. Sacraments were only administered by clergy, but laypeople could preach or at least read a published sermon of a clergyperson. This was even more frequently the case in the frontiers of North America. Circuit riding clergy brought the sacraments several times a year, and the rest of the time, worship was a **Service of the Word**.

The heritage of the pattern of Gathering, Proclamation, Response (without Table), and Sending Forth, therefore, has dominated much of Mainline Protestantism until recent decades. Lately, as part of the liturgical renewal efforts that have arisen in the twentieth century, there has been an ecumenical movement to return to weekly communion, thus reclaiming the centrality of Word and Table in the fourfold ordo. In what follows, we will try to honor both versions of the fourfold patterns.

THE FOUR MOVEMENTS OF THE ORDO

In terms of our practical theology of worship, the reason we need to attend closely to the ways we structure the time during which the church gathers for worship is to give unity and movement to the sacred conversation we plan to moderate. A conversation that has no thematic focus potentially rambles into small talk, ending without significance. A conversation without a clear flow becomes either stagnant (without movement) or lost (with random movement and no clear destination).

There are many different actions that are or could be part of the liturgical conversation. Consider the following alphabetical list:

Acclamation

Altar Call

Anointing

Announcements

Apostolic
    Greeting

Assurance of
Pardon

Baptism

Benediction

Blessing

Call and
    Response

Call to Worship

Chant

Children's
    Sermon

Charge

Choral Anthem

Collect

Commission

Confession

Countdown

Creed

Dance

Decalogue

Dedication

Dismissal

Doxology

Drama

Genuflexion

Gloria Patri

Greeting

Hymn

Invitation to
    Discipleship

Invocation

Introit

Joys and
    Concerns

Kyrie

Lighting the
    Candles

Laying on Hands

Lord's Prayer

Meditation

Offering

Offertory

Passing the Peace

Postlude

Praise Song

Prayer for
    Illumination

Prayers of the
    People

Prelude

Procession

Reception of
    New Members

Recession

Responsive
    Reading

Salutation

Scripture
    Reading

Sermon

Sign of the Cross

Silence

Special Music

Table

Testimony

Video Clip

Some of these actions comprise the **ordinary** of worship, that is, the elements of worship that remain the same week after week (e.g., the Lord's Prayer or Gloria Patri), regardless of variable factors, such as the theme for the day, the liturgical season, and so on. These elements are stable in terms of language and often in terms of placement in the service. This does not mean that different congregations might not place the items in different locations in the order of worship. For example, one congregation might always have the recitation of a creed during the Gathering as part of establishing the identity of the community, whereas another might always place it as part of the Response after the sermon so that the congregation can affirm the breadth of the faith in light of (or in contrast to) the more narrow element of the faith with which the preacher dealt.

Other liturgical actions comprise the **propers** of worship, those elements that change week to week (e.g., the call to worship, hymns, scripture readings). These should be chosen or developed in ways that focus on the central theme of the worship service. Usually this theme is derived from a scripture reading (or set of readings, for instance from the **Revised Common Lectionary**) that is chosen first and upon which the sermon focuses. While some of the propers are anchored to a specific location in the liturgy by virtue of their function, even though the language changes week to week (e.g., an introit or a benediction), others can (and should!) be moved to help shape the unfolding of the theme across the plot of worship for a particular service.

Consider, for instance, the *choral anthem*. Many congregations with traditional services keep the anthem located in the same spot in the liturgy week after week, regardless of the content of the song's lyrics. Perhaps the most popular position in the liturgy is during the offering. The benefit of this placement is that it combines two liturgical actions into a single time period, thus shortening the service and filling the silence during the offering. While there is nothing wrong with the anthem taking place during the offering, the reason stated above is a terrible one. Practical needs should certainly play a role in the shaping of worship but not to the point that they overshadow sound liturgical theology.

Some anthems are expressions of praise, representing the congregation's voice speaking to God, and are best for the opening of worship. Others are songs drawn from or based on the scripture text for the day and belong in the Proclamation section of worship. Still other choral pieces might name a congregation's thankful posture in light of God's grace and calling through Jesus Christ and best serve the flow of worship by being sung during the Response portion of the service. And, finally, some anthems are blessings set to music and belong in the Sending Forth.

As noted earlier, different Mainline denominations weigh the relationship between form and flexibility in liturgy differently. Even traditions that value flexibility must be careful not to change the order of worship so radically week after week that worshipers are unsure what they are to be doing and lose a sense of the significance of worship as a patterned ritual. That said, in relationship to liturgical actions and speech that a tradition allows to be moved about, congregations and worship planners must be careful not to adopt (usually by habit) an idolatrous attachment to the order of worship, such that a logical and experientially meaningful enactment of the ordo is lost. In fact, helping a congregation have attachment to the overarching fourfold movement of Christian liturgy (for instance through using the headings in bulletins) is a way to free them from any legalistic approach to the specific details of the order of worship.

Liturgical choices concerning order should be made in terms of how individual liturgical actions, as well as the relation of the various actions to each other, shape the unity and flow of the liturgical conversation. Which voice does this action represent, and is this the appropriate time in the development of the conversation for that voice to speak this content?

Let us turn, then, to each of the four movements of the ordo individually and explore their theological and experiential purposes and potential.

Gathering

The Gathering is the opening of the service, in which the church is called out (*ek-klesia*) from serving God in the world to serving God in communal worship. This overarching purpose is fulfilled in several ways. First, **the conversation is called to order**, if you will. The conversation partners, or at least the two primary ones, are called together. This is most evident in the *call to worship* or *opening sentences* (usually of scripture), calling the congregation to attention and the *invocation* or *collect of the day* and the *lighting of candles*, inviting and claiming God to be present. Of course, since God is omnipresent, God is already present in the worship event, just as much as those who have parked their cars and taken their seats are already present. The symbolic act of inviting the divine presence is really the request that God reveal God's presence to the gathered community, and that all conversation partners attend to one another.

Second, in terms of God's being present, the Gathering is characterized by **praise**. Certainly other actions take place in the Gathering but this one is dominant. The first response to the revelation of God's presence is adoration, especially since the declaration of God's worthiness is central to the meaning of worship itself. The praise and worship movement clearly emphasizes this aspect by singing numerous *praise songs* in sequence right at the beginning of the service. In traditional styles of worship this aspect can be seen in music as well—*hymns* that are sung by the congregation in the Gathering are usually characterized by lyrics/texts that express adoration to one or all of the persons of the Trinity and by music that is upbeat and strong as opposed to hymns that might be used later in worship that are quieter and more contemplative in content and tone.

Third, in terms of the congregation's being present in worship, the Gathering **shapes and names the identity of the community** in various appropriate ways. It binds individual worshipers into the body of Christ—a community that sings, speaks, and serves in unison. *Calls to worship* often highlight or imply some aspect of the church's identity that relates to the central theme of the day. Corporate *prayers* *of confession* can be offered, which, on the one hand, acknowledge our unworthiness to be in God's presence, were it not for God's grace made known to us through Jesus Christ, and, on the other, name something of the moral, ethical, and spiritual goals of the Christian life. To this end, some traditions include a unison reading of the *Decalogue* (Ten Commandments) in the Gathering. As mentioned above, some congregations recite an *affirmation of faith* or *creed* during the Gathering in order to claim and remind the congregation right from the beginning that this expression is central to our faith and thus central to who we are as a community of faith. Although not as common as it used to be, some congregations include *prayers of the people* (usually in the form of a *pastoral prayer*) in the opening of worship as well. Having been called to worship and having offered praise in unison, the community is bound all the more tightly together by offering their concerns to the God who is our ultimate concern. Even less common than it used to be is the inclusion of the *offering* in the Gathering. When placed here, the offering symbolically gathers individuals into a community that uses its gifts in service to God, the Church, and the world and reminds the congregation that all that follows in worship is an offering (liturgy—work of the people) as well. Finally, there are even some congregations that place the *Lord's Supper* during the first movement of the service. While this might seem to many an odd (and even inappropriate) reversal of the core movement from word to table, there is an interesting historical reason for this practice that we will discuss in the chapter reviewing **Table Practice**. For our current purposes, we need only to recognize that these congregations are ones that view the meal as an ordinance to be fulfilled instead of as a sacrament in which God acts. As the Church's meal, then, the Lord's Supper in the Gathering establishes the identity of the Church in a way no other liturgical action does.

A fourth function of calling the church out from serving God in the world as individuals to serving God communally in worship is to **set the tone for the service as a whole and foreshadow the theme(s)** that will come increasingly to the fore in the later movements of the liturgy. This can occur with all of the acts of worship in the Gathering, including the *prelude*. Recall the analogy of the hook in a plot for the Gathering. In the hook, the narrator does not give away the whole direction of the story to follow but somehow introduces and hints at what is to come. The Gathering likewise, makes a sort of subtle promise about what the congregation will be doing through the rest of the service without having to be in complete lockstep with the focus for the day. Rarely do worship planners find an opening *hymn of praise* that says exactly what they want said explicitly later in the scripture readings, sermon, and prayers. Instead, they find a hymn that overlaps and converses with the focus of the day. If the central text for the service is Genesis 1 and the theme centers on a specific aspect of a theology of creation, one might not be able to find a hymn that expresses that specific theological perspective but can easily find a hymn that praises God for creation as opposed to singing a hymn praising Christ for our redemption.

59

Proclamation

The second movement of the ordo is focused on one purpose: **speaking and hearing a word of God's good news for humankind and the world**. In the conversational model, then, this movement primarily represents the voice of God speaking to and with the congregation, Church, and world. God's voice is lifted up in two primary ways. The first is the *reading of ancient scripture*. The second is the offering of a message, which is usually called a *sermon*, *homily*, or a *meditation*. In some traditions, there are technical differences between these labels, but in most Mainline traditions, they simply indicate something about length (a sermon is longer than a homily) or tone (a meditation is less authoritative than a sermon). All these forms of proclamation should include interpretation of the scripture reading(s) as central to their composition. Too often it seems that the reading of scripture serves the sermon as its prelude, when it should be that the sermon serves the reading of scripture.

Even though we have only named two liturgical actions as part of the Proclamation movement of the service, compared to the larger number of possible options for the other three movements, it is noteworthy that Proclamation is often the longest portion of the service in terms of duration. Protestantism's emphasis on the word translates into great weight being placed on the sermon, and it is thus usually the longest single liturgical action in the service.

Moreover, while reading and preaching on scripture anchors this movement, other liturgical elements can be included. As with the sermon, any other liturgical actions taken in the Proclamation should serve scripture. A *prayer for illumination* before the scriptures (or a similar prayer before the sermon) asks God to reveal God-self and God's will through the reading of the text (or the message). Congregational, choral, or praise band *singing* is appropriate when it proclaims what the scripture proclaims and especially if a song is directly related to the text(s) for the day. For congregations that use multiple readings of scripture, a hymn, anthem, or piece of special music is sometimes placed between readings to break the monotonous feel produced by a long series of uninterrupted readings. While there is some practical wisdom behind this rationale, it is not a good enough reason theologically or liturgically for including music at this point. It is only justified if the song appropriately highlights themes from the reading it follows or precedes.

Finally, we should mention the relatively new development—that is, from a historical perspective—of the *children's sermon*. The inclination to be hospitable to children and make sure proclamation is extended to them has strong theological and liturgical support. Too often children's sermons, however, have nothing to do with the rest of the service, much less the scripture for the day. And sometimes, this element is moved early in the service so kids can be sent off to children's church as soon as possible. (It is ironic to send the children away during the portion of the service designated for Gathering the body of Christ.) We must be careful lest bringing the children forward becomes little more than children showing up on our favorite talk shows to break the monotony of adult guests. Avoid practices in which the children's sermon is more about the cuteness of the children and less about the word for the day.

Table/Response

After Proclamation comes Response. God speaks, and we reply. This does not mean that God's voice does not continue to be represented in the third movement of the ordo (especially in the traditions that view baptism and Table as sacraments), but the dominant character of the movement is that of **the congregation actively responding to the word proclaimed on this particular liturgical occasion**. In our analogy of the ordo to an underlying plot structure, the Response is related to the climax. This is not meant to diminish the role that the sermon, as the longest liturgical action, plays in the service, so much as to remind us that worship is, as Kierkegaard made so clear, at its core our offering to God.

As we have already noted, from very early times in church history, the ordo was focused on the movement from word to table. Thus the *Eucharist* is and should be the dominant liturgical action of this portion of the worship service. Having heard the word proclaimed, the community responds to God's invitation to be in communion with Christ and fellow Christians by feasting at the meal in which we remember together Christ's death and resurrection.

Similarly, having heard the word proclaimed, people in attendance who are not members are invited to enter into the fellowship of this worshiping community, indeed into the body of Christ itself. *Baptism* is often placed during the Gathering to get it out of the way. For traditions that baptize infants, this placement allows the parents to get the baby to the nursery as quickly as possible and avoid it crying throughout the service. For traditions that practice believers' baptism, this early placement gives everyone involved in the baptism a chance to get dry and return to worship. But baptism properly belongs as a response, not as a prelude to God's good news. So all rituals related to initiation—not only baptism but also *confirmation, transfer of membership, renewal of commitment*, and *remembering one's baptism*—belong in the third movement. This is why sermons in some traditions are so often followed by *invitations to discipleship* or *altar calls*. While the Response is anchored by the Table, when some element of the rituals of Christian initiation are involved, they should precede the Meal. That way the movement within the Response is from the font to the table.

Of course, there are responsive elements of the liturgy that are not sacramental in nature. These can be part of the Response when the Eucharist is observed but are all the more important in services of the word that do not include the Table. An *affirmation of faith* is often included after the sermon in most creedal traditions. After having heard a particular aspect of God's word proclaimed, the congregation responds by affirming the core content of the overarching story of the Christian faith. Congregants may or may not have agreed with what the preacher said, so the creed gives everyone a chance to come together in reciting ancient words that name the core of Christian doctrine (although ancient creeds, of course, require interpretation and elicit multiple interpretations, just as ancient scripture does).

While, as we noted above, the *prayer of confession* is most often found in the Gathering portion of worship, sometimes congregations include it here, particularly when Baptism or Table is included at this point in the service. Theologically, the rationale is that having heard God's calling proclaimed, we recognize our shortcomings and seek a word of assurance and thus confess our sins before we approach the table/altar. Or having heard God's grace proclaimed, we recognize our sinfulness. We do not confess our sins to convince God to forgive us. We confess our sins in light of God's having forgiven us.

Passing the peace is often included during the Response, especially as a community moves toward the Table. This practice grew out of the Matthean passage in which Jesus says, "So when you are offering your gift at the altar, if you remember that your brother or sister has something against you, leave your gift there before the altar and go; first be reconciled to your brother or sister, and then come and offer your gift" (Matt 5:23-24).

Singing is especially appropriate as part of the response to the word proclaimed. Hymns, anthems, and contemporary music can be found to express a whole range of responses from celebration for a gift received from God to commitment to God's mission in the world.

Similarly, the *prayers of the people* best fit as a response to the Proclamation. Whether the prayer is written in advance or offered extemporaneously, the one leading the prayer can intertwine the theme of the Proclamation with the broader adoration, confession, thanksgiving, supplication, and intercessions offered to God in prayer.

Finally, the *offering* best fits in the Response movement of the liturgy as well. Some congregations resist placing the offering late in the service because they feel like they are paying for the sermon, but the giving of money at this point is symbolic of the giving of one's whole self in response to the gospel. In many traditions, the monetary offering is brought forward at the same time as the bread and wine for Communion, so that the meaning of offering is expanded beyond just money.

Sending Forth

The heritage of evangelistic frontier religion shared by much of the Mainline Protestant church in North American has meant that sermons were oriented toward the individual hearers' being called to make a decision for Christ. The Response has thus often been limited to an altar call during a *hymn of dedication* and the service ended with a quick *dismissal* to which was given little thought. As the liturgical renewal movement, however, led to a renewed appreciation of the Meal at the center of the Response, so has the Sending Forth come to be seen as an important part of the liturgy in its own right, instead of simply as the way to let people know the service was over.

In a word, the purpose of the fourth and final movement of the ordo is to **dismiss the congregation with a sense of purpose and direction as well as a sense of being under God's providential care**. Two liturgical elements are essential for this to occur. The first is a *commission* or *charge* extended to the congregation. These are words that send the congregation out to do something during the week: "Go forth and _____." The second is the *benediction* or *final blessing* prayed over the congregation. Often traditional biblical blessings are used for this (e.g., Num 6:24-26). Also in most churches, the benediction involves the use of a Trinitarian formula (e.g., 2 Cor 13:13), but not always.

In most traditions, the commission and benediction are combined, and in printed bulletins, congregants only see "Benediction" or "Dismissal" listed. It is better to separate them, because too often, preachers give only one or the other. To be charged but not blessed at the end of worship results in a loss of grace. To be blessed but not charged results in a loss of vocation. The charge and the blessing are usually spoken by the preacher for the day. She will offer a charge and need barely take a breath before raising her hands over and blessing the congregation.

In addition to the commission and benediction, congregations usually *sing* a closing hymn or song during the Sending Forth. This can certainly still be a hymn of dedication as mentioned above, but a wider range of themes and tones of closing congregational singing is also appropriate. Worship planners should choose songs with language that relates the theme of the day to life beyond the walls of the church. As the opening music foreshadows the themes to be proclaimed and responded to, the closing song should echo back to and reaffirm those themes in some way. Also, sometimes the benediction itself is sung, or a short response (such as an Amen) is sung after it.

Some traditions include a *closing prayer* alongside or in place of a benediction. Instead of the preacher pronouncing God's blessing upon the congregation, in this prayer the congregation prays for God's blessing in the coming days, in relation to the word for the day.

Also, some churches close with the *passing the peace* so that, in a sense, everyone offers the benediction to everyone else. More often, this liturgical act occurs earlier in the service as we have already noted, but certainly an informal greeting time occurs at the end of most Christian worship services that resonates with the passing of the peace.

Finally, if the service began with a prelude, it will likely end with a *postlude*. This piece should be appropriate to the themes and tone for the day. But here at the end of the service, the postlude is usually (but not always need be) an upbeat song that lifts the feet of worshipers as they head out the door and into the world.

Sample Ordo

The basic Lord's Day liturgy of **Reformed Church of America** below (copyright © Reformed Church Press; used by permission) will serve well as a case study for the fourfold ordo described above. As you read through the resource that follows, note how the denomination adapts the fourfold ordo, and identify features that are different from those described above as well as those feature that the denomination prescribes as essential versus those that are optional.

The basic services offered by other denominations can be found in the following:

The African Methodist Episcopal Zion Book of Worship, 1, 9–15

AMEC Book of Worship of the African Methodist Episcopal Church, 9–15

Book of Common Prayer (Episcopal Church, USA), 323–44

Book of Common Worship (Presbyterian Church (USA), 18–30

Book of Ritual (CME), 2–3, 9

Book of Worship: United Church of Christ, 31–54

Celebrate God's Presence (United Church of Canada), 1–8

Chalice Worship (DOC), 5–10

Evangelical Lutheran Worship (ELCA), 92–93

The United Methodist Book of Worship, 13–32

CONGREGATIONAL SERVICES

ORDER OF WORSHIP FOR THE LORD'S DAY

The service of worship ordinarily begins with the Votum, Sentences, and Salutation. Or it may begin with the Hymn, especially if it is a processional, followed by the Votum, Sentences, and Salutation.

THE APPROACH TO GOD

VOTUM

Our help is in the name of the Lord,
who made heaven and earth.
Amen.   *Psalm 124:8*

SENTENCES

The following, or other appropriate portions of Scripture, may be used.

O come, let us worship and bow down,
let us kneel before the Lord, our Maker!
For he is our God,
and we are the people of his pasture,
and the sheep of his hand.   *Psalm 95:6-7*

And/or

Psalm 33:1-5	*Psalm 100*
Zechariah 8:7-8	*Psalm 43:3-4*
Exodus 15:2	*John 4:24*
Psalm 96:1-3	*Isaiah 55:1, 6-7*

SALUTATION

Grace to you and peace from God our Father and the Lord Jesus Christ.
Amen.

Or

Galatians 1:3-5	*2 Peter 1:2*
Jude 2	*1 Timothy 1:2*
2 John 3	*Revelation 1:4-5*
Titus 1:4	

HYMN

PRAYER OF CONFESSION

The minister may introduce the prayer with the following, or another suitable call to confession.

Let us confess our sins to almighty God. Let us pray.

All shall join in one of the following prayers or another appropriate confession.

Have mercy upon us, O God,
according to your steadfast love;
according to your abundant mercies,
blot out our transgressions.
Wash us thoroughly from our iniquity,
and cleanse us from our sin.
For we know our transgressions,
and our sin is ever before us.
Create in us a clean heart, O God,
and put a new and right spirit within us.
Cast us not away from your presence,
and take not your Holy Spirit from us.
Restore to us the joy of your salvation,
and uphold us with a willing spirit.
Through Jesus Christ our Lord. Amen.

Adapted from Psalm 51

Or

Most holy and merciful Father,
we acknowledge and confess before you our sinful nature,
prone to evil and slow to do good;
and all our shortcomings and offenses.
You alone know how often we have sinned:
in wandering from your ways, in wasting your gifts,
in forgetting your love.
But, O Lord, have mercy on us,
who are ashamed and sorry for all wherein we have displeased you.
Teach us to hate our errors;
cleanse us from our secret faults;
and forgive our sins;
for the sake of your dear Son.

2 / LORD'S DAY

And, O most holy and loving God,
help us to live in your light and walk in your ways,
according to the commandments of Jesus Christ, our Savior. Amen.

A brief period for silent prayers may be allowed. The following or another
suitable response may then be said or sung.

Lord, have mercy upon us.
Christ, have mercy upon us.
Lord, have mercy upon us.

ASSURANCE OF PARDON

One of the following scriptural assurances or one drawn from other portions
of Scripture may be used to convey an assurance of God's promise freely to
pardon all who come to him in repentance and faith.

The Lord is merciful and gracious,
slow to anger and abounding in steadfast love.
He does not deal with us according to our sins,
nor repay us according to our iniquities.
For as the heavens are high above the earth,
so great is his steadfast love toward those who fear him;
as far as the east is from the west,
so far he removes our transgressions from us.

Psalm 103:8, 10-12

Or

With everlasting love I will have compassion on you,
says the Lord, your Redeemer.
I, I am he who blots out your transgressions for my own sake,
and I will not remember your sins.
Return to me, for I have redeemed you.

Isaiah 54:8; 43:25; 44:22

Or

Can a woman forget her nursing child,
or show no compassion for the child of her womb?
As a mother comforts her child,
so will I comfort you, says the Lord.

Isaiah 49:15; 66:13

LORD'S DAY / 3

67

Or

For God so loved the world that he gave his only Son,
so that everyone who believes in him may not perish
but may have eternal life.
Indeed, God did not send the Son into the world to condemn the world,
but in order that the world might be saved through him.

John 3:16-17

Or

Psalm 130:3-4, 7   *Isaiah 44:21-22*
John 8:34-36   *Psalm 145:18-19*
Luke 1:68, 77-78   *Colossians 1:11-14*

At the conclusion of the scriptural assurance, the minister shall add:

Believe this Gospel and go forth to live in peace. **Amen.**

THE LAW OF GOD

The Law may be read or sung, or the service may proceed to the reading of
the Summary.

Then God spoke all these words:
I am the Lord your God,
who brought you out of the land of Egypt,
out of the house of slavery;

you shall have no other gods before me.

You shall not make for yourself an idol,
whether in the form of anything that is in heaven above,
or that is on the earth beneath,
or that is in the water under the earth.
You shall not bow down to them or worship them;
for I the Lord your God am a jealous God,
punishing children for the iniquity of parents,
to the third and the fourth generation of those who reject me,
but showing steadfast love to the thousandth generation of those
who love me and keep my commandments.

You shall not make wrongful use of the name of the Lord your God,
for the Lord will not acquit anyone who misuses his name.

4 / LORD'S DAY

Remember the sabbath day, and keep it holy.
Six days you shall labor and do all your work.
But the seventh day is a sabbath to the Lord your God;
you shall not do any work—
you, your son or your daughter, your male or female slave, your livestock,
or the alien resident in your towns.
For in six days the Lord made heaven and earth, the sea,
and all that is in them,
but rested the seventh day;
therefore the Lord blessed the sabbath day and consecrated it.

Honor your father and your mother,
so that your days may be long in the land
that the Lord your God is giving you.

You shall not murder.

You shall not commit adultery.

You shall not steal.

You shall not bear false witness against your neighbor.

You shall not covet your neighbor's house;
you shall not covet your neighbor's wife,
or male or female slave, or ox, or donkey, or anything
that belongs to your neighbor.

Exodus 20:1-17

And/or

Hear what our Lord Jesus Christ says:
"You shall love the Lord your God
with all your heart,
and with all your soul,
and with all your mind."
This is the greatest and first commandment.
And a second is like it:
"You shall love your neighbor as yourself."
On these two commandments
hang all the law and the prophets.

Matthew 22:37-40

or as it is recorded in Mark 12:29-31.

Lord's Day / 5

PSALTER AND GLORIA PATRI

A selection from the Psalms and the Gloria Patri or another appropriate hymn may be sung to express gratitude to God.

THE WORD OF GOD IN PROCLAMATION AND SACRAMENT

PRAYER FOR ILLUMINATION

This prayer or another petition may be offered.

Guide us, O Lord,
by your Word and Holy Spirit,
that in your light we may see light,
in your truth find freedom,
and in your will discover peace;
through Jesus Christ our Lord. **Amen.**

LESSONS

There will ordinarily be two or three lessons, one from the Old Testament, one from the portion of the New Testament other than the Gospels, and one from the Gospels. The Psalm for the day may be said or sung following the first lesson. A hymn or anthem reflecting the Scriptures of the day may be sung between the lessons. The lessons may be announced as follows:

The Word of the Lord from _____.

After the reading of the lesson there may be the response:

This is the Word of the Lord.
Thanks be to God.

The Gospel may be announced as follows:

The Gospel of our Lord Jesus Christ according to _____.

The following may be used as a response to the Gospel:

This is the Gospel of the Lord.
Praise to you, O Christ.

SERMON

The minister shall deliver a sermon proclaiming the Scripture of the day.

PRAYER FOR BLESSING

Almighty God,
grant that the words we have heard this day
may, through your grace, be so grafted within our hearts
that they may bring forth in us the fruits of the Spirit,
to the honor and praise of your name;
through Jesus Christ our Lord. **Amen.**

The minister shall move to the table.

When worship includes only the grace of the Word in Proclamation, then the
Creed, Offering, Doxology, Prayers of Thanksgiving and Intercession,
Hymn, and Benediction may be understood as the congregation's Response
to God.

CONFESSION OF FAITH

The minister shall call the people to join in an affirmation of the Christian
faith.

Let us confess our Christian faith using the Nicene [or Apostles'] Creed:

When all have risen, the minister shall say:

Let us say what we believe.

A   THE NICENE CREED

We believe in one God,
 the Father, the Almighty,
 maker of heaven and earth,
 of all that is, seen and unseen.

We believe in one Lord, Jesus Christ,
 the only Son of God,
 eternally begotten of the Father,
 God from God, Light from Light,
 true God from true God,
 begotten, not made,

of one Being with the Father;
through him all things were made.
For us and for our salvation
he came down from heaven,
was incarnate of the Holy Spirit and the Virgin Mary
and became truly human.
For our sake he was crucified under Pontius Pilate;
he suffered death and was buried.
On the third day he rose again
in accordance with the Scriptures;
he ascended into heaven
and is seated at the right hand of the Father.
He will come again in glory to judge the living and the dead,
and his kingdom will have no end.

We believe in the Holy Spirit, the Lord, the giver of life,
who proceeds from the Father [and the Son],
who with the Father and the Son is worshiped and glorified,
who has spoken through the prophets.
We believe in one holy catholic and apostolic Church.
We acknowledge one baptism for the forgiveness of sins.
We look for the resurrection of the dead,
and the life of the world to come. Amen.

Or

B   THE NICENE CREED

We believe in one God,
   the Father almighty,
   maker of heaven and earth,
   and of all things visible and invisible;

And in one Lord Jesus Christ,
   the only-begotten Son of God,
   begotten of his Father before all worlds,
   God of God, Light of Light,
   very God of very God,
   begotten, not made,
   being of one substance with the Father;
   by whom all things were made;
   who for us and for our salvation
   came down from heaven,
   and was incarnate by the Holy Ghost of the Virgin Mary,

and was made man;
and was crucified also for us under Pontius Pilate;
he suffered and was buried;
and the third day he rose again according to the Scriptures,
and ascended into heaven,
and sitteth on the right hand of the Father;
and he shall come again, with glory,
to judge both the quick and the dead;
whose kingdom shall have no end.

And we believe in the Holy Ghost, the Lord and giver of life,
who proceedeth from the Father and the Son;
who with the Father and the Son together is worshiped
and glorified;
who spake by the Prophets,
and we believe in one holy catholic and apostolic Church;
we acknowledge one baptism for the remission of sins;
and we look for the resurrection of the dead,
and the life of the world to come. Amen.

Or

A   THE APOSTLES' CREED

I believe in God, the Father almighty,
creator of heaven and earth.

I believe in Jesus Christ, God's only Son, our Lord,
who was conceived by the Holy Spirit
born of the Virgin Mary,
suffered under Pontius Pilate,
was crucified, died, and was buried;
he descended to the dead.
On the third day he rose again;
he ascended into heaven,
he is seated at the right hand of the Father,
and he will come to judge the living and the dead.

I believe in the Holy Spirit,
the holy catholic Church,
the communion of saints,
the forgiveness of sins,
the resurrection of the body,
and the life everlasting. Amen.

Or

B   THE APOSTLES' CREED

I believe in God, the Father almighty,
    maker of heaven and earth;

And in Jesus Christ, his only Son, our Lord;
    who was conceived by the Holy Ghost,
    born of the Virgin Mary,
    suffered under Pontius Pilate,
    was crucified, dead, and buried.
    He descended into hell.
    The third day he rose again from the dead.
    He ascended into heaven,
    and sitteth on the right hand of God the Father almighty.
    From thence he shall come to judge the quick and the dead.

I believe in the Holy Ghost,
    the holy catholic Church,
    the communion of saints,
    the forgiveness of sins,
    the resurrection of the body,
    and the life everlasting. Amen.

PEACE

The minister may introduce the Peace with these, or other appropriate words
of Scripture:

Let the peace of Christ rule in your hearts, to which indeed you were called
in the one body.

Colossians 3:15

The peace of Christ be with you.
And also with you.

The congregation may then exchange the Peace using the same greeting and
response or through other appropriate words and actions.

OFFERING

As the offerings are gathered there may be an anthem or other musical offering. The elements for the Lord's Supper may be brought forward with the offering.

DOXOLOGY

This hymn, or another ascription of praise, may be used as the offerings are brought forward.

MEANING OF THE SACRAMENT

Beloved in the Lord Jesus Christ,
the holy Supper which we are about to celebrate
is a feast of remembrance, of communion, and of hope.

We come in remembrance
that our Lord Jesus Christ was sent of the Father into the world
to assume our flesh and blood
and to fulfill for us all obedience to the divine law,
even to the bitter and shameful death of the cross.
By his death, resurrection, and ascension
he established a new and eternal covenant of grace and reconciliation
that we might be accepted of God and never be forsaken by him.

We come to have communion with this same Christ
who has promised to be with us always, even to the end of the world.
In the breaking of the bread he makes himself known to us
as the true heavenly Bread that strengthens us unto life eternal.
In the cup of blessing he comes to us as the Vine
in whom we must abide if we are to bear fruit.

We come in hope,
believing that this bread and this cup
are a pledge and foretaste of the feast of love
of which we shall partake when his kingdom has fully come,
when with unveiled face we shall behold him,
made like unto him in his glory.

Since by his death, resurrection, and ascension
Christ has obtained for us the life-giving Spirit
who unites us all in one body,
so are we to receive this Supper in true love,
mindful of the communion of saints.

Most righteous God,
we remember in this Supper
the perfect sacrifice offered once on the cross by our Lord Jesus Christ
for the sin of the whole world.

In the joy of his resurrection and in expectation of his coming again,
we offer ourselves to you as holy and living sacrifices.

Together we proclaim the mystery of the faith:

Here all shall say or sing:

Christ has died!
Christ is risen!
Christ will come again!

Send your Holy Spirit upon us, we pray,
that the bread which we break
and the cup which we bless
may be to us the communion of the body and blood of Christ.
Grant that, being joined together in him,
we may attain to the unity of the faith
and grow up in all things into Christ our Lord.

And as this grain has been gathered from many fields into one loaf,
and these grapes from many hills into one cup,
grant, O Lord, that your whole Church
may soon be gathered from the ends of the earth
into your kingdom.
Even so, come, Lord Jesus!

COMMUNION

The minister shall declare the Words of Institution.

In full view of the people the minister shall take the bread and say:

The Lord Jesus, the same night he was betrayed, took bread;
and when he had given thanks,
he broke it

The minister shall break the bread.

LORD'S DAY / 13

and gave it to them, saying,
"Take, eat;
this is my body which is given for you:
do this in remembrance of me."

Lifting the cup, the minister shall say:

After the same manner also, he took the cup when they had supped,
saying, "This cup is the new testament in my blood:
this do, as often as you drink it, in remembrance of me."

In partaking of the bread it shall be said:

The bread which we break
is the communion of the body of Christ.

In partaking of the cup it shall be said:

The cup of blessing which we bless
is the communion of the blood of Christ.

THE RESPONSE TO GOD

THANKSGIVING AFTER COMMUNION

Brothers and sisters,
since the Lord has now fed us at his Table,
let us praise God's holy name with heartfelt thanksgiving!
Bless the Lord, O my soul,
and all that is within me, bless his holy name.
Bless the Lord, O my soul,
and do not forget all his benefits—
who forgives all your iniquity,
who heals all your diseases,
who redeems your life from the Pit,
who crowns you with steadfast love and mercy.
The Lord is merciful and gracious,
slow to anger and abounding in steadfast love.
He does not deal with us according to our sins,
nor repay us according to our iniquities.
For as the heavens are high above the earth,
so great is his steadfast love toward those who fear him;
as far as the east is from the west,
so far does he remove our transgressions from us.

14 / Lord's Day

As a father has compassion for his children,
so the Lord has compassion for those who fear him,
who did not spare his own Son,
but gave him up for us all,
and will also give us all things with him.
Therefore shall my mouth and heart show forth the praise of the Lord,
from this time forth forevermore. Amen.

From Psalm 103, with additions

INTERCESSION

The following prayers may be used. Intercessions may be selected from
other sources or may be in the minister's own words. The intercessions shall
conclude with the Lord's Prayer.

Let us pray.

We praise and thank you, O Lord,
that you have fed us at your Table.
Grateful for your gifts and mindful of the communion of your saints,
we offer to you our prayers for all people.

God of compassion,
we remember before you
the poor and the afflicted,
the sick and the dying,
prisoners and all who are lonely,
the victims of war, injustice, and inhumanity,
and all others who suffer from whatever their sufferings may be called.

Silence

O Lord of Providence,
who holds the destiny of the nations in your hand,
we pray for our country.
Inspire the hearts and minds of our leaders
that they, together with all our nation,
may first seek your kingdom and righteousness
so that order, liberty, and peace may dwell with your people.

Silence

O God the Creator,
we pray for all nations and peoples.

LORD'S DAY / 15

Take away the mistrust and lack of understanding
that divide your creatures;
increase in us the recognition that we are all your children.

Silence

O Savior God,
look upon your church in its struggle upon the earth.
Have mercy on its weakness,
bring to an end its unhappy divisions,
and scatter its fears.
Look also upon the ministry of your church.
Increase its courage, strengthen its faith,
and inspire its witness to all people,
even to the ends of the earth.

Silence

Author of grace and God of love,
send your Holy Spirit's blessing to your children here present.
Keep our hearts and thoughts in Jesus Christ, your Son, our only Savior,
who has taught us to pray:

Our Father in heaven,
  hallowed be your name,
  your kingdom come,
  your will be done,
  on earth as in heaven.
Give us today our daily bread.
Forgive us our sins
  as we forgive those who sin against us.
Save us from the time of trial,
  and deliver us from evil.
For the kingdom, the power,
  and the glory are yours,
  now and forever. Amen.

Or

Our Father, who art in heaven,
  hallowed be thy name,
  thy kingdom come,
  thy will be done,

on earth as it is in heaven.
Give us this day our daily bread.
And forgive us our debts,
   as we forgive our debtors.
And lead us not into temptation,
   but deliver us from evil.
For thine is the kingdom,
   and the power, and the glory,
   forever. Amen.

HYMN

BENEDICTION

Facing the congregation, the minister shall give the blessing:

The grace of the Lord Jesus Christ,
the love of God,
and the communion of the Holy Spirit be with all of you.
Amen!

2 Corinthians 13:13

Or

Numbers 6:24-26	*Luke 2:29-32*
2 Thessalonians 3:16	*Psalm 67:1-2*
Romans 15:5-6	*Hebrews 13:20-21*

THE LITURGICAL YEAR

We began our study of liturgical time with an exploration of the general, theological understanding of time in Judeo-Christian traditions. From this broad orientation, we looked at the way the Church structures the actual time when the community gathers for worship—first in terms of worshiping weekly on the Lord's Day and then in terms of the Christian ordo. Now we turn our attention to the church calendar, that is, the liturgical construct of the annual liturgical cycle.

Remember that we said one of the earliest liturgical innovations as Christianity evolved from a movement within first-century Judaism into an independent religion was the move from worshiping on the Sabbath to worshiping on the Lord's Day. The Christian calendar of seasons and holy days, however, evolved much more slowly, and the process was messy. The evolution revolved around two celebrations of key moments in the story of the Christ event: resurrection and nativity. We are going to begin by looking at this historical development, and then we will revisit the church calendar and walk through the course of a year as it currently stands.

HISTORICAL SKETCH OF THE EVOLUTION OF THE LITURGICAL CALENDAR

From Pascha to Ash Wednesday through Pentecost

If the movement from Sabbath to the Lord's Day was the first major liturgical innovation in relation to time, the second was the creation of **Pascha**. *Pascha* is the Greek word for the Jewish Passover, and its verb form means "to suffer." This holy day name may be unfamiliar to readers, but some may have heard of a "paschal candle" or heard Christ referred to as the "Paschal Lamb." The early church came to use *Pascha* the Christian Passover. *Pascha* was a unitive celebration of the center of the story of the Christ Event—Christ's suffering, death, resurrection, and glorification—which the Gospels set as occurring in relation to Passover.

But over time this celebration spread out and broke into multiple separate commemorations. The evolution went something like this. First, out of *Pascha* came what we now call **Easter**, celebrating the resurrection, **Good Friday**, marking Jesus's death, and **Maundy Thursday**, remembering Jesus's Last Supper and washing of the disciples' feet. This set of holy days is called the Triduum. The term may not be familiar to many Protestants, but it is an important concept. The term refers to the three-day period that extends from Thursday evening through Sunday evening. These three days are key to understanding Christianity's historically rooted identity and values.

From the Easter celebration of the resurrection emerged the celebration of the gift of the Spirit on **Pentecost** and from it the celebration of the **Ascension**. The timing of these celebrations (Ascension Day occurring forty days after Easter Sunday and Pentecost fifty days after Easter Sunday) is rooted in the chronology established in Acts 1–2.

In sum, *Pascha*—a one-day commemoration of the suffering, death, resurrection, and glorification—grew into Easter *as a season*. The season is usually simply called Easter (as in "the Third Sunday of Easter") but is sometimes referred to as **Eastertide**. It also appropriately is called **the Great Fifty Days**.

Because part of the celebration of Easter included baptism into the faith, a period of preparation and catechism developed leading up to the initiation. In different regions, this period lasted different lengths of time, even as long as three years. But a period just before Easter developed where the instruction and preparation intensified. It eventually became a **forty-day** period modeled on Jesus's forty days being tempted in the wilderness. The period is called **Lent** today. Lent begins on **Ash Wednesday**, lasts forty days (not counting Sundays), and goes through **Holy Week**.

Thus in terms of the liturgical calendar, the first historical development was the evolution of Pascha into the seasons Lent and Easter, with Easter Sunday as the most important day of the series.

EXCURSUS: THE DATING OF EASTER SUNDAY

One of the oddities of the evolution of the church year is the dating of Easter. While Christmas is anchored on December 25, Easter Sunday changes from year to year. Every year some parishioner will ask, "Why does Easter move around?" Or "Why is Easter so early (or late) this year?" Here is what pastors can tell them (or what they can bring up at really boring dinner parties). It is a complicated story, but the basics can be told in brief form.

In the early church, there were two primary competing methods of dating Easter, both in relation to Passover. Some churches celebrated Easter on the day of Passover, on *Pascha*, according to the Jewish calendar. The

Jewish calendar is a lunar calendar that differs from the solar calendar that became the primary construct for determining the length and monthly divisions of the year, so each year Passover falls on a different day in the solar calendar. Still, the date of Passover according to the **Hebrew calendar** is always on the fourteenth day of the month of Nisan. So Christians who observed Easter on this date were labeled **Quartodecimans** (from the Latin word for "fourteen").

But since Passover fell on different days of the week, others argued that Easter should always be celebrated on Sunday as the day of resurrection. So these people celebrated Easter on the Sunday after Passover. In the second century, this latter option took the lead.

There were still regional differences, however. So, in the year 325, the **Council of Nicea** regulated the dating of Easter using the most complex formula anyone could imagine: *Easter is the first Sunday after the ecclesiastical full moon following the vernal equinox (set as March 21)*.

No astronomy professor ever mentioned an "ecclesiastical" full moon. The *astronomical full moon* occurs when you look up in the sky and see that the whole moon (or technically all of one hemisphere) is visible. An *ecclesiastical full moon* comes from a fictional calendar that mathematically determines when the full moon occurs. To be able to answer a parishioner who asks *why* Easter changes, one need not know that mathematical formula. We just need to know that it was set in the ancient church so that Easter could be determined forever and ever. Similarly, the vernal equinox can actually occur on either March 20 or 21, but in the church formula it is set as March 21 for the sake of consistency.

But even that is not the end of the story. Printed and online calendars that list holidays will often place Easter on one Sunday and "Orthodox Easter" on another. Why is that? Well, as astronomy became more sophisticated, errors in the **Julian calendar** were better understood. Thus, in 1582, the **Gregorian calendar** was established (which is what we use today). Even though the Gregorian calendar was adopted by almost every country over the next few centuries, the Eastern Orthodox Church continued to use a form of the Julian calendar for determining *liturgical* dates (similar to Judaism continuing to use the lunar calendar to determine liturgical dates). So sometimes the East and West celebrate Easter on the same day (that is, when the Julian and Gregorian calendars agree), and sometimes they do not.

From Epiphany to Advent through Christmas

Whereas the first set of holy days and seasons to evolve in church history dealt with the end of Jesus's earthly life, the next set dealt with the beginning. In the Eastern part of the Roman Empire, a celebration called **Epiphany** developed. The Greek root of *epiphany* means "revelation," and the day of Epiphany was a celebration of the revelation of Christ. Like Pascha, Epiphany was a unitive celebration. It did not focus on a single event in Jesus's life but on a range of events, in which God revealed the true nature of Christ to the world. Central to these revelations was the nativity of Jesus, especially the visitation of the Magi found in Matthew 2:1-12, because this story was traditionally interpreted as the first revelation of Christ to the Gentiles. Included in the celebration as well was Jesus's baptism, during which the heavens open, and the Spirit descends upon him (Matt 3:13-17; Mark 1:9-11; Luke 3:21-22; John 1:29-34); Jesus's first sign, the turning of water into wine at the wedding in Cana (John 2:1-11); and the transfiguration, in which Jesus's true glory was revealed when Moses and Elijah appeared with him on the mountaintop (Matt 17:1-8; Mark 9:2-8; Luke 9:28-36). This celebration was held on **January 6**.

In the Western part of the Empire, a different celebration that came to be called **Christmas** (Christ + mass) developed independently of Epiphany. It came along later than Epiphany developed, and unlike the Eastern holy day, Christmas was not a unitive celebration. It was a celebration focused solely on Christ's birth, especially as narrated in Luke's Gospel with its emphasis on Mary, and the angelic appearance to the shepherds (Luke 2:1-20). The celebration was held on **December 25**, assimilating the timing and practices of celebrating the winter solstice.

As the two celebrations of Epiphany and Christmas spread throughout the Empire, they came into conflict, because both celebrated Christ's nativity but in different ways. Instead of one winning out and the other disappearing, Christmas on December 25 became the celebration of the birth proper, and Epiphany broke apart, if you will, with January 6 celebrating the visitation of the Magi, the Sunday after Epiphany celebrating Jesus's baptism, the Sunday after that becoming the traditional day for recalling the wedding at Cana, and the transfiguration later. Christmas Day to Epiphany became the season of Christmas (sometimes called **Christmastide**), the **Twelve Days of Christmas**.

This is not the last of the developments related to this period, however. Over time a season of penitence and preparation developed before Christmas and Epiphany. Baptisms were associated with Epiphany, so it was natural to have a period of catechism here that paralleled Lent. The season came to be called **Advent**. Early on Advent lasted five weeks (like Lent), but over time it was reduced to four.

Completing the Church Year

Out of these two stages of historical development has evolved the whole of the liturgical year as we know it today. The annual cycle of seasons and holy days is not a circle but an ellipse that revolves, as we have seen, around two foci: Christmas (Christ's nativity) and Easter (Christ's resurrection).

- The Church year begins with Advent, the four Sundays prior to Christmas.

- The season of Christmas is quite short, the twelve days from Christmas—really Christmas Eve—to Epiphany.

- After Epiphany, there is a break before thematic seasons begin again. This period is considered Sundays in **Ordinary Time**. Ordinary does not mean "normal" so much as Sundays numbered using "ordinals." When we count using cardinal numbers, we use whole numbers to name quantity—1, 2, 3, and so on. When we count using ordinal numbers, we do so to name relational order—first, second, third, and so on. Thus, in bulletins, Sundays in this series are usually listed as, for example, "Third Sunday after Epiphany" or "Fourth Sunday after Epiphany." (Although we continue to count the Sundays after Epiphany in the manner of Ordinary Time, in recent years, this stretch of time has come to be celebrated in some ways like a season, extending from Epiphany and Baptism of the Lord to the celebration of Transfiguration.)

- After Ordinary Time, or the Season of Epiphany, Lent starts with Ash Wednesday and runs for forty days (not counting Sundays) through Holy Week.

- Lent prepares for the Season of Easter that runs from the Easter Sunday (or really from the Easter Vigil on Saturday night) through Pentecost Sunday.

- Like the Sundays after Epiphany, the Sundays after Pentecost are Sundays in Ordinary Time. Although there are some thematic days in this period, it is not a thematically focused season. It extends from Pentecost to the Reign of Christ Sunday (the last Sunday of the liturgical calendar before the beginning of Advent in a new liturgical year) and lasts nearly half the calendar year.

Having examined the historical development of the liturgical year in broad strokes, we now need to explore each season individually in the order in which the year unfolds.

EXCURSUS: LECTIONARIES

Before we turn to our chronological exploration of the liturgical year, we need to pause to recognize that alongside the evolution of the Church's holy days and seasons is the evolution of the **lectionary**. So closely tied are the liturgical year and the lectionary that one can only fully appreciate the current shape of the liturgical calendar if one understands the development and shape of the Church's lectionaries.

The word *lectionary* comes from the Latin *lectio* meaning "to read." The lectionary approach was traditionally called *lectio selecta*, that is, selected readings (*lections*) in a specific order. Some Jewish communities pre-dating the Church seem to have followed lectionary readings through the Torah and the Prophets over a set period of time. With this practice in its background, the Church associated specific readings with specific holy days as they developed and evolved. Slowly the set of readings was filled out to cover the entire year, but there were significant differences in tables of readings across the regions. It was not until the **Catholic Reformation** that the **Council of Trent** (1545–63) standardized the lectionary for the whole Roman Catholic Church. This lectionary prescribed an Epistle and Gospel reading for every Sunday on an annual cycle. While there were a few exceptions, such as when a reading from the Hebrew Bible would be substituted for the Epistle reading, the Hebrew Bible was for the most part neglected. Psalms, or really portions of psalms, did continue to be used liturgically as **graduals**—responses chanted following the Epistle reading—but not as a reading for its own sake. This **Tridentine lectionary** continued to be authoritative for the Roman Catholic Church for four hundred years.

Of course, the churches of the Protestant Reformation(s) were in no way bound by this lectionary. Still, because they all grew out of the medieval church, they shared some readings with the Tridentine lectionary, especially on holy days. Protestant reading of scripture in worship, however, often followed a pattern of the preacher working through a book of the Bible, verse by verse, passage by passage, week after week. This practice is referred to as *lectio continua* (Latin, "continuous reading") and was also a practice with a precedent in the early church. Across the next four hundred years, some Protestant denominations, especially those with more formal liturgical practices (e.g., Anglican and Lutheran) developed their own lectionaries. For many congregations, however, choices were made Sunday by Sunday, based on what the preacher felt called to preach on.

It was not until the **Second Vatican Council** (1962–65) that the Roman Catholic Church reformed its lectionary as part of reforming the liturgy more broadly. The document defining liturgical reforms was entitled the **Constitution on the Sacred Liturgy**, and it decreed that "the treasures of the Bible be opened up more lavishly so that richer fare might be provided for the faithful at the table of God's word and a more representative portion of sacred scripture be read to the people over a set cycle of years." From that decree came the **Lectionary for Mass** of 1969. It expanded the readings for each Sunday over a three-year cycle to include a reading from the Hebrew Bible, a responsorial Psalm, an Epistle reading, and a reading from the Gospel.

Each year of the cycle focused primarily on one of the Synoptic Gospels: Year A, Matthew; Year B, Mark; Year C, Luke. John is read here and there throughout the three years. While the liturgical calendar determined the choices of lections for Advent through Pentecost, during Ordinary Time the Lectionary for Mass utilized (as one of two options) a modified *lectio continua*, providing semicontinuous readings for the Epistle and Gospel lections.

Various Mainline Protestant denominations immediately adapted the Lectionary for Mass for their own congregations. The result was a wide array of lectionaries being used in Mainline Protestantism. An ecumenical lectionary would grow out of this diversity. In 1969, the **Consultation on Common Texts** (CCT), an ecumenical group formed in response to Vatican II's liturgical reforms, began working on English-language liturgical texts to be shared across traditions. Because of the growing popularity of lectionaries among Mainline Protestant denominations and congregations, in 1978, the CCT took up the charge to harmonize the different lectionaries into a single ecumenical version. The result was the Common Lectionary that began being used in 1983.

After extensive use and feedback provided by sponsoring denominations, the lectionary was revised in 1992, resulting in the **Revised Common Lectionary** (RCL) that is used in most Protestant denominations and congregations that follow a lectionary today. For example, one of the changes that can be seen between the Common and Revised Lectionaries is the inclusion of more biblical texts about or involving women. A second change is that during Ordinary Time, alternate readings were selected from the Hebrew Bible and the Psalter that follows the semicontinuous pattern being used in the Epistle and Gospel lections. While the Lectionary for Mass improved over the Tridentine Lectionary by including readings from the

Hebrew Bible, these readings were subordinate to the Gospel readings, in that they were chosen to support the themes of those New Testament texts. The semicontinuous readings in the RCL invite the reading of the First Testament and the Epistles on their own terms.

The liturgical year and lectionaries exist in a symbiotic relationship. They evolved together throughout church history, with each shaping the evolution of the other. And, more recently, Mainline Protestant interest in the lectionary arose in the latter part of the twentieth century, along with a reclamation of the liturgical year in many traditions. For many North American Protestant denominations, much of the liturgical calendar beyond Christmas and Easter, perhaps with a slight nod of the head to Lent and Advent, had been intentionally rejected or unintentionally neglected over time. While the causes for this loss of the liturgical cycle and the use of lectionary were many, three of the most obvious are the frontier, evangelical heritage of these denominations, a Protestant emphasis on a theology of the word, and an anti-Catholic sentiment found among many Protestants. The confluence of the rise of historical liturgical scholarship early in the twentieth century, Vatican II's reformation of Catholic worship, and the emphasis on ecumenism in the mid-twentieth century, however, led to renewed practices involving the liturgical calendar and the lectionary among Protestants.

SKETCH OF THE CHURCH CALENDAR IN ITS CURRENT SHAPE

Advent

We begin our walk through the liturgical year as it is currently observed with the season of Advent, which involves the four Sundays before Christmas. Advent begins on the last Sunday of November or the first Sunday in December, depending on what day of the week December 25 falls. The word *advent* comes from the Latin *ad* (to) *venire* (to come). In secular idiom, the "Christmas season" is the time of preparation leading up to December 25. It begins with the appearance of Santa Claus at the close of the Macy's Thanksgiving Day Parade and ends on Christmas Day. Thus, sometimes laity mistakenly see Advent as a pre-Christmas season in the same fashion as this secular season.

Advent, however, is not just a time for preparing for Christ's birth; it is a time of preparing for the coming of God-in-Christ to us more broadly—past, present, and future. The season reverses chronology, in order to set theological priorities for the year as a whole.

Thus, the Christian year begins at the End, with a capital E, if you will. The *First Sunday of Advent* focuses eschatologically on the *parousia,* commonly referred to as "the rapture" or "Christ's second (or final) coming."

After starting with Christ's final coming, on the *Second and Third Sundays of Advent,* the lectionary backs the Church up to prepare for the coming of Christ's ministry by focusing on John the Baptist's role as the one who prepares the way for the Messiah.

Then, finally, on the *Fourth Sunday of Advent* we back up in time again and prepare for the coming of the Christ child, by focusing on stories in which an angel foretells the birth. Only on the Fourth Sunday of Advent does the season turn toward a pre-Christmas emphasis.

During the medieval period, different colors began to be assigned to the various liturgical periods. At first, black was the color assigned to both Advent and Lent for the associations of the season with affliction and abstinence. **Violet**, however, was also connected to the seasons and came over time to dominate them because it was interpreted to represent both our need for repentance and Christ's royalty. In recent years, many churches have switched to a **royal blue** during Advent, emphasizing the royalty of Christ but de-emphasizing the theme of penitence, sharpening the distinction between Advent and Lent.

One of the more popular rituals of the season developed in recent decades is the **Advent wreath**. On each of the four Sundays, a different candle is lit. These candles, with the exception described below, are the same color as the **paraments**, violet or blue. And then finally a white **Christ candle** in the center is lit on Christmas Eve/Day.

Many of the wreaths have one candle that is **rose** (pink). This is antiquated and ought to be omitted in most Protestant churches. It is the candle for the Third Sunday, called "**Gaudete Sunday**." Gaudete is Latin for "rejoice," and it was the first word of the Latin Mass for this Sunday: "Rejoice in the Lord always." When Advent was a five-week period of penitence, the third Sunday was a hump day of sorts, celebrating that the fast was halfway over. The primary remnant of this theme in Protestant practice, besides the pink candle, is that lectionary readings for the day often emphasize the call to rejoice. (The background of Gaudete Sunday with its focus on joy has led some to assign similar themes such as love, hope, and peace to the other three candles on the outside of the wreath. While there is nothing inherently wrong with such assignments, worship planners should recognize that, first, these themes are neither part of the tradition of Advent or the Advent wreath and, second, these themes may compete with the thematic focus of the lectionary reading assigned for the first, second and fourth Sundays of Advent.)

Christmas

Christmas is not only a day; it is a season. The word *Christmas* is a compound of Christ + Mass. Early on, the nativity of Christ was celebrated with three masses: one on Christmas Eve, one on Christmas morning, and one on Christmas evening. (We will see a similar pattern at Easter.) These were not different times from which congregants chose to attend one; all three were attended by all. In some sense, the current practice of gathering for worship on Christmas Eve but not on Christmas Day is giving in to secular pressures that view Christmas as a secular, family, gift-giving holiday more than a religious holy day. In another sense, though, it reflects the ancient practice of celebrating the first worship service of Christmastide on Christmas Eve, a remnant of our Jewish heritage of viewing the day as beginning at sundown.

While there are always twelve days of Christmas, the number of Sundays in the Christmas season varies year to year based on two factors—on which day of the week Christmas falls and whether a congregation celebrates **Epiphany**, the day of the Magi's visit to the Christ child, on January 6 or on the Sunday before January 6 (as **Epiphany Sunday**) if it falls on a day other than Sunday. There is always at least one Sunday between December 25 and January 6, and the Gospel lection designated focuses on one of the few stories from Jesus's childhood.

For churches that celebrate Epiphany *on* January 6 regardless of what day of the week it is, there is sometimes a Second Sunday of Christmas, for which the Gospel reading is always John's prologue celebrating the incarnation (John 1:1-11). For churches that celebrate Epiphany Sunday in any year that January 6 falls on another day of the week, there is never a Second Sunday of Christmas.

Epiphany itself serves as a hinge day, if you will. It is the last day of Christmastide and, at the same time, sets the season of Epiphany into motion.

The color for the season of Christmas, including the day of Epiphany, is **white**, which is usually retained for the holiest of days and seasons in the Christian year.

Sundays after Epiphany

As we mentioned earlier, the Sundays after Epiphany are hard to get a handle on. In one sense, they are part of **Ordinary Time**, split between this period and the period after Pentecost and standing in between the clearly defined cycles of Advent-Christmas on the one hand and Lent-Easter on the other. In another sense, they comprise a somewhat thematically focused season. Let's explore how these dynamics unfold across these Sundays.

The word *epiphany* comes from the Greek word *epiphainein* meaning "to reveal." Special days in this season celebrate scenes within the story of Jesus's life and ministry in which his being God's son is revealed in unique ways. The first such day, of course, is **Epiphany** or **Epiphany Sunday** itself. On this day, the Church celebrates the first revelation of Christ to Gentiles, that is, to the Magi (Matt 2:1-16). On the First Sunday after Epiphany, the Sunday after January 6, we celebrate the Baptism of the Lord, when the heavenly voice declares Jesus to be God's son (Matt 3:13-17; Mark 1:9-11; Luke 3:21-22). Then on the last Sunday after Epiphany, that is the Sunday before Ash Wednesday, most Mainline Protestant churches celebrate the Transfiguration, when the heavenly voice again declares Jesus as God's son (Matt

17:1-8; Mark 9:2-8; Luke 9:28-36). In other words, the voice of God speaking about Christ as God's son bookends the season. (Until the recent development of the ecumenical lectionary, churches that celebrated the transfiguration did so on the second Sunday in Lent and/or on the Feast of the Transfiguration on August 6. Different denominations today may celebrate a combination of these three different dates in relation to the transfiguration.)

The Sundays between Baptism of the Lord and Transfiguration Sunday are more of the nature of Ordinary Time with lectionary readings progressing through texts in semicontinuous fashion. (This semicontinuous progression is picked up again after Pentecost.) The focus of the Gospel readings during this first portion of Ordinary Time is usually on the beginning of Jesus's ministry. The number of these Sundays varies based on whether Easter comes early or later in the year.

Even though the color for the special days focusing on revelation (Epiphany, Baptism of the Lord, and Transfiguration) is **white** as it was during the season of Christmas, the dominant color for the season as Ordinary Time is **green** (the color associated with growth).

Lent

Lent began as a period of intense catechism and fasting for converts to be baptized on Easter. The season is composed of the forty days before Easter, not counting Sundays. Because Sunday is the Lord's Day and commemorates the resurrection, sometimes people refer to every Sunday as a **little Easter**. We do not fast on Easter, big or little. We do not fast on the day of resurrection. Thus, Sundays during this period are usually referred to as Sundays *in* Lent instead of Sundays *of* Lent and do not count toward the forty days of Lent. (In contrast, in the Eastern Church, Sundays are counted as part of the forty days.)

The name *Lent* originally had no theological meaning. It comes from an Old English word, *lencten*, simply meaning "spring." In the fourth century, the Council of Nicea simply referred to the season as "**the Forty Days**," which is of course followed by the Great Fifty Days.

The season begins on **Ash Wednesday**. Worshipers are reminded of their mortality with the imposition of ashes on their forehead in the sign of the cross and with words such as, "From dust you came, and to dust you shall return. Repent and believe in the gospel." They are then invited to take on a Lenten discipline of abstinence, prayer, study, and almsgiving.

The number forty is a symbolic length of time, showing up repeatedly throughout scripture. Lent has especially come to be associated with Jesus's forty days of fasting in the wilderness when he was tempted (Matt 4:1-11; Mark 1:12-13; Luke 4:1-13). Therefore, the **First Sunday in Lent** every year uses this story to set the tone of season.

The season progresses through five Sundays before Holy Week begins. Themes and imagery in the scripture readings for these Sundays include baptism and salvation through Christ's death. The First Testament lections usually follow a pattern sketching a schema of salvation history.

As noted earlier in the discussion of Advent, originally the color for this season was black (signifying mourning) but later came to be **violet**. Violet/purple was an expensive dye in the ancient world and so was associated with royalty and is fitting for a season leading to Christ's exaltation. The deep tone of the color also evokes the experience and depths of human penitence.

The last of the forty days of Lent make up **Holy Week**. Most Mainline Protestant denominations continue to use violet during this period but some traditions switch to **red**, because the color evokes the memory of Christ's blood that was shed.

Holy Week begins on the Sixth Sunday in Lent, which is commonly known as **Palm Sunday**, the celebration of Christ's triumphal entry into Jerusalem, when crowds lined Christ's path with palm branches. More and more Mainline Protestant congregations, however, are combining the celebration of Palm Sunday with a remembrance of the Passion so that the day is called **Palm/Passion Sunday**. The reason for this contemporary combination is that many people do not come to worship on the weekdays of Holy Week, and it is inappropriate to move from the joyous entry into Jerusalem to the joyous departure from the tomb without experiencing the cross in-between. Thus, on this Palm/Passion Sunday, the service is filled with lengthy readings from the Synoptic Gospel assigned to the year in the lectionary cycle that walk the congregation through Jesus's last week.

The Church, then, walks through Jesus's last week in a slower manner and with more depth, using readings from the Gospel of John throughout Holy Week. Each day of the week is called Holy Monday, Holy Tuesday, and so forth. Although we might wish they would, few Protestant congregations worship on each day of Holy Week. Many do, however, hold worship on the three days of the **Triduum**, even if the term is not common among Mainline Protestants. Triduum is the "three days" of Maundy Thursday, Good Friday, and Easter Vigil. As the day of Epiphany is a hinge between Christmastide and the Sundays after Epiphany, the Triduum is the hinge between Lent and the season of Easter. Maundy Thursday evening through Easter Sunday evening takes us through Jesus's Last Supper, arrest, trials, crucifixion, burial, and resurrection.

Holy Thursday, often referred to as **Maundy Thursday**, is thus named because, according to the Gospel of John, on Jesus's last Thursday, after he washed his disciples' feet (**John 13:31-35**), Jesus commanded ("Maundy" comes from the Latin *mandatum*, the root for "mandate" and "command") his disciples to love one another.

In contrast, according to the Synoptic Gospels (Matt 26:26-28; Mark 14:22-24; Luke 22:14-23), this was the day on which Jesus had his last meal with the disciples and instituted the **Lord's Supper**. Maundy Thursday worship, then, often commemorates these two stories in a harmonizing fashion, marked with a foot washing and the Eucharist. Sometimes this is done as part of a **Tenebrae**. *Tenebrae* is the Latin word for "shadows." Tenebrae services, which can be performed on Good Friday but also on Maundy Thursday, involves reading through the final scenes of the last two

92

days of Jesus's life and extinguishing a candle following each reading, increasing the darkness and shadows. When the reading of Jesus's death is completed, a loud sound is made (e.g., crashing cymbal or slamming close of a large Bible) and the final candle is extinguished. Ending this way makes this service especially appropriate for a congregation that does not gather again for worship on Good Friday. Often the conclusion of the Maundy Thursday service involves the **stripping of the altar**, a practice in which all purple or red paraments and implements on the table are removed, sometimes draping the table and/or cross with **black** or gray cloths. The chancel area is left in this stark representation of death until the Easter Vigil or Easter Sunday morning.

Holy Friday, better known as **Good Friday**, is the day on which the Church commemorates Jesus's crucifixion and death. The liturgical practice of labeling the day of Jesus's death "good" may seem inappropriate, but it is not. While the Church mourns Christ's death, and especially the sinful state of the world that brought about that death, we also claim that the cross is salvific. The tension between grief and gratitude reminds us that the liturgical tone for the day should be somber but not morose.

The lectionary readings for Good Friday focus on the crucifixion and death, but there are other structures used to focus the liturgy and proclamation on Good Friday at times. Although not common across much of Mainline Protestantism, some traditions observe the **stations of the cross** on Good Friday. This is a devotional practice involving fourteen images of moments of Christ's last day (drawn from scripture and tradition). Worship might involve meditations and prayers related to each station. Another way some traditions structure Good Friday worship involves the **Seven Last Words** of Christ from the cross, as recorded in the different Gospels; again, meditations and prayers might be offered after the reading of each.

Easter

In most languages, the celebration of the resurrection is named with some version of the word ***Pascha***, but in English it came to be called **Easter**. As with "Lent," the etymology of "Easter" has no theological link. The obvious connection is with the word *east*, which originally meant "dawn." Austron was the goddess of fertility and sunrise, and her feast was celebrated on the spring equinox. Anglo-Saxon Christians adopted her name for the spring celebration of the resurrection, which was itself discovered by women at dawn.

As it is the holiest of seasons, Easter uses **white** paraments, as does Christmas. And like Christmas, Easter was traditionally celebrated with three Masses on Easter eve, Easter morning, and Easter evening. The **Easter Vigil** on Easter eve traces salvation history through scripture from the creation to its apex in the resurrection. This celebration represents the final review, if you will, before converts undergo the baptism of initiation into the faith. Most Protestant churches do not keep the vigil, which is a shame. It is a powerful and meaningful worship service tracing the history of salvation leading to the resurrection of Christ. In place of a vigil, many congregations have a **sunrise service** early on the morning of **Easter Sunday** before the regular service later in the day.

Thematically speaking, the season of the **Great Fifty Days of Easter** is divided into two parts. In the first part, the Gospel lections for Easter Sunday through the Third Sunday of Easter focus on the resurrection appearances. The second part of the season, the fifth through seventh Sundays, focus on Jesus's departure to glory. As a transition between the two parts, the Fourth Sunday of Easter is **Good Shepherd Sunday**, focusing on imagery of Jesus as the Good Shepherd found in **John 10**.

According to the book of Acts (from which lections are used in the place of Hebrew Bible readings during Eastertide), forty days after Jesus was raised from the dead, he ascended into heaven (Acts 1:3-11). Thus on the fortieth day of Eastertide, the Thursday between the sixth and seventh Sunday, the Church celebrates **Ascension**. Many churches, however, move this celebration to the seventh Sunday as **Ascension Sunday**.

The last day of the Easter season is **Pentecost**. In the place of Christ, who rose from the dead and ascended into heaven, comes the Holy Spirit who gives birth to the Church (Acts 2). The color for the day is **red**. In addition to resembling blood and thus being used in Holy Week and on days honoring Christian martyrs, red recalls the symbol of fire that represents the gift of the Holy Spirit in the story of Pentecost and thus becomes the color for the Church. This is why the Church uses red for ordinations and why some churches paint their doors red.

Sundays after Pentecost

The Day of Pentecost is a hinge drawing the season of Easter (and really the whole of the christologically focused liturgical cycle beginning on Advent 1) to a close and opening the season of the Church, if you will. This time is called **Ordinary Time**, again, because it is counted using ordinals in relation to Pentecost—for example Eighteenth Sunday after Pentecost, Nineteenth Sunday after Pentecost, and so on. The length of this season is about half the year, although the specific number of Sundays varies based on whether Easter is early or late. Although the color for the day of Pentecost is red, the color for the Sundays after Pentecost (as with the Sundays in Ordinary Time following Epiphany) is **green**, the color of growth.

While Advent through Pentecost is focused around themes and chronology related to the Christ Event, the season after Pentecost is in no way thematically focused. Instead, the lectionary progresses through different books of the Bible in a *lectio continua* fashion, that is, reading through biblical works in a semicontinuous fashion. Each year of the three-year lectionary cycle focuses on a different Gospel, and during Ordinary Time, lectionary-based worship reads through parts of the Gospels not read during the other seasons. There are two options for non-Gospel lections during Ordinary Time. In the first option, the Hebrew Bible, Responsive Psalm, and Epistle readings are chosen to relate to the theme of the Gospel reading. In the second option, the readings from the Hebrew Bible and Epistles are read in a semicontinuous fashion like the Gospels, without intending for the different readings to relate at all (with the exception that the Psalm is usually a response to the Hebrew Bible lection). The second option offers congregations a potentially wider experience of the Christian canon and is to be preferred. In this option the Epistle readings work through various letters in the Pauline corpus and the Catholic Epistles across the three years:

Year A: Romans, Philippians, 1 Thessalonians

Year B: 2 Corinthians, Ephesians, James, Hebrews

Year C: Galatians, Colossians, Hebrews, Philemon, 2 Thessalonians,
    1 and 2 Timothy

In the semicontinuous approach, the lessons from the Hebrew Bible work through the first testament in a sort of historical progression across the three years of the lectionary cycle:

Year A: Creation through Conquest

Year B: The Nation of Israel and Wisdom Literature

Year C: Prophetic Materials

Although the Sundays after Pentecost are not focused around liturgical holy days, there are special days that occur at different times in the season that Protestants celebrate.

Trinity Sunday is the first Sunday after Pentecost and celebrates the doctrine of the Trinity.

All Saints falls on November 1 or the first Sunday in November. On this day, congregations honor members of the Church who have died during the previous year and celebrate the communion of saints across history.

The last Sunday after Pentecost is the **Reign of Christ**, also called Christ the King. The last few Sundays in the liturgical year have an eschatological theme, similar to the way the first Sundays of Advent do. So the year ends where it began, and the celebration of Christ's eschatological reign is the pinnacle of the emphasis.

There are two other days that are not part of the historical liturgical calendar but are important throughout much of Mainline Protestantism. The first is **World Communion**, which celebrates the communion of saints around the world and falls on the first Sunday of October. The second is **Reformation Day**, commemorating the story of Martin Luther posting the Ninety-Five Theses on the door of the Wittenberg Church on October 31, 1517. The day is celebrated on October 31 or the last Sunday of October (as Reformation Sunday).

Most service books from denominations that follow the liturgical calendar (and use the RCL)contain liturgical resources for the various seasons and special days throughout the liturgical year. Those tasked with designing worship in such liturgical traditons where there is also some flexibility in how the individual service is shaped are served well by using their own denomination's, other tradition's worship books, and ecumenical (including international) resources. Below are sample pages from ***Chalice Worship*** (Chalice Press, 1999, used with permission) the service book for the Christian Church, Disciples of Christ (DOC). The first page comes from the table of contents to illustrate the range of liturgical resources the book offers for the whole calendar. The subsequent pages are a small sample from that collection, specifically resources for the Day of Pentecost. After these sample pages, a list of resources in other denominational service books is provided.

FURTHER READING

The African Methodist Episcopal Zion Book of Worship, 50–210

Book of Common Prayer (Episcopal Church, USA), 159–298

Book of Common Worship (Presbyterian Church (USA), 157–400

Book of Ritual (CME), 7–8

Book of Worship: United Church of Christ, 169–243

Celebrate God's Presence (United Church of Canada), 79–217

Evangelical Lutheran Worship (ELCA), 14–65

"Seasonal Worship Resources" Liturgy of the Reformed Church of America

The United Methodist Book of Worship, 225–444

III. $\mathcal{W}$ORSHIP SERVICES FOR THE CHRISTIAN YEAR

IV. $\mathcal{W}$ORSHIP ON SPECIAL SUNDAYS

PENTECOST

Pentecost is an annual festival of the Christian church occurring on the seventh Sunday after Easter, to celebrate the descent of the Holy Spirit upon the disciples. The Pentecost service of worship usually adheres to a congregation's regular pattern of worship. It becomes a festival through an emphasis upon the Pentecost theme in words and music augmented by flowers, colors, banners and other joyous expressions. The celebration of those gathered for the first Pentecost in which they understood one another despite barriers of language may be highlighted by the reading of scriptures or praying in various languages. Another possibility is to assign various persons to read the appropriate passage from Acts, beginning at intervals, so as to elicit a feeling of unity and understanding despite the confusion of many tongues.

The materials below are intended for possible use at various points within the congregation's ordinary pattern of worship. Additional resources may be found in this book under the heading Worship Resources. *There each aspect of worship includes resources for special days of the Christian year.*

CALL TO WORSHIP

The Lord said:
> You shall receive power when the Holy Spirit has come upon you,
> and you shall be my witnesses to the ends of the earth.

**Come, Holy Spirit, fill the hearts of your faithful
and kindle in them the fire of your love. Alleluia!**

OPENING PRAYER

Kindling Spirit, build well the fire in our hearts this day.
Fan us to flame that all will see
    the Christ-presence of love blazing in our midst.
Burn the witness on our tongues: Christ's Spirit moves among us.
Jesus Christ, our risen Lord has set his church on fire
    with strength and boldness and power.
Kindling Spirit, build well the fire in our hearts this day.

A PRAYER OF CONFESSION

**Almighty God, we confess that we have sinned against you:
    for we have denied your saving presence in our lives,
    and we have grieved your Holy Spirit.
Come to us in the fire of your love,
    and set our minds on the things of the Spirit,
    that we may bear the Spirit's fruit in love and joy and peace;
    through Jesus Christ our Lord. Amen.**

A PENTECOST LITANY OF AFFIRMATION

At Pentecost the Holy Spirit was given to the church.
In pouring the Spirit on many people
    God overcomes the divisions of Babel.
Now people from every tongue, tribe, and nation
    are gathered into the unity of the body of Christ.

Jesus stays with us in the Spirit,
    who renews our hearts, moves us to faith,
    leads us in the truth, stands by us in our need,
    and makes our obedience fresh and vibrant.

The Spirit thrusts God's people into worldwide mission,
    impelling young and old, men and women,
    to go next door and far away
    into science and art, media and marketplace
    with the good news of God's grace.
The Spirit goes before them and with them,
    convincing the world of sin and pleading the cause of Christ.

The Spirit's gifts are here to stay in rich variety,
    fitting responses to timely needs.
We thankfully see each other
    as gifted members of the fellowship
    that delights in the creative Spirit's work.
More than enough the Spirit gives to each believer
    for God's praise and our neighbor's welfare.

OFFERTORY PRAYER

God of wind, word, and fire, we bless your name this day
    for sending the light and strength of your Holy Spirit.
We give you thanks for all the gifts, great and small,
    that you have poured out upon your children.
Accept us with our gifts to be living praise and witness
    to your love throughout all the earth;
through Jesus Christ, who lives with you
    in the unity of the Holy Spirit, one God, forever. Amen.

Or:

Lord our God, send down upon us your Holy Spirit, we pray you, to
cleanse our hearts, to hallow our gifts, and to make perfect the offering
of ourselves to you; through Jesus Christ, your Son, our Lord. Amen.

DISMISSAL

The blessing of God, whose love creates new life and whose fire burns
away our impurities, be with you in your journey of life.

The blessing of God, whose love has the power to transform our living from old habits into new hope, be with you always.

The blessing of God, whose Spirit blesses our spirit with wisdom and vision, embolden you to proclaim the good news of God's love to all.

PART THREE
SPACE

Space comprises the three dimensions of height, width, and depth in which all things exist and move. It is a key concept in physics, engaging everything from geometric explorations of the properties and relationships of points, lines, and shapes within space to examining the distance and relationships between subatomic elements. Part of our fascination with outer space and the evolving shape of the universe has to do with the basic human drive to understand and master space as the environment in which we live and act.

All ritual occurs in given spaces. While this sounds like an obvious statement, it also implies that space is not neutral. Every ritual occurs in a *given* space and is shaped by that *particular* space. Different groups assume different kinds of space are appropriate or inappropriate for their rituals. The Church's sense of what is appropriate for its ritualistic space has evolved and continues to evolve. In this section we will examine a number of issues related to the leadership role of interpreting, changing, and using the physical and visual aspects of worship space. We will divide the material into two main chapters: the first focuses on the actual architectural configuration of Christian worship spaces and the second on the kinds of liturgical art and symbolism often employed in those spaces.

WORSHIP SPACE

We usually take the space in which we worship for granted. The worship space has been there forever; it has been the way it is forever. Except for replacing the carpet and painting the walls every few years or the rare times when a building project or renovation is scheduled, church leaders do not think about worship space much.

We should think about it, however. Those who design and lead worship on a weekly basis need to lead the church in interpreting and using the worship space appropriately and effectively on a weekly basis. Worship space shapes and expresses elements of the community's identity and theology while inviting some new uses of the space and hindering others.

In this chapter, we focus on the architectural structures and styles of the worship space. We will begin with a broad historical survey of what lies behind contemporary Mainline Protestant worship spaces. This review will serve as a backdrop for theological and practical considerations.

At root our driving question for this chapter is, **"What makes space appropriate for sacred worship?"** The wording of this question is important. It is not, "What makes a space sacred enough for worship?" In Christian theology, God is considered omnipresent and thus the presence of God has never been viewed as localized. In this sense, Protestant church buildings are not temples in which God resides. They are, instead, places in which the people of God gather to converse with and about God, the world, and the historic and global Church. And it is through these conversations that congregations believe God at times reveals God's self in these spaces.

Neither God nor Mainline Protestant tradition requires specific architectural structures for sacred conversation to take place. Nevertheless, over the course of Christian history, the Church has developed certain architectural patterns that have proven to facilitate Christian rituals. In other words, Christian spaces may not be holy in and of themselves, but they are sanctified by ritual practice and are designed to serve those sacred practices. As the practices and theologies of worship evolve, so do the spaces in which worship occurs.

HISTORICAL SKETCH OF THE EVOLUTION OF CHRISTIAN WORSHIP SPACES

Anyone who has spent time driving through the streets of Anytown or Everycity, North America, has likely noted a wide range of architectural styles of churches. On the same block of a county seat town, one could easily see a small white clapboard church next to a large Neo-Gothic church building next to a medium redbrick Georgian-style church that is just down the road from a prefabricated church building. Such diversity is nothing new. Across the history of the Church, there has been a great deal of variation in chapels, churches, and cathedrals based on the geographical location, population of the area, financial resources, and tastes and aspirations of different congregations and patrons of congregations. We will concern ourselves less with taking account of such nuanced differences and instead focus on major trends that still influence the design and use of worship spaces today.

House Church

The first Christians worshiped in people's homes, and thus the architectural designs and purposes of residential structures influenced worship space and practices. Often these were larger homes of wealthy patrons but not always. Christianity initially developed primarily in urban centers, so the types of homes used for worship were those found in highly populated areas. That is, many would have been analogous to modern-day apartments (numerous residences in a single building) or brownstone-type homes (single family dwellings attached to other single family dwellings).

Before we examine a specific example of an ancient house church, there are two other factors of ancient home life we need to keep in mind. First, a clear line between family residence and family business often did not exist, especially when we are talking about tradespeople who were not significant landowners. A family who made a living off fish, for instance, might involve the men of the family out fishing while the women salted and sold fish out of the front of the home. The living quarters, then, would be upstairs or behind the working quarters. This is worth mentioning because it shows that the boundaries between public and private life, in relation to space, could be quite fluid.

Second, many homes in the Greco-Roman period—both Jewish and Gentile—would have had a space dedicated to family worship. Meals (and the spaces in which the family ate) often included ritualistic elements and implements related to the family's religion. Moreover, Greco-Roman families would likely have an altar of some sort in the home near the hearth. The point of mentioning this fact is that there was little in the way of boundaries between worship and family life.

All of this is to say that it should come as no surprise that the burgeoning new religious movement of Christianity in its first few centuries would primarily gather in small groups to worship in people's homes. As the Church grew, but before it was accepted enough to establish public buildings as places of worship, residential spaces were adapted to serve the liturgical needs of the worshiping community.

The oldest archaeological example of a house church was discovered in **Dura Europos**, Syria. It is a house converted into a church that is part of a row of buildings that included a synagogue and Greco-Roman temple. It dates to the mid-third century (ca. 230–40), a time at which the population of the city would have been six to eight thousand. It is likely that this was a domestic structure that a wealthy patron converted to serve fully as a church building. The walls were covered with frescoes depicting biblical scenes and characters, although most of the paintings have been lost. The layout of the parts of the building that can be reconstructed from the archaeological dig is sketched in the diagram.

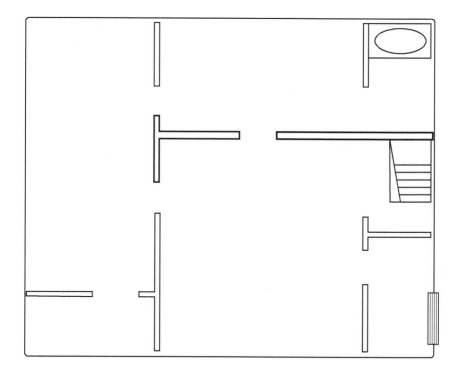

Basilica

As Christianity became more accepted and legalized in the fourth century, the Church could move out of dwellings and begin to use public buildings for worship and other communal functions. One of the most prominent architectural structures that had been around for centuries in the forum of Roman cities was the basilica. The word *basilica* comes from the Greek *basileus*, which means "king." A basilica, then, represented imperial authority and was a large secular structure used for legal functions and commerce.

One later example of this type of secular architecture of which there are still substantial remains is the massive **Basilica of Maxentius and Constantine** in the Roman Forum. Construction began during the reign of Maxentius in 308 and was completed by Constantine in 312, just before this type of structure would have begun being used for church buildings.

We can imagine what the inside of the Basilica of Constantine looked like with Constantine's statue standing in the apse, as we know it did at one time. The building functioned as a governmental administrative building and a shopping mall all wrapped into one. In the aisles down the side, mercantile trading might have taken place, and in the apse at one end a throne could be set up on a raised platform where a local ruler would adjudicate court cases.

It was not difficult to adapt this structure for churches, although most early Christian basilicas would not have been large as the Basilica of Maxentius and Constantine. Some secular basilicas were transformed into church buildings and other basilicas were built for Christian worship. **Santa Sabina** is a basilica in Rome built between 422 and 432. It has been maintained and restored and is still in use today. We can use it to illustrate how the floor plan of the basilica was Christianized.

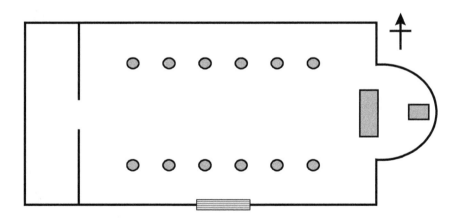

As Christianity evolved from its origins in the Roman Empire to its medieval form that spread throughout Europe, the basilica also evolved. To be sure, such evolution was rooted in new architectural technologies that developed—these need not concern us here. The architectural evolution of worship space, however, was also related to the evolution of liturgy and vice versa. During the Middle Ages, worship became more observation than participation for laity. This practice was related in part to the development of the theology of the Eucharist, which saw the meal as a sacrifice. Thus the altar, at which Christ is being sacrificed, was seen as deserving of being set off. An analogy is the Holy of Holies in the Jerusalem temple.

Development Beyond the Basilica

While architectural styles range greatly in modern Christianity, the basic floor plan found in the basilica is still dominant in Western Christianity today. The design is often called the **Western Plan**, or the **Longitudinal Plan**, referring to the long center aisle running east and west. A majority of Catholic, Anglican, and Protestant worship spaces represent some variation of this floor plan. The diagram represents what this plan looks like in simplified form.

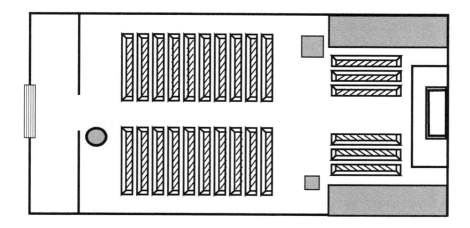

Since the altar had moved to the east wall, most churches no longer had a rood screen. In fact such screens were frowned upon at the Council of Trent in the Catholic Reformation. They are still found in some older Anglican churches, but most Protestants never included them in their worship spaces. In their place, though, is often found a **communion rail** surrounding the altar. This separates the altar, or table, from the rest of the worship space and provides a place for worshipers to kneel when receiving the Lord's Supper.

The primary areas of the basilica are still represented in this floorplan. The **narthex** is the primary entrance into the worship space. The **nave** with **pews** is where the congregation of laity gathers. While there is rarely a choir of clergy in such settings, there may be a **split loft** of seating for the musical choir and other liturgical leaders. And the **chancel** is still the area at the front from which worship is led.

Notice that although this floor plan does not have transepts, the central aisle leading into the chancel and the perpendicular aisle dividing the nave and the chancel still take a **cruciform** shape.

In the Middle Ages, **baptisteries** were often a different part of the church building than the worship space or a separate building altogether. This architectural element reflected liturgical practice, as baptisms took place as soon after birth as possible apart from regular worship. The Reformers, however, viewed baptism as initiation into the worshiping community and thus returned it to Sunday morning worship, requiring that accommodations in the worship space be made for the ritual. Sometimes the **font** was placed near the chancel so that baptisms could be viewed by those in the pews, but often it was placed at the rear of the nave or the doorway of the narthex to symbolize that baptism was the ritual entrance into the community.

While earlier churches had a single **ambo**, or raised platform, from which scripture was read and other types of liturgical speech were offered in worship, the split choir of basilicas in the Middle Ages led to dual reading places. In a **split chancel** arrangement of the Western Plan, speaking before the congregation takes place at two primary pieces of furniture.

The first is the **lectern**. The word *lectern* (as with the words *lectionary* and *lection*) comes from the Latin word for "read." So the lectern was originally the place where scripture was read, especially the Epistle reading, back when the lectionary had only an Epistle and a Gospel reading. (The "Epistle side" was traditionally on the right when facing the altar.)

The second place of speech is the **pulpit**. In Latin, the word *pulpit* simply refers to a platform for actors. At the pulpit the Gospel lesson was traditionally read. So the lectern side of the chancel was called the Epistle side and the pulpit side was called the Gospel side.

The pulpit is usually larger than the lectern, reflecting the authority granted to the Gospel over other scripture readings in a day before historical criticism gave us better understanding of the development of the Gospels.

As Protestants adopted and adapted the Western Plan and worship evolved into forms focused primarily on proclamation of the word, the lectern and pulpit were retained but their unique functions as places related to different types of lectionary readings were lost. Often the pulpit became the locus of proclamation and the lectern was used for all other liturgical actions. Or liturgical leaders just stepped up to the desk to which they were seated closest. Or the pulpit was reserved for clergy and the lectern used by laity.

While there is no single approach to using the lectern and pulpit today, worship planners and leaders should think about them in theological terms. When the two pieces of furniture are different sizes, a hierarchy of importance is symbolized. This hierarchy should not be expressed in terms of persons or office, such as a division between clergy and laity, since Protestants affirm the priesthood of all believers. Instead, the more important liturgical functions should take place at the pulpit. For example, in terms of our conversational model of worship, the two speaking desks can indicate different voices in the liturgical conversation. When worship leaders (clergy or lay) speak on behalf of the congregation, such as in prayer addressed to God, they stand at the smaller lectern. When they (laity or clergy) speak on behalf of God, in the reading of scripture and preaching the sermon, they stand at the pulpit.

With the liturgical renewal movement of the twentieth century and especially Vatican II, congregations decided to reclaim the symbolism of gathering *around* the table during the Eucharist so that those presiding would stand behind the table facing the congregation instead of standing with their backs to the people.

This required some adjustments to the Western Plan. Redesigning the worship space went something like this. The **altar** was moved out from the wall toward the nave. Sometimes this would simply be at the front of the chancel, but other times it was placed on the floor, level with the congregation. Those traditions that had a kneeling rail could still use one.

In some churches, the altar against the wall was built in, so it became a stand for holding flowers, candles, and offering plates, among other things, and a new table was brought in. Some Protestant traditions had moved the altar away from the wall as early as the Reformation(s) and had reclaimed the piece of furniture as a **table** instead of altar, since their theology stressed the Lord's Supper as a meal and not a sacrifice as in the Mass.

When redesigning instead of building a new worship space, the placement of the **choir** often depended on the architectural limits. Changing the choir arrangement was helpful to the quality of music. Music had evolved far beyond antiphonal chanting where clergy sang to themselves to four-part harmonization. Such music, much less acoustics, is not served well by a split choir. Sometimes the choir is placed in the **balcony** at the back of the nave so the choir leads the congregational singing instead of performing for them. And sometimes the choir is brought together at the **back of the chancel**. While this diminishes the cruciform design of the Western Plan, it does do a better job of symbolizing the community gathered around the table. The split chancel, or at least the split lectern/pulpit, is usually retained in spite of these other adaptations, but they are now placed to either side of the table, often set back a little because of space issues. This simply depends on architectural limitations.

Traditions that emphasize word more than table sometimes demonstrate this emphasis with a central pulpit instead of a split chancel. In this configuration, the pulpit usually stands behind and above the table. Because the pulpit separates the table from the raised platform, if you will, this area loses any sense of being a sanctuary or chancel, and is more properly called a **dais**.

Many, but not all, of the churches that use this floor plan have a lower view of the sacraments and may pass the communion elements through the pews instead of having congregants come forward to receive. In this configuration of the worship space, then, these churches usually do not have a communion rail around the table.

Many of these traditions also practice baptism by immersion so instead of a font standing somewhere in the worship space they have a **baptismal pool** built into the worship space. This is often located at the rear of chancel so that the whole congregation can witness the baptism.

This adaptation is only a step away from floor plans related to what is sometimes called the **Central Plan**. In worship spaces using some form of this design, the seating is shaped in a fashion similar to a theater. The worship space is usually wider and shorter. The floor may slope toward the dais. And balconies may wrap around the back and even sides of the worship space. The central aisle often disappears and any sense of a cruciform shape is lost. But the intimacy of the community and the idea of the community gathering around the word or around the table is highlighted.

Congregations that embrace a praise and worship style of liturgy can occur in Western or Central Plans, but usually arrange the furniture in ways more like the Central Plan. They struggle in traditional spaces to make room for music that is different than a choir accompanied by an organ or piano. The use of a band with multiple instruments and a lead singer often results in replacing the chancel or dais with more of an actual **stage**. Thus, often praise and worship services occur in auditorium settings. There may or may not be a permanently placed pulpit, but proclamation usually occurs from the center of the stage. The presence and placement of a table and baptismal font or pool vary depending on the sacramental orientation of the praise and worship community.

Developments in North America

North America inherited the architectural history we have sketched above. There are, however, a few historical influences on worship space that are specific to our location and culture. This first is the fact that North American Christianity, especially Protestantism, has a history as a **frontier religion**. A lot of the worship practices on the continent, and thus the space that developed for them, were shaped by the combination of evangelical fervor and conquering a new land. This meant that many churches were built in a utilitarian fashion related to meeting the needs of people on the frontier in as simple a way as possible.

A second historical influence stands at odds with the first. It involves the **revival of classic architectural styles** (e.g., Neo-Gothic). As a new nation, the United States wanted to prove its connection with older civilization and at times church buildings reflect this. This was especially true early in the nation's history in established cities on the east coast.

In contrast to this desire to legitimize the new nation in terms of older traditions, another factor influencing the building of churches related to the youth of the United States was the drive to be all things **modern**. So while some American churches reflect, say, a Neo-Gothic approach influence by medieval church structures of Europe, others were built to look like anything but a dusty old traditional church building.

A fourth influence is the **ecumenical dialogue** in which most American churches participated in the mid-twentieth century. As denominational practice became more and more similar, so did their worship spaces. We have already commented on this influence, for example, in relation to moving the table away from the back wall of the chancel toward the nave.

Finally, there is the influence of three pillars of North American culture: **entertainment**, **consumerism**, and **individualism**. While the Reformation(s) represented a shift away from observing worship to participating in it, much of recent practice in Protestantism is returning to an observing mentality, especially as influenced by megachurch trends—such as the use of projection technology or the congregation being sung to by or singing along with a praise band as opposed to being led in its singing by a choir. Congregations embracing this approach design worship space to feel and function like a theater hall or stadium in which anonymous individual seekers "pay" for their ticket and come to a show with expectations of being entertained while having little asked of them. Worship space is being designed to invite these "seekers" into the fold of the Church.

INFLUENCES ON WORSHIP SPACE DESIGN

We have been discussing the evolution of Christian worship space primarily in terms of **liturgical function** and **liturgical traditions** as if the evolution occurred in a vacuum. This history continues to influence the design, shape, and use of worship space in ways that congregations are often unaware or take for granted. Education is needed to help those who design and lead worship as well as those who attend in order to both appreciate and critique elements of this heritage.

Still, we should also be aware that there are significant considerations outside of this history that play a role in the congregational practices related to worship space. There are (and always have been) many internal and external factors that influence choices in worship space design. Let us mention just a few such influences that shape the way we interpret, design, and use worship spaces today.

First and foremost is **theology**. By "theology" in this context, we mean the theology of the community that gathers for worship as well as the theology of the ecclesial leaders and architects who designed the space. In terms of "theology of worship," Protestant worship space usually reflects a stronger emphasis on either word or sacrament. Consider, for instance, the way that the relative position, visibility, and size of the pulpit, baptismal font/pool, and communion table in a particular space expresses what seems to be held as more important.

Or consider the difference between an ornate worship space filled with liturgical art and symbolism and a simple worship space that is built more like a lecture hall or meeting house; those who build the first type of space consider the space itself to be an offering to God, and those who worship in the second assume God cares naught for space but only what occurs in them.

Theological commitments beyond a theology of worship also influence the design and use of worship space. Long linear worship space with high ceilings that sends your eyes upward makes us aware of God's *transcendence* whereas intimate spaces where people are seated in the round looking at each other across the communion table emphasizes divine *immanence* as found in the community of faith.

111

Art or symbolism in the space might emphasize one person of the Trinity over the others. Stained glass windows usually highlight particular elements of the Christian story over others. Where clergy leading worship are situated—a great deal higher and apart from the gathered community or at the same physical level and stepping out of the congregation for different liturgical acts—says something about the view of authority granted to the clergy.

The **size of the congregation** also influences the design of worship space. There are two sides to this. The first is that a worship space must accommodate the size of the gathered community. There must be enough seats for everyone in the nave, and all must be able to see and hear the various liturgical acts occurring in the liturgy. For larger congregations, this can require the chancel or dais to be raised, projection screens to be larger, and/or expensive sound systems to be installed. The second side of this issue is that the size of the congregation often reflects the economic capabilities of a congregation. A smaller congregation is less likely to be able to build or maintain worship space that makes use of elaborate ornamentation or expensive AV equipment than a larger congregation. This problem is especially seen in congregations that were once larger and have shrunk in size but are still required to pay for utilities and upkeep on larger spaces.

Issues of **taste** also influence the design of worship spaces. Architectural and design aesthetics vary among different individuals, communities of faith, geographical regions, and cultures. What one community considers inspiring and beautiful another can see as ugly and kitschy.

Finally, concerns for **accessibility** and **hospitality** play a role in the way worship spaces are designed. How does the space hinder or help people with physical disabilities in fully participating in the whole of the liturgy? Are there aids for those with hearing problems? Can those with mobility issues sit in the nave or get to the table and chancel easily? How does the worship space invite visitors to feel welcome in the community, participate in worship, and explore the possibility of becoming a member? Is the space designed in a way that multigenerational needs are met?

PRACTICAL CONSIDERATIONS

Too often worship occurs in a congregation week after week, year after year, with little consideration of the worship space itself beyond exchanging the flowers and replacing the candles until the paint or the carpet needs refreshing, the sound system breaks, or the congregation grows too large or too small for the nave. This should not be the case.

Both those in a congregation responsible for worship and those responsible for the building—pastors, worship leaders, altar guilds, worship committees, building committees, trustees, and the like—need some awareness of the history of Christian worship space to value appropriately the arrangement of a congregation's space and the furniture within it.

As we stated at the outset, most Protestant communities do not consider worship space to be sacred in and of itself. There is nothing sacrosanct about the Western Plan. The table is not a holy relic that must be positioned in a certain way to protect its holiness. That does not mean, however, that there is not significant meaning to be accounted to such architectural and design traditions. Consider a congregation that shrinks, and the pastor rightfully encourages the congregation to sit closer together to better perform the liturgical "work of the people." But one seventy-six-year-old woman refuses to move from the pew where she has sat her entire adult life even though she sits a good distance away from any of her fellow worshipers. She refuses to move because this is the pew in which she taught her children to observe the faith. This is the pew in which she sat beside her husband for forty-three years until his death. That pew is not holy, but it is meaningful because something holy has taken place there over the years and to abandon or move from it has meaning as well.

Describing the woman's commitment to "her" pew is not to imply that we should hold on to worship space traditions for the sake of those traditions. There may not be clear rights and wrongs when it comes to building, arranging, and using worship spaces; but at different times in the life of a congregation, decisions about the worship space carry different kinds of weight of significance to be considered. Congregations need to weigh many factors any time changes are made to or in the use of worship space. Calling on the history of worship space helps avoid discussions or decisions that only involve matters of taste—what someone with influence "likes" or "dislikes."

The history of worship space also should enhance weekly worship. Holding in tension practical, theological, and historical considerations while considering how to "set" and use the space for each worship service will lead to more vibrant and meaningful liturgy. One way of bringing together the practical, theological, and historical is to consider use of the space in terms of the primary liturgical actions that occur in Christian worship.

Protestants observe two sacraments or ordinances: **baptism** and **communion**. There needs to be distinct areas and furnishings in the worship space for both of these worship practices. There needs to be room for baptism and table practices to be performed appropriately. Moreover, even though baptism is practiced only occasionally and Eucharist may not be weekly in some congregations, these two worship practices are central to Christian identity. The presence and honoring of the font or bath reminds worshipers every week of our initiation into the faith and of the calling and ministry of the baptized. The presence and honoring of the table reminds us of the center of the Christian story even when the Meal is not served.

Central to the Protestant understanding of the purpose of worship is the proclamation of the **word**. There needs to be a distinct area and furniture in the worship space for this worship practice. The placement of the podium(s)—pulpit and/or lectern—should contribute to communication of reading scripture and preaching between speaker and hearer. But the placement also speaks symbolically about how God's word and those who deliver it are understood theologically. Indeed, even in the

113

worship space outside the time of worship, the appearance and location of the pulpit says something about the congregation's view of how God speaks to God's people.

Music has been a key element of Christian worship since the beginning of the Church. Adequate space needs to be provided for musicians and singers to lead the congregation in the musical aspects of worship. A tension exists between setting up a distinct area and furniture (including instruments) for music to occur in worship and avoiding the slippery move toward the space being set as if it were a musical performance in the sense of entertainment.

It goes without saying that there must be distinct space and furniture for the **work of the people**, that is, for the gathering of the congregation. In addition to supplying enough seating for all who gather, this area expresses something about the nature of *koinonia* in the community. In other words, the design of the seating space not only allows the congregation to see and hear what occurs in the front of the worship space, it also places individuals next to each other in a specific way, inviting them to participate in worship in a specific way.

Finally, good worship spaces provide for plenty of **movement** amongst and between the five different areas named above. While the liturgical spaces should be distinct to promote them and their symbolic meaning, there should also be a fluidity to worship space to indicate symbolically the relatedness of the different liturgical actions. Moreover, we often think about worship in terms of our intellect or emotions. But there is also a kinesthetic dynamic in worship seen in standing, sitting, bowing heads, laying on of hands, lifting up of hands, passing the peace, genuflecting, kneeling, dancing, and so on. (See the chapter entitled Embodied Worship.)

LITURGICAL ART AND SYMBOLISM

In the previous chapter, we began asking the question, **"What makes space appropriate for sacred worship?"** We continue that discussion in this chapter by recognizing that one of the most significant ways communities of faith designate space to be used for sacred worship is by the visual art and symbolism that is employed in the space.

Different Christian denominations and communities, however, have quite different views concerning the appropriateness of visual art and symbolism in worship and worship space. Their understanding of God, theology of worship, sacramental theology and theology of proclamation, relationship to wider culture, communal identity, and understanding of the role of physical space in framing worship all play a role in shaping their positions. In other words, a community's particular ritual life and approach to the sacred conversation that is Christian worship determines their approach to art and symbolism. But the converse is also true: the art and symbolism in Christian space influences the community's rituals and sacred conversation.

Perhaps, then, we should keep two guiding questions in our minds as we examine types of art and symbolism in worship space.

- What is the role/function of art/symbolism in worship space?

- What criteria should be used to determine appropriateness?

HISTORICAL SKETCH

Having taken an intuitive survey of our appreciation of art and symbolism in worship, let's see if we can frame and advance those thoughts a little. A little history and a brief overview to aesthetical issues will help us begin to formulate critical answers to the questions above.

The **early church** inherited the commandment against graven images from its parent Judaism (Exod 20:4-6). We might imagine, then, a great reluctance to use art or symbolism in the first centuries of Christianity. The earliest extant synagogue, however, discovered in **Dura Europos** (the same locale for the earliest extant house church discussed in the previous chapter) is filled with frescoes of biblical scenes. Similarly, mosaics are found on the floors of synagogues in the early centuries of the Common Era. So it would seem that Jewish communities in the years that the Church was developing did not interpret the commandment against graven images as banning all art, but only forbidding representations of God.

Additionally, Greco-Roman religions had long used lots of art in their temples, including representations of their gods. Thus the early church, which grew out of Judaism and became more and more Gentile, seemed primed to use art in worship space.

As we noted before, such use of art is exactly what we find in the **house church in Dura Europos**. The baptistery is filled with images presenting the biblical stories in ways that would inspire those participating in baptism (and presumably other parts of the building were filled with similar images as well). Moreover, in this house church, we find images of Jesus as the center of the faith. This image of Jesus as the Good Shepherd was already a traditional image in the Church. It is found, for instance, in the catacombs. While this image draws on biblical metaphors in John 10, it is more than just a remembering of the biblical story. It expresses christological values that inspire worship of Jesus. This is the beginning of **iconography** in the Church. While Jewish heritage would have led early Christians to resist making an image of God, the incarnation invited making images of Christ.

In addition, we find the artistic use of **symbolism** in early Christian worship spaces. When Christianity was persecuted, the symbol of the **fish** was used to identify fellow Christians. Because the fish had been used as a symbol in Greco-Roman traditions, it would not have drawn attention from persecutors. In fact, some argue that it functioned as sort of a secret handshake. In conversation with someone a person thought might be a Christian but was not sure, he could draw an arch in the dirt with his foot. If the person did nothing, he knew he was not safe to talk about his faith. But if the person drew an accompanying arch and made a fish, he knew he was in the company of a brother or sister in the faith.

A fish was used as a symbol in worship because of the role fish played in various biblical stories—the miraculous catch of fish, the miraculous feeding of the five thousand with bread and fish, and Jesus calling the disciples to become fishers of people. But the symbol was also an acronym: Once the Church was no longer persecuted, the fish became part of the Church's symbolism and was artistically rendered and stylized in Christian worship space.

Throughout the **Middle Ages**, the use of art and symbolism in worship space evolved as the Church and its wealthy, influential patrons built more elaborate buildings and as technologies and artistic techniques themselves evolved. The art created a sense of the space being set apart from other kinds of spaces. In this view, worship space is sacred space dedicated to sacred ritual and therefore requires sacred art. Creating a beautiful worship space filled with beautiful art and symbolism was considered in and of itself an act of worship.

At the same time, some of the art had a utilitarian function. The Church used art to teach the faith to the illiterate masses who could not read and to encourage piety and devotion in all who came into the worship space and examined the art.

There were movements within the Church (e.g., in the eighth century) that resisted the extensive use of visual art and symbolism that evolved throughout this period because, they claimed, veneration of such symbols as those of Mary and the Trinity were forms of idolatry. Overall, however, a theology of incarnation won the day and stained glass windows, statues, and other visual art continued in great use.

During the **Reformation**(s) and the rise of the Enlightenment, however, much of the Protestant church rejected any extensive use of art. To be more specific, while Lutheran and Anglican Protestants continued to value art and symbolism in worship spaces, Zwinglians, Calvinists, and Anabaptists rejected much of visual art and symbolism in worship space. These Protestants emphasized the oral/aural event of the word as the center of worship and rationality in religion over aesthetic and emotional dimensions of faith.

Some of these communities were, literally, **iconoclastic**. They removed and/or destroyed images of saints from churches that became Protestant. They broke stained glass windows and replaced them with plain glass. As worship moved from laity observing to laity participating, from watching to hearing, such things were considered distractions from the real purpose of worship, from conversing with God.

Thus, as Protestantism spread and built new church buildings, these buildings were often much plainer than their medieval predecessors. These Protestants saw the church building less as a sacred temple constructed as part of the worship of God and instead as a **meeting house** where the church gathers to worship God with sacred speech.

In the **twentieth century**, however, there has evolved a significant interest in the aesthetic and experiential/emotional side of worship among Protestants across a much wider theological spectrum than in the past. This interest has led many communities to reintroduce liturgical colors, paraments, art, and symbolism into the worship space. Thus today, if one visits a range of Protestant churches in any city, even a range of churches within a single denomination, she or he may find a spectrum of approaches to visual art within their sanctuaries.

AESTHETICS FOR PROTESTANT WORSHIP SPACE

In the introduction to this chapter we posed two questions:

- What is the role/function of art/symbolism in worship space?
- What criteria should be used to determine appropriateness?

Our quick survey of the historical development of the use of art in Christian worship space gives worship leaders some data to help answer these questions in relation to their particular worship space and worshiping community. While our contemporary practices should be informed by tradition, however, the past need not dictate current practice. Some basic aesthetic considerations approached from a theological perspective will also help as congregations consider the appropriateness of visual art and symbolism for Protestant worship spaces today.

A first consideration deals with a basic understanding of God and specifically how we experience God as engaging humanity. At one end of the theological spectrum (e.g., Catholic, Orthodox), Christians hold a sacramental worldview. God is present in everything, everywhere, and liturgical art celebrates an incarnational understanding/expression of that. In other words, liturgical art and symbolism proclaims God as **immanent**. At the other end of the spectrum (e.g., Neo-Orthodox), Christians view God as Totally Other. The word comes from outside of creation and speaks to it. Orality/proclamation is lifted up, and art is seen as distracting. This view emphasizes divine **transcendence**.

In truth, most Mainline Protestants lie somewhere in between these two extremes. They hold God's transcendence and immanence in paradoxical tension, and their use of visual art and symbolism reflects this tension. So there is more visual art used in most Mainline Protestant worship spaces these days than in traditional meeting house worship spaces but less than in many Roman Catholic churches.

Given this tension (as well, frankly, as different tastes within a congregation), it is helpful for worship leaders to ask a few questions of a congregation that is using or considering using visual art in the worship space.

First, **is this art/symbol simply decoration or is it integral to the ritual(s) being enacted in the space?** When we are talking about liturgical art, we are not talking about interior design. Interior design for the worship space is concerned with the color of the carpet, the pew cushions, the tone of the wood, and the acoustical quality of the space. Interior design is not unimportant. It can be hard to enter into sacred conversation in an ugly environment. But, visual art in worship space is more than mere decoration. We do not hang pictures in the chancel to fill in the space of an empty wall the way might in our living rooms at home or even the way we might in the fellowship hall in the church. If any pictures, plants, banners, statuary, or furniture are placed in the worship space, it should be because those items appropriately enhance the sacred conversation between God, the congregation, the historic and universal Church, and the world. Another way of putting the question is: Does the object help focus attention on the ritual actions of the worshiping community or does it focus attention on itself?

Second, even though we may not all view the worship space as in and of itself an act of worship, we should ask of any object we place in the worship space: Is this something we are willing to offer to God as an act of worship in the same way we would offer the sermon, anthem, table prayer, or what we put in the offering plate to God? In other words, we may not consider the space holy or the objects within them as inherently sacred, but we do consider our ritual use of the space and the objects as sacred. Therefore, **does the object properly glorify God?** Is it tasteful and appropriate to the liturgy the community intends to perform in the space, or is it tacky or kitschy? Beauty challenges and provokes, lifting the hearts and minds of worshipers to lofty places where God dwells, whereas kitsch is sentimental and invites people into being comfortable where they are and how things are. It is the difference between a picture that is worth a thousand words and clip art that includes words in it. It is the difference between an empty cross evoking the passion and resurrection of Christ and a felt banner of the Last Supper mimicking DaVinci's masterpiece but possessing and evoking none of its wonder.

A third question involves the interpretation of the visual object. **Is meaning of the art piece or symbol accessible to worshipers?** Good art is multivalent, inviting a range of responses and interpretations. By this question, then, we do not mean to imply that the visual image in the worship space must elicit in everyone the exact same understanding. On the other hand, many of the symbols found in worship space, as we will see in a minute, are ancient and based on Latin or Greek words and letters. We do not want to discard these nor limit them, but to use them without explanation transforms them into mere decoration. Worship leaders can explain the origin of these ancient symbols that are part of our communion with the saints in brochures, sermons, newsletters, or bulletins. While the arena of the explanations can vary, it is important to give congregants some common framework to interpret the art, furniture, and symbols in the stained glass windows in the worship space.

Fourth, assuming the meaning of a symbol or piece of visual art is accessible, we still have to ask: **Do the potential meanings of the piece resonate with the Christian gospel and traditions of the Church as well as bring new insights to bear on them?** The Church as an expression of the communion of saints reminds us that we are here as a community of faith because many have gone before us and passed down the faith across the generations. Like our music, proclamation, and prayers, our physical and visual elements in the worship space should connect us to understandings of the faith we have inherited.

Not all that has been passed down in the traditions of the Church, however, has been faithful to the core of the gospel. The **Protestant Principle** insists that Church is reformed and is always to be reforming itself. This principle applies to liturgy and worship space as much as to theology. In terms of our worship practices (including our worship space), we never start from scratch but neither should we simply continue practices of the past without critical evaluation. Visual imagery and symbolism can be a significant part of helping communities rethink and re-experience the faith. So we must ask how the artwork offers experiences of God's grace and call while inviting us to move beyond oppressive structures such as patriarchy and racism. For example, if all of our pictures present God as an old white man with white hair and Jesus as white, blond-haired, and blue-eyed, what are we saying to persons of color and to women when we speak of humans being made in the *imago Dei* or call Christians to be conformed to the image of Christ?

A final question to ask concerns the relation of the specific congregation's identity and the artwork. **Does the art express something of the community's theological, missional sensitivities or only those of the artist?** Visual imagery in the

119

worship space must be appropriate to the community's self-understanding in both cultural and religious terms. We should not be surprised to find very different visual dimensions in the worship space of an Orthodox church in Ukraine, a social justice-oriented congregational church in New England, a Pentecostal church in Appalachia, and an immigrant, Catholic community in southern Texas. Some of the same symbols and liturgical colors may be present across this spectrum, but the manner in which they are used and what they express will and should be quite different.

SURVEY OF SYMBOLISM USED IN WORSHIP SPACES

In addition to understanding the basic architectural design of worship spaces and some basic theological and aesthetic principles for evaluating the use of visual art, worship leaders need to have at least an elementary grasp of traditional symbolism and imagery in order to help a congregation best interpret and use their space in worship. Let's survey some of the most common types.

The **cross** is the central visual symbol of the Christian faith and the primary symbol used to designate space as Christian worship space. In days past, worship spaces were at times filled with multiple crosses. In recent years, there has been a move to place one cross of significant size in a central visible spot in the chancel or near the communion table.

While the **crucifix** is used in Catholic and Episcopal worship spaces in relation to the meal as a sacrifice, many Protestants argue for an **empty cross** because Christ is not sacrificed over and over again in the Eucharist and because the empty cross recalls both the crucifixion and the resurrection—Christ died once for all and then was raised from the dead.

There is an inherent tension in the scandal of the cross and the ugliness of sin and suffering that it represents, on the one hand, and the beauty of the salvation toward which it points, along with the artistic beauty of many sanctuary crosses, on the other. Instead of being resolved, this tension should be highlighted. Various styles of crosses are meant to symbolize different doctrinal emphases.

Because the content of the **Bible** is considered to be an expression of God's self-revelation and the source of the Church's proclamation, the book itself is a symbol used in worship space. Images of Bibles can appear, then, in artwork such as stained-glass windows. The Bible is a visible sign of the impact of the Word of God on the life of the Church and of the significant role proclamation plays in worship.

However, there are problems with using an actual Bible as a symbol alone. Congregants can be tempted into a *biblolatry*—idolatry of the Bible. The Bible should never only be on display in the worship space. A Bible on the communion table when the meal is not being served, for example, may confuse a congregation about the function/role of both the table and the Bible. A Bible displayed in the worship space should be a Bible read in worship.

Stained glass has long been used to help designate space for the purpose of Christian worship. Our knowledge of the history of stained glass is filled with gaps.

The first multi-pieced colored glass window of which we know is from a British monastery in the seventh century. In the Middle Ages, stained glass windows included pictures of biblical stories and saints of the faith to inspire worshipers who were illiterate and unable to read the Bible. Often the windows are also filled with a range of other traditional symbols from the faith. But abstract, colorful designs are also found.

Another visual aspect in many worship spaces that follow the liturgical calendar involves the use of **paraments**. The word *parament* comes from a Latin root meaning "to adorn or prepare." Paraments are the textile hangings that adorn the walls, table, lectern, pulpit, and even worship leaders (in the form of **liturgical vestments**). These can involve representations of the denomination or culture of the congregation, but they usually involve colors and symbols or imagery related to the different liturgical seasons and celebrations of the church year. We discussed the different colors in more detail in the earlier chapter on the **liturgical calendar**, but it is worth listing them here:

Advent: Violet or blue

Christmas: White and gold

Lent: Violet

Easter: White and gold

Pentecost: Red

Ordinary Time: Green

One type of parament that is not used in many Protestant churches but ought to be reclaimed is the **pall**. The word *pall*, as in pall bearers, comes from the Latin *pallium*, meaning "cloak." A pall is a cloth used to cover a coffin at a funeral. Today we more often cover a coffin with a spray of flowers (although military funerals use the flag as a pall). The costs of caskets and flowers become a status symbol even when we are dealing with the great equalizer: death. When a congregation uses the same pall for every member who dies, usually with colors and symbols from Eastertide, it reminds us that the promise of resurrection is extended to *all* through Christ's death and resurrection.

Having discussed textile paraments, and having mentioned the use of the flag as a pall, we should discuss the use of a **national flag** in worship spaces given how common it is to find the American flag in churches of various denominations throughout the United States. A national flag is inappropriate in worship spaces because it competes with God for our ultimate concern, thus becoming a form of idolatry. This is not to claim that Christians can or should not love their country or honor the flag in other settings. Nor is it to assert that congregations should not be engaged in activities of a civic nature. As the body of Christ gathered to worship, however, we are citizens of the reign of God. We honor God as creator of the whole world in which all people are our sisters and brothers. Any national flag in worship space calls for a

121

loyalty to something much narrower than these kinds of commitment. Nationalistic flags invite allegiance to the reign of "Caesar" instead of the reign of God. Still, pastors and worship leaders must act in a pastorally sensitive manner when attempting to remove a national flag from a worship space. We humans are very loyal to our various idolatries, which we, of course, do not recognize as idolatry; and there are few stronger loyalties than the patriotism expressed in civil religion.

Many Christian worship spaces include images related to the **Trinity**, even if the congregation does not express trinitarian theology much beyond singing some trinitarian hymns and some formulaic benedictions. On the one hand, a worship space can include symbols of the different persons of the Trinity. For example, the Seeing Eye calls forth the omniscient Creator. The victorious lamb is an image of Christ drawn from the book of Revelation. And the dove is a symbol for the Holy Spirit.

In addition to symbols for the different persons of the Trinity, there are traditional symbols representing the whole of the Triune God. A common example is three interlinked circles. The circle, used in many symbols, represents God's eternal being. Another example is the symbol of the hand of God descending from the heavens. In the example to the right, the hand is formed in the shaped sometimes used by clergy blessing congregations. Different traditions configure the fingers differently, but when they are placed in sets of two and three, the two are said to represent the dual nature of Christ—fully human and fully divine—which is central to trinitarian theology, and the Trinity itself is represented by the other three fingers.

Christograms (monograms for Christ) appear in many worship spaces—carved on chancel furniture or crosses, in stained glass windows, on light fixtures, and so on. A monogram is a combination of two or more initials of someone's name used to represent the person. There are several common monograms for Christ.

One of the oldest monograms for Christ is the *Chi-Rho*, the first two letters of the Greek word *Christos*. The chi, which is transliterated as "*ch*," is shaped liked an English X. The rho, transliterated as "*r*," is shaped like an English P. The letters are often stylized and/or overlapped in monograms. If not provided with an explanation, parishioners may well wonder why in the world there are P's with X's over them in the sanctuary. At times the Chi-Rho is connected with other symbols, especially the Alpha and Omega.

Alpha (A, α) *and Omega* (Ω, ω) are the first and last letters of the Greek alphabet and are often combined in a monogram in worship spaces. Several times the book of Revelation uses these letters to refer to Christ as the beginning and end of history.

Perhaps the most common Christogram in the West is the *Iota-Eta-Sigma*. Iota = I,ι. Eta = H,η. Sigma = Σ,σ/ς. This monogram can take several forms depending on how the Greek letters are stylized or transcribed. Iota-Eta-Sigma are the first three letters of the Greek form of Jesus. Many congregants fail to recognize that this is a Greek monogram and think that it means something in English like "In His Service." Or worse, it results in vulgar slang like "Jesus H. Christ."

122

Another common Christogram, especially in the East, is *Iota-Sigma, Chi-Sigma*, with the sigmas written in the shape of C's. This monogram takes the first and last letter of both Greek words in the name Jesus Christ, *Jēsous Christos*.

Finally there is the Latin acronym *INRI*. It takes the first letter of each word in the Latin inscription, *IESVS NAZARENVS REX IVDÆORVM*, meaning "Jesus the Nazarene, King of the Jews," which according to John 19:19, Pilate posted on Jesus's cross.

There are some other traditional symbols and images that show up in worship spaces with which worship leaders and their congregations should be familiar.

The emphasis on the Church as being in succession or continuity with the **apostles** has resulted in representing them in worship space. This can be in the form of carvings, stained glass pictures, or statues of the Twelve. Often they are represented by traditional symbols that relate usually either to their work before they followed Jesus, some incident in their ministry, or their martyrdom.

Along with the apostles, the *Four Evangelists* (or Gospel writers) are often symbolized in worship with pictures of the four "living creatures" that surround God's throne in Revelation 4:6-9 (which is an image borrowed from Ezek 1:4-12). Matthew is the winged human; Mark, the winged lion; Luke, the winged ox; and John, the eagle.

If the apostles and evangelists are the parents of the Church, as it were, then the **Hebrew Bible** is the grandparent. Symbols from the First Testament are found regularly in Christian worship space. The most common one is the *Decalogue*, or the Ten Commandments, usually represented by two tablets.

Of course, we not only find symbols of the ancient influences on the Church, but ancient symbols for the Church itself in worship space. We mention in the lesson on architecture and design that the gathering space for the sacred assembly is called the nave, related to the ship being a symbol for the Church. We should not be surprised, then, to find **nautical imagery** in worship spaces. *Boats* show up symbolizing the Church, often with a cross as the mast. And Jesus is represented as an *anchor* composed of a cross, since Jesus anchors the Church.

Finally, the **sacraments** or **ordinances** of the Church are often artistically symbolized in the space, reminding the Church of its central ritual actions even when they are not being performed.

Interestingly, some churches that have historically used imagery sparsely in the worship space have been among the first to embrace the use of **visual projection** during worship. This may be a way of providing the congregation with song lyrics, biblical readings, or even sermon notes, but it is also a way of projecting artwork in the worship space. There are many online services that can provide professional photograph and graphic designs as backgrounds, but anyone with camera or, for that matter, anyone who can search the internet can find images that fit with worship themes for the day. Worship planners must be careful when downloading images from the internet, however, to make sure the pictures are not copyright protected. We cannot exhort our congregants to live ethical lives while not being ethical in leading worship.

LITURGICAL VESTMENTS

To close our discussion of symbolism, we need to look at liturgical garb because such clothing plays a symbolic role in Christian worship. Two of the primary reasons for the use of liturgical garb are to designate the office of the worship leader and to designate the person's role in the worship service.

Originally clergy wore what everyone else in the Roman Empire wore—a basic robe. As tastes in clothes changed however, medieval clergy continued wearing robes as unique clerical garb. The earliest form was the **alb**. The word *alb* comes from the Latin (*albus*) for "white." The alb is usually worn with a rope tied around the waist that is called a *cincture* or a *girdle*.

In most Protestant traditions, the alb can be worn by anyone leading worship although it is often worn only by clergy. In traditions that have different orders of ministry, those ordained as deacons to the ministry of service usually wear an alb with a **stole** hung over their left shoulder and attached on their right hip. The word *stole* comes from the Old English meaning "long robe" or "scarf" and referring to a band of cloth. The stole is usually the color of the liturgical season, matching the paraments hanging on the liturgical furniture.

In higher, more formal liturgical traditions, those ordained to the ministry of word and sacrament wear the alb in worship with a **chasuble** covering all other garb. The word *chasuble* comes from the Latin *casual* meaning "cloak." The chasuble is basically a liturgical poncho, if you will. Like the stole, the colors and symbols on the chasuble change from season to season.

In most Mainline Protestant worship traditions in which clergy robe, ordained pastors (i.e., ordained to ministries of word and sacrament) who robe usually wear a stole and no chasuble; whereas deacons wear the stole over one shoulder, those ordained to word and sacrament wear it over both shoulders.

Instead of wearing an alb, many Protestant ministers wear a **pulpit robe**, technically called a **Geneva robe** or a Geneva gown. The name refers to the Reformed origin of this garb. Until recent years, most Protestant pastors who robed in worship wore some form of this robe instead of an alb. Albs have been reclaimed as part of the liturgical renewal movement. The Geneva robe obviously has similarities to academic robes (which used to be worn daily by teachers) and emphasizes the teaching role of the preacher that goes with the Protestant liturgical focus on the proclamation of the word.

One adaptation of the Geneva robe is the **Wesley robe**, so named because John Wesley made the adaptation. Story has it, although it may be apocryphal, that since Wesley often preached outside, he tired of his stoles flapping in the wind. So he sewed black velvet strips down the front of the robe instead of wearing the loose scarf.

Some clergy who wear a preaching robe have **bars on the sleeves** to indicate that he or she has obtained a doctorate. While such decoration is a key element in academic regalia, it should not be used in the pulpit. One of the things liturgical garb does is to symbolically cover, if you will, the individual personality, tastes, and

124

achievements of the person leading worship and emphasize instead her or his ecclesial role and office. To add doctoral bars to the robe is to distort this symbolic purpose of the robe, accentuating personal achievement and misplacing authority in that individual achievement instead of in the office itself.

Of course, as mentioned earlier not only clergy wear robes in worship. The robe worn symbolically by all Christians and literally by some is the **baptismal robe**. In the ancient church when converts were baptized, they would disrobe, be immersed naked, and then rise from the font to be clothed in a new white robe to symbolize rebirth. In traditions that baptize by immersion, white robes are often worn by the one being baptized. These robes usually have small weights in the hems to keep the robe from floating in the water. A derivation of this practice is the **baptismal gown** often worn by infants being baptized in traditions practicing infant baptism.

Another robe worn by laity are **acolyte robes**. Acolytes are often older children who assist the celebrant in the service. In most Protestant churches that have acolytes, one of their main responsibilities is **lighting the candles** to signify God's presence in the service. Acolytes usually wear a **cassock**, a long robe (often black but here red) with a white **cotta** (or waist-length **surplice**). Unlike the chasuble, which is a sleeveless cloak, the cotta has wide sleeves.

In some traditions, even where the clergy do not robe, choirs do. **Choir robes** remind all that the choir is not performing, as in a concert. They are up front to *lead* the congregants in singing, and they do so as one body.

In some denominations, it is very clear what worship leaders are to wear. In other traditions, it may vary from congregation to congregation or even from minister to minister. Those who are in a position to choose should think carefully about the culture of the congregation and what claims need to be made about the worship leaders' roles in the congregation. Women have often found that robing helps them gain acceptance and authority in a role that has been dominated by men throughout the history of the Church.

PART FOUR
MATTER

As a scientific category, *matter* refers to any and all physical elements and objects in the universe. Matter has mass and occupies space. All matter is made of atoms, which in turn are made of protons, neutrons, and electrons. Thus matter is related to but distinct from energy. We experience matter in the form of the solid, liquid, and gaseous "stuff" of the universe.

The primary elements of physical matter used in Protestant worship are water, bread, and wine. (Sometimes oil is used in anointing and healing rituals.) In this section, we will explore the sacraments or ordinances of baptism and meal. The rituals of bath and Table are central to Christian identity and liturgical practice. Before turning to them individually, however, it is important to have a handle on the preliminary concepts of rites of passage on the one hand and sacraments or ordinances on the other. Then we will explore the history, theology, and practice of baptism and communion.

RITES OF PASSAGE AND SACRAMENTS/ORDINANCES

As we noted in an earlier chapter, when a community declares its devotion and service to a concern that it considers to ground the whole of existence and ritualizes that devotion as being ultimate, we can properly call the devotion "religious" and the ritual "worship." When a community devotes itself ritually to that which it considers worthy of ultimate concern, it is natural that it ritualizes major movements through human life so that the meaning of those transitions is understood in relation to its Ultimate Concern. In other words, Christianity has developed a number of rites of passage to name the different phases of human life in relation to the Christ Event. In this chapter, we are going to explore the concepts of "rites of passage" and "sacraments" or "ordinances" that are part of the Christian life extending from birth to death to set up our in-depth examinations of baptism and Eucharist in this section of the book and weddings and funerals in the section called Chaos Theory.

RITES OF PASSAGE

Pastors accompany their parishioners from the waters of new birth to dying in Christ and feed them at the Lord's Table all along the way. The story of Christ's birth, ministry, death, resurrection, ascension, and promise to return is never more meaningful to people than when they are transitioning from one state of being to another. Worship leaders worth their salt never allow these rituals to become stale or rote.

In the opening chapter we defined *ritual* as *the patterned, symbolic enactment of a community's historically rooted identity and values*. In ritualized action and speech, a community performs and actualizes an interpretation of some aspect of its core values, stories, symbols, and beliefs. At this point we need to examine more narrowly rituals by which a community marks different social stages of life. It is important for Christian worship leaders to understand such **rites of passage** with some sophistication because they play such an important role in Christian life.

All communities, cultures, and religions have rites of passage that express something important about the core meanings of human existence and what is most important in life within that community as it marks individuals' transition from one state or stage of life to another. **Arnold van Gennep** first defined rites of passage in the early twentieth century in a book written in French—*Les rites de passage* (1909). It was not until sixty years later—when the book was translated into English (*The Rites of Passage*, trans. Monika B. Vizedom and Gabrielle L. Caffe [Chicago: University of Chicago Press, 1960]) and then was reinterpreted by **Victor W. Turner** (*The Ritual Process: Structure and Anti-Structure* [Chicago: Aldine Publishing, 1969])—that the theory gained popular influence in North America.

Van Gennep used a spatial metaphor to describe rites of passages, as the word *passage* itself implies. At the root of his description is the Latin word **limen**, which means threshold. A rite of passage, then, is *a process by which someone ritually passes through a doorway and is changed in the process.*

Van Gennep argued that rites of passage have three elements: *separation, transition*, and *inclusion*; or *the preliminal, liminal*, and *postliminal*. In different rites of passages and in different communities, these three elements can be weighted in different ways.

There are two ways to think of the three stages of a rite of passage. Both ways are really saying the same thing but from slightly different perspectives.

The first is to focus on *the change in the individual* undergoing the rite. This is a linear view of change—the threshold is like a tunnel, if you will, that takes someone from one kind of existence to another.

Another way to interpret the rite of passage is to focus on *the relationship of those undergoing the rituals with the wider community.* In this case the threshold is viewed more like a revolving door. Someone is taken out of the community *in order* to be returned to the community in a new role.

Rites of passage occur all around us. Consider the following alphabetical list of some common and familiar ones:

Baptism	First Communion
Bar/Bat Mitzvah	Gang Tattoos
Basic Training	Graduation
Binge Drinking	Hazing
Birth/Parenthood	Induction into Office
Circumcision	Initiation
Citizenship Ceremony	Marriage/Wedding
Coming Out	Ordination
Confirmation	Promotion
Death/Funeral	Quinceañera
Driver's Test	Retirement

130

Some are major life transitions, and some minor. Some are nearly universal in a culture, and others are chosen. Some are healthy, some are not. Some are religious, some cultural, and some political. Some are institutionally sponsored and some happen unofficially or off the record, if you will. In the context of studying Mainline Protestant worship, we are going to examine three major rites of passage that are part of the Church's liturgy: baptism, marriage, and death.

SACRAMENTS OR ORDINANCES

In addition to rites of passage, in this section of the book, we are also going to look at the Table (aka Eucharist, Communion, Lord's Supper). It is not a rite of passage. It is not a once-in-a-lifetime transition. Table is celebrated repeatedly. It is, however, related to a rite of passage in that generally the Church and its members move from the font to the table. Indeed, many traditions require one to be baptized in order to share in the Meal. Thus baptism and Table are intimately related as sacraments or ordinances of the Church. Before we turn to examine either, then, we must explore what makes a ritual a sacrament or ordinance.

As we saw in the chapter on worship space, good Christian worship keeps in constant tension the transcendence and immanence of God, never letting one eliminate the other. High ceilings, a lofty organ, and grand theological claims/doxologies lift our eyes to heaven, to God as totally Other. Proclamation, passing the peace (with human touch), and intercessory prayer remind and help us experience God-with-us. At the center of this tension is also our use of bread and wine and of water. We use these everyday, physical elements to proclaim and experience abstract, divine mysteries. But what precisely is the relationship between the physical elements and that to which they point?

SIGN VERSUS SYMBOL, ORDINANCE VERSUS SACRAMENT

One way to explore how different Christian traditions answer this question is to think about the difference between a **sign** and a **symbol**. In common parlance, these words are synonyms, but in theology and philosophy they are often used as technical terms with an importance difference between them.

As background to this discussion, we can recall our earlier introduction to **speech act theory**. Most speech is considered referential—the word *table* refers to a piece of furniture external to the speaking of the word itself. Some speech, however, enacts what it says instead of referring to something else. For instance, when someone says, "I bet . . ." the speech *is* the making of the bet; it is not a reference to a bet external to the speech. Using this distinction as analogy, sign can be thought of as referential communication and symbol as speech act.

Carl G. Jung, a psychologist who viewed humans as essentially religious, argues that signs have fixed meanings constructed by social agreement whereas

131

symbols are multivalent and evocative of deeper realities (e.g., see "Approaching the Unconscious" in *Man and His Symbols* [New York: Doubleday, 1964], 20). Signs simply point to something we know (the way the word *tree* points to a certain kind of plant), but symbols require interpretation and through them we make meaning (e.g., "the tree of life").

Twentieth-century theologian **Paul Tillich** offers a similar view, but with an added nuance (see "The Symbols of Faith" in *The Dynamics of Faith* [New York: Harper and Row, 1957]). He argues that a sign is something that points to the other. A symbol, on the other hand, does not just point, it *participates* in the other.

Perhaps a crude illustration of the difference between sign and symbol will help show what is at stake in drawing the distinction. Consider a warning sign on the side of the road. The shape and color of the traffic sign are arbitrary. They are simply a convention of our culture that a yellow diamond warns a driver that something ahead demands their attention. We could have chosen another shape or color. In fact, other cultures have. In Europe most road signs are triangular or round and are white with a red border. The symbol on the sign, however, is not arbitrary. The curving arrow indicates the shape of the curvy road ahead. The arrow on the warning sign participates in the reality of the curving road ahead.

When we apply this distinction between sign and symbol to baptism and Table in Christian worship, we are asking whether the physical elements and ritual actions participate in that to which they point. Are baptism and communion signs (pointing to a reality beyond the matter and rituals employed) or symbols (matter and rituals that participate in a reality that lies beyond the ritual and matter themselves)? Christian denominations answer this question differently.

Traditions such as Catholic, Lutheran, Presbyterian, Reformed, United Church of Christ, Episcopalian, and Methodist call these two rituals "**sacraments**" because they hold a more symbolic view of them. (Orthodox traditions fit here as well but call the rituals "**mysteries**.") These groups follow Augustine, who defined a sacrament as "an outward and visible sign of an inward and invisible grace." Augustine, writing in the early fifth century, was not using the word *sign* in the technical fashion that arose in the twentieth century. His more "symbolic" approach is signaled by the participatory language of outward and inward, or visible and invisible—in other words, of physical and spiritual. In different ways or another, denominations that use Augustine's view as a starting point for defining the sacraments view God as active in these rituals in a special way. In other words, although the denominations nuance the meaning of the sacraments differently, they would all agree that sacraments are **means of grace**.

Ecclesial traditions such as Anabaptists, the Stone-Campbell movements, and Baptists, on the other hand, view the rituals as signs and have traditionally referred to baptism and Table as "**ordinances**." In this view, the rituals point to God's work and God's grace that have been active and experienced *elsewhere*. God is present in the rituals only in the same sense that God is present everywhere. The ritual actions and their physical elements may make worshipers more aware of God's presence and grace, but divine presence and grace is not revealed or offered in any special way in baptism and the Lord's Supper.

Yet another way to think about the difference between ordinance and sacrament is in relation to our conversational model of Christian worship. In a sacramental view, God's voice is the primary one speaking in baptism and Table, and our voices are spoken in response. In an ordinance view, our voices are the primary ones speaking the rituals is response to God have spoken before—that is, we take this bath and eat this meal as testimony to what God *has* done.

HISTORICAL SKETCH OF SACRAMENTAL PRACTICE AND THEOLOGY

We can see how these two basic views and different variations of them came to be in the different theo-liturgical traditions with a quick review of liturgical history.

Early Church. As early as the New Testament—primarily in Paul's letters and the Gospels—it is clear that there are already differences about how baptism and table practice occurred in the early church. We will look at some of these specific differences when we turn to examine baptism and Eucharist individually. For now we can say that even with those differences we do not really have any record of developed sacramental theologies in the first century.

It is important to note, however, that some terminology developed in the early centuries that came to be commonly used throughout the history of the Church. In Greek writings of the second and early third centuries, baptism and Eucharist were each called a ***mystērion*** (mystery); and as we noted earlier, this term is still used in Eastern traditions today. The Christian use of this term likely paralleled the reference to secret, sacred rituals in Greco-Roman mystery religions as "mysteries." As the Church began shifting from speaking Greek to speaking Latin, *mystērion* was replaced with a very different word: ***sacramentum***. In common Latin, *sacramentum* is a "vow" or an "oath." In baptism, some have said, God and the Church make an oath to the one being baptized and the one being baptized makes an oath to God and the Church. At first neither *mystērion* nor *sacramentum* were technical terms limited to referring to what we call sacraments or ordinances today. That use evolved over time.

Medieval Church. Definitions and theology of the sacraments began to develop as the Middle Ages approached. Augustine's understanding of the sacraments as "visible words" that expressed "invisible grace" shaped sacramental theology significantly during this period. An instrumental view of the sacraments developed: God works through them. This elevated the role of clergy as officiating over the sacraments, but the emphasis on invisible grace also evolved into the idea that God works through the sacraments ***ex opere operato***, literally, "from the work having worked." This doctrine means that the performance of the sacrament achieves what God intends regardless of any human agency. Thus the character of the priest and of the communicants cannot diminish the sacraments *if* they were performed correctly. In other words, God is present and active in the sacraments, and humans cannot distort or thwart God's work.

This early sacramental language would slowly evolve into debates about how the physical elements (visible words) embody or do not embody God's (invisible) grace and what ritual actions and language are essential for the efficacy of the sacraments. In other words, sacraments were seen as means by which God gives divine grace to worshipers, but not all agreed about how this happened.

Accompanying these debates was the question of which rituals of the Church count as sacraments and which do not. Through which ritual acts does God convey God's grace? In the twelfth century, **Peter Lombard** (in Book 4 of *Sentences*) named the developing consensus that there are seven sacraments. This list was not meant to limit God only to acting in seven ways. Instead, it was an assertion that God gifted the Church with seven sacraments through which God's grace was especially and repeatedly mediated.

See a picture of a fifteenth-century altarpiece by Flemish painter Rogier (raw-GEER) van der Weyden (vän d*uh*r VĪ-dun) at https://www.artbible.info/art /large/757.html. In this painting, van der Weyden presents all seven sacraments as if they were occurring at one time in a basilica. Above each of the enactments of the sacraments is an angel in liturgical colors with a streaming scroll explaining the sacrament.

Protestant Reformation(s). As the Middle Ages passed, sacramental views slowly evolved into a consensus position, if you will. There were certainly underground, dissident voices along the way, but the political and economic situation would have to change before such voices could find support to withstand the threat of the medieval church's power.

That change came in the early sixteenth century. In 1517, **Martin Luther**, as the legend goes, posted his Ninety-Five Theses on the door of the Wittenberg Church. This has been claimed as the starting pistol of the Reformation(s). One of the things that had troubled Luther greatly was the way the Mass was celebrated in rote fashion.

It was three years later (1520) that he published **The Babylonian Captivity**. The title is a metaphor for Luther's assertion that Rome held the Church in captivity. One of the major, lasting contributions of the work was to add a new element to the definition of sacraments. This definition was an extension of the key Protestant doctrine, *sola scriptura* (scripture alone). The added element was that a sacrament was something that the Bible tells us Jesus *commanded* the Church to do. Because Christ only commanded his followers to baptize and share the Lord's Supper, Luther reduced the number from seven to **two sacraments**. It was not that Luther thought the other five rituals should have no role in church life—he valued them. He did not, however, view them as being of the same rank and type of ritual as baptism and Eucharist.

Luther nevertheless retained the sense of divine presence and activity in the sacraments, although (as we will see in the chapters on baptism and Table) he rethought how this presence was manifested. Broadly speaking for now, in the sacraments God makes a *promise* of salvation to those receiving the sacrament. Luther rejected *ex opere operato*, claiming that sacraments convey grace only to the point that they are received by faith. After all, central to Protestant theology was the claim that we are justified by faith alone (*sola fide*)—thus the sacraments could not be salvific in and of themselves.

Luther's reforms quickly spread from Germany to Switzerland. They took strongest hold in Zurich, where **Ulrich Zwingli** had become the people's priest, the head Roman Catholic clergy in the city, in 1519. He convinced the city officials to switch to Protestantism in 1523.

He took the critique of Catholic sacramental practice and theology a step further than Luther. He did not reject completely the idea that the sacraments were a means of grace, but he did reject the idea that God is present in them in some way that God is not present elsewhere. He claimed the sacraments are **signs** or ceremonies of the individual's and the Church's faith. In other words, they are something we do more than something God does.

As we will see, this sacramental disagreement between Luther and Zwingli was never reconciled and continues to shape much of the denominational division in Protestantism today.

In Zurich there was a group that had been supportive of Zwingli's reforms but thought he did not go far enough in reforming sacramental practice. They argued he had not drawn out the implications of his own theology, especially in relation to baptism. If the sacraments were a testimony of the Church's faith and thus *required faith*, children could not appropriately partake of them. So infant baptism was considered illegitimate, which meant their own baptisms were illegitimate. In January 1525, **George Blaurock** asked Conrad Grebel to baptize him as an adult. Blaurock then baptized others in the group. When word got out that this had happened, people began deriding them by labeling them **Anabaptists**, or re-baptizers. This group was the first to drop the Latin term sacrament for the term **ordinance** (the root of which is "ordain"). We baptize and share the Lord's Supper because Christ "ordained" them.

As Protestantism moved from its first to its second generation, **John Calvin** became its premier spokesperson. Geneva, Switzerland, started moving toward Protestantism in the third decade of the sixteenth century but really only made the move fully in 1535. The city leaders quickly invited the lawyer, John Calvin, there to build a reformed Church. With conflicts over what it meant to have a Christian society and the moral codes that go with it, he was run out of town within a few years. But once new leaders emerged, he was invited back and stayed there the rest of his life.

It was during this time that he began writing the **Institutes of the Christian Religion** (first published in 1536), which he would revise over and over again throughout his career. His sacramental language in the *Institutes* stands in-between that of Luther and Zwingli, and can be seen as a compromise between their positions (although it is unlikely that was Calvin's intent).

He focuses his discussion of sacraments through the lens of anthropology: God gives us the sacraments not because they are some magical way to dispense grace, but because in our human fallibility we *need* symbols of God's grace to bolster our feeble

135

faith. In other words, the rituals are symbols by which God seals on our consciences the promises of divine goodwill in order to sustain the weakness of our faith.

English Reformation. The Church of England began for political reasons with Henry VIII in 1529, not for theological/liturgical reasons. And the Church of England swung back and forth between Catholicism and Protestantism a number of times. We need not retrace the whole complicated history in detail, but the pendulum effect did have sacramental implications. Henry VIII continued to understand the sacraments in a Catholic manner.

In 1549, after Henry VIII's death, while the teenager Edward was on the throne, the **Act of Uniformity** was passed. This meant that full-blown Protestantism was brought in, and **Thomas Cranmer**'s *Book of Common Prayer* became the liturgical law of the land. The church and its worship at this time were thoroughly Calvinist, thus including only two sacraments.

When Edward died, Mary ("Bloody Mary," 1553–58) became queen, got rid of the *Book of Common Prayer*, brought back Catholicism, and persecuted Protestants.

When Elizabeth I took over, she returned the land to Protestantism but tried to create a version that was more of a compromise between Catholicism and Protestantism than under Edward. This **Religious Settlement of 1559** is often called the "middle way" (***via media***). This compromise retained a higher, Catholic view of the sacraments but took seriously Protestantism's definition of sacraments as commanded by Christ in the Gospels. Thus the tradition held on to seven sacraments but practiced baptism and Eucharist as central to the faith (**major sacraments**) and the other five as optional (minor or **lesser sacraments**).

Catholic Reformation. The Catholic Reformation responded both to the Protestants and to reform movements within the Roman Catholic Church's own structures with the **Council of Trent** (1545–63). The Catholic Reformation tried to rid the Roman Catholic Church of corrupt practices while also undergirding and reaffirming the theology (especially the sacramental theology) of the medieval church.

Quakers. One final movement that developed yet another view of the sacraments is that of the Quakers, or Friends. **George Fox** was raised an Anglican, but as a young adult he had a religious experience that led him to question much of the established state church. Based on such religious experience, he and other dissenters emphasized the presence of Christ, over against views of Jesus as historical or exalted in heaven. This emphasis on Christ's immanence resulted in questioning the validity of the whole discussion about the presence of Christ in the sacraments. Eventually the Quakers drew the conclusion that there is no biblical mandate for "sacraments" at all other than the **spiritual sacrament** of knowing/experiencing Christ's presence.

Current Situation. By the end of the Reformation(s) period, the lines in the sacramental sand were pretty much drawn as they stand even today. This does not mean that there have been no developments in sacramental theology or practice since the seventeenth century. Throughout the eighteenth and nineteenth centuries, different denominations developed their sacramental theologies in ways that cohere with other strains of their theology and practice. In the twentieth century, liturgical historical research, the **liturgical renewal movement**, **Vatican II**, and ecumenical discussions sponsored by the **World Council of Churches** have brought churches much closer in theology and practice than they have been since the Reformation(s). But both of these types of changes represent movements within the already defined trajectories of sacramental theology instead of radical departures from them.

SYMBOL OR SIGN?

With this overview in hand, we can return to the question with which we started: "**What is the relationship between the ritual elements and actions on the one hand and that to which they point on the other?**" This is the question of sacrament versus ordinance that we laid out as we distinguished between signs and symbols. What is evident from our historical survey, however, is that the answer is rarely a clear either/or. The initial answers we have explored in this historical overview offers a spectrum of possible sacramental theologies.

- Catholics (and although we have not discussed them, Orthodox Christians) hold the highest sacramental position, viewing all seven sacraments as means of grace that function *ex opere operato*.

- Anglicans, with their *via media* of two major scaraments and five minor ones have the highest sacramental theology among Protestants.

- While Lutherans retain much of the participatory emphases of Catholic sacramental theology, they do so in a very different way and limit the sacrmanets to baptism and Table.

- With Calvin the sacramental nature of baptism and Table is affirmed but with much less at stake in the discussion of "presence" than the others on the sacramental side of the spectrum.

- Zwingli interpreted baptism and Table as human actions instead of means of God's grace basically making them ordinances.

- Anabaptists explictly referred to the rituals as ordinances, rejecting Zwingli's willingness to continue to baptize infants.

- And, finally, Quakers are off the chart in viewing these rituals as human actions that are unnecessary.

THE HISTORY AND THEOLOGY OF BAPTISM

There are two ways for students of Protestant worship to reflect on the theological and existential meaning of Christian initiation, specifically baptism. The first is to locate oneself and one's tradition in the historical debates about baptism. The second is to examine actual practices/liturgies and locate oneself (and one's tradition) in relation to them and what they mean. In this chapter, we'll offer a historical sketch allowing readers to do the first. (A reminder about the nature of this textbook as a *basic* introduction, however, is needed at this point. In the historical sketch provided, much of the complexity and diversity of practices in different historical periods and geographical regions is ignored for the sake of viewing the main developments that have shaped contemporary baptismal thought and practices.) In the next chapter, we will examine contemporary baptismal liturgies allowing readers to do the second.

BACKGROUND

In the ancient Mediterranean world, bathing (that is, for personal hygiene) was a communal or social activity. The **Romans** inherited the idea of public baths from the Greeks, but were able to extend the practice significantly by building public baths across the Empire, thanks to their aqueduct system. These baths could be immense—with some accommodating hundreds and even thousands of bathers at one time. In addition to this cultural practice, public baths have been found in temples or at religious sites that were assumed to have therapeutic or healing qualities. Moreover, some Greco-Roman religions used immersions for ritual purification.

As with so many of the rituals of the Christian Church, however, the primary antecedent to Christian baptism seems to be found in the practices of our **Jewish** forebears. Baptism can be traced to a number of backgrounds in Judaism. First is the *mikveh*, or the Jewish practice of bathing as ritual cleansing. In ancient Judaism, purity laws specified a range of ways people would become unclean: getting certain skin blemishes, having a monthly menstrual period, or caring for a dead body. Various rituals were used to return to normalcy, including washing.

Second, the story of the Christ Event begins with **John the Baptist**. Scholars debate how much John's baptism was an innovation versus how much it reflected other Jewish practices of the time. Regardless, the New Testament texts (that is, Christian interpretations of John the Baptist; e.g., see Mark 1:2-8) interpret his baptism as having three related emphases:

- John calls his audience to repent of their wrongdoing before he baptizes them.

- John described his baptism as being for the forgiveness of sins.

- John views his baptism eschatologically as related to the baptism of the Holy Spirit yet to come.

Finally, part of the heritage of Christian baptism is the Jewish practice of **circumcision**. On the eighth day of a boy's life, he would be circumcised as a sign of participating in the covenant between God and Israel. Obviously, circumcision is not a water ritual, but we will see below how later Christian theologians interpreted baptism in relation to circumcision.

EARLY CHURCH

First Century. As we turn from backgrounds to the Church itself, we begin with texts concerning baptism found in the New Testament. We need to move through this early material fairly thoroughly because it is different interpretations of the language, stories, and images here that influence all of what follows in the evolution of theology and practice. We do not need a full exegetical exploration of each passage so much as we need to attend to different elements of the passages that tell us about the author's view of baptism.

Paul. We begin with a passage from the opening of 1 Corinthians:

> For it has been reported to me by Chloe's people that there are quarrels among you, my brothers and sisters. What I mean is that each of you says, "I belong to Paul," or "I belong to Apollos," or "I belong to Cephas," or "I belong to Christ." Has Christ been divided? Was Paul crucified for you? Or were you baptized in the name of Paul? I thank God that I baptized none of you except Crispus and Gaius, so that no one can say that you were baptized in my name. (I did baptize also the household of Stephanas; beyond that, I do not know whether I baptized anyone else.) For Christ did not send me to baptize but to proclaim the gospel, and not with eloquent wisdom, so that the cross of Christ might not be emptied of its power. (1 Cor 1:11-17)

Paul has written to address divisions in the Corinthian house churches, which arise at least partly due to allegiances to different ministers. Notice what the text says (and implies) about baptism. First is the issue of **belonging**. While some Corinthians argue that they belong to different apostles based on who baptized them, Paul implies that the baptized belong to Christ because they were baptized *in his name*. Second, Paul emphasizes proclamation over baptism. It is unclear what theological claim he would make about the relation of preaching and baptism if he were not addressing churches in conflict.

Nowhere in his corpus does Paul offer a theology of baptism, but he does refer to baptism while writing theologically. In Romans, Paul is explaining his understanding of justification as God's free gift when he raises the logical question: If God is graceful in response to our sin, should we sin more so God can be more graceful? The answer is obviously no, but Paul uses baptism to explain why.

> What then are we to say? Should we continue in sin in order that grace may abound? By no means! How can we who died to sin go on living in it? Do you not know that all of us who have been baptized into Christ Jesus were baptized into his death? Therefore we have been buried with him by baptism into death, so that, just as Christ was raised from the dead by the glory of the Father, so we too might walk in newness of life. For if we have been united with him in a death like his, we will certainly be united with him in a resurrection like his. We know that our old self was crucified with him so that the body of sin might be destroyed, and we might no longer be enslaved to sin. (Rom 6:1-6)

As with the 1 Corinthians reading above, Paul here asserts that baptism is *into* Christ. This is **participatory language**. In baptism we *have* participated in Christ's death. But the participation is not just in reference to a past salvific act. It is also eschatological: through baptism we *will be united* with Christ in resurrection. Paul is not as direct as we might like, but here seems to imply that baptism is a means by which Christ's death and resurrection is effective in people's lives.

Notice also that when Paul speaks of baptism as participating in Christ's death he uses the metaphor of being buried with Christ. Some interpreters assume this metaphor refers to the practice of *immersion*—in other words, being buried under water.

In his letter to the Galatians, Paul reminds his readers of the gospel he preached to them. The reminder is intended to keep them from thinking that they must from submit to circumcision (become Jewish) to be Christian. As he tries to explain the correct understanding of the relationship of the Hebraic law and salvation in Christ, he reminds them of the meaning of their baptism.

> As many of you as were baptized into Christ have clothed yourselves with Christ. There is no longer Jew or Greek, there is no longer slave or free, there is no longer male and female; for all of you are one in Christ Jesus. (Gal 3:27-28; cf. 1 Cor 12:13)

Paul again asserts that baptism is participation in Christ. In the opening line, Paul uses the image of being clothed with Christ as a metaphor for this participation. This language likely relates to the early church practice of baptizing people naked and then clothing them in a **white robe** as a sign of their new life.

Most scholars consider verse 28 to be a traditional baptismal formula—in other words, it is a line Paul is quoting, not creating. Specifically, he is quoting a line his readers know by heart. Participation in Christ erases lines of distinction, division, and social hierarchy. Baptism unites us with Christ and with all who are in Christ.

Matthew. When we turn from Paul in the mid-first century to the Gospels, written in the latter third of the first century, we find scenes in which Jesus himself is baptized. Each of the Gospels present Jesus's baptism differently, but they must all deal with two problems. The first is that if Jesus was baptized by John it would appear that John was greater than Jesus, even that Jesus was John's disciple. And second, if baptism was for repentance and the forgiveness of sins, why did Jesus have to be baptized? Let's look at how Matthew deals with these questions.

> Then Jesus came from Galilee to John at the Jordan, to be baptized by him. John would have prevented him, saying, "I need to be baptized by you, and do you come to me?" But Jesus answered him, "Let it be so now; for it is proper for us in this way to fulfill all righteousness." Then he consented. And when Jesus had been baptized, just as he came up from the water, suddenly the heavens were opened to him and he saw the Spirit of God descending like a dove and alighting on him. And a voice from heaven said, "This is my Son, the Beloved, with whom I am well pleased." (Matt 3:13-17)

Matthew deals with the two problems we mentioned by having John himself say that he should not be baptizing Jesus. And then Matthew shows Jesus giving a different reason for being baptized than we heard in Paul: to fulfill all righteousness. Jesus is baptized in response to his call. This call is confirmed in what follows in the scene. The baptism functions as an epiphany and anointing in which God **sends the Holy Spirit** upon Jesus and claims Jesus as God's own.

As Matthew begins the story of Jesus's ministry with baptism, so he ends his Gospel with a reference to baptism when Jesus gives the **Great Commission** to the apostles:

> Go therefore and make disciples of all nations, baptizing them in the name of the Father and of the Son and of the Holy Spirit, and teaching them to obey everything that I have commanded you. And remember, I am with you always, to the end of the age. (Matt 28:19-20)

Although Matthew never presents Jesus as baptizing others himself, the post-resurrection Jesus here commands the disciples to baptize others as they **make disciples**. In other words, baptism is related to conversion and initiation. Notice Matthew does not assume that baptism is the end of the process of Christian discipling—instruction follows. So there is **teaching/catechism** both before and after baptism.

Also important in this text is the **trinitarian formula** Matthew offers for baptism. Whereas Paul had talked about being baptized in the name of Jesus, Matthew asserts that baptism is to be performed in the name of the Father, Son, and Holy Spirit.

Acts. Following Peter's Pentecost sermon in Acts, we find Luke offering a view of baptism that connects several of the themes we have seen elsewhere in the New Testament.

142

> Now when they heard this, they were cut to the heart and said to Peter and to the other apostles, "Brothers, what should we do?" Peter said to them, "Repent, and be baptized every one of you in the name of Jesus Christ so that your sins may be forgiven; and you will receive the gift of the Holy Spirit. For the promise is for you, for your children, and for all who are far away, everyone whom the Lord our God calls to him." And he testified with many other arguments and exhorted them, saying, "Save yourselves from this corrupt generation." So those who welcomed his message were baptized, and that day about three thousand persons were added. They devoted themselves to the apostles' teaching and fellowship, to the breaking of bread and the prayers. (Acts 2:37-42)

This passage implies that baptism **requires repentance** and is for **the forgiveness of sins**. It is performed **in the name of Jesus Christ**, not the Trinity. It is a means of **receiving the Holy Spirit**, which has been promised by God. And it is **incorporation into the community of faith** where members continue to receive instruction.

In texts we have read that have mentioned the Holy Spirit, it has been assumed that baptism is a means for receiving the Spirit. But this is not always the case in the New Testament. In Acts 8, Philip baptizes Samaritan converts but it is not until apostles come and **lay hands** on them that they receive the Holy Spirit.

> But when they believed Philip, who was proclaiming the good news about the kingdom of God and the name of Jesus Christ, they were baptized, both men and women. . . . Now when the apostles at Jerusalem heard that Samaria had accepted the word of God, they sent Peter and John to them. The two went down and prayed for them that they might receive the Holy Spirit (for as yet the Spirit had not come upon any of them; they had only been baptized in the name of the Lord Jesus). Then Peter and John laid their hands on them, and they received the Holy Spirit. (Acts 8:12, 14-17)

Or in Acts 10, Cornelius's household receives the Holy Spirit while Peter is preaching without being baptized. In fact, they are baptized *in response* to have received the Spirit.

> While Peter was still speaking, the Holy Spirit fell upon all who heard the word. The circumcised believers who had come with Peter were astounded that the gift of the Holy Spirit had been poured out even on the Gentiles, for they heard them speaking in tongues and extolling God. Then Peter said, "Can anyone withhold the water for baptizing these people who have received the Holy Spirit just as we have?" So he ordered them to be baptized in the name of Jesus Christ. (Acts 10:44-48a)

Second and Third Centuries. By the end of the first century and the middle of the second, baptism had come to involve a time of fasting and preparation beforehand, and baptism was required for access to the Lord's Supper. In ***The Didache***, or the Teaching of the Twelve Apostles, which was an early church order likely written near the end of the first or beginning of the second century (although some scholars now argue for an earlier provenance), the author follows Matthew in instructing baptism to be done using a **trinitarian formula**:

143

> Now about baptism: this is how to baptize. Give public instruction on all these points, and then baptize in running water, in the name of the Father and of the Son and of the Holy Spirit. If you do not have running water, baptize in some other. If you cannot in cold, then in warm. If you have neither, then pour water on the head three times "in the name of the Father, Son, and Holy Spirit." Before the baptism, moreover, the one who baptizes and the one being baptized must fast, and any others who can.

Moreover, we see that discussions of **modes of baptism** had already arisen in the Church by this point. The *Didache* proposes a hierarchy of modes: immersion in running water, in cold water, in warm water, and pouring water over the head.

By the third century, baptismal rituals seem to have become more defined and more complex. One example, found in *The Apostolic Tradition*, is a church manual incorrectly attributed to Hippolytus of Rome (170–235). This text was discovered in the mid-nineteenth century and has been quite influential in the twentieth-century discussions in the liturgical renewal movement concerning initiation, Eucharist, and ordination. The document was likely written sometime in the early to mid-third century and gives the earliest complete description of or prescription for a baptism ritual. We are going to look at a few excerpts, because the ritual is quite long.

> Let catechumens spend three years as hearers of the word. (17.1)
>
> At cockcrow prayer shall be made over the water. The stream shall flow through the baptismal tank or pour into it from above when there is no scarcity of water, but if there is a scarcity, whether constant or sudden, then use whatever water you can find. (21.1-2)
>
> They shall remove their clothing. And first baptize the little ones; if they can speak for themselves, they shall do so; if not their parents or other relatives shall speak for them. Then baptize the men, and last of all the women; they must first loosen their hair and put aside any gold or silver ornaments that they are wearing; let no one take any alien thing down to the water with them. (21.1-5)

The document prescribes three years of **catechetical preparation** with intense instruction in the days just before baptism. The Easter Vigil, which lasted from 2:00 a.m. through sunrise, became the primary time of baptisms, although Pentecost was also used.

Just before the bath itself, the catechumenates go through intense **moral examination**, renunciation of the devil, and exorcisms. The one being baptized is stripped naked, **anointed** with the laying on of hands (first children, then men, then women). Notice that the children being baptized here include **infants** who cannot speak for themselves.

> When he has renounced [Satan and all Satan's servants and all Satan's works], the presbyter shall anoint him with the oil of exorcism, saying: Let all spirits depart from thee. Then, after these things, let him give him over to the presbyter who baptizes,

and let the candidates stand in the water, naked, a deacon going with them likewise. And when he who is being baptized goes down in the water, he who baptizes him, putting his hand on him, shall say thus: Dost though believe in God, the Father Almighty? And he who is baptized shall say: I believe. Then holding his hand placed on his head, he shall baptize him once. (21.10-18)

Once the baptizand is standing in the water naked, she or he is examined again, specifically being asked to **profess faith** in the Triune God, using questions that reflect language that grew into the **Apostles' Creed**. The mode of baptism is immersion with the one officiating standing outside the water and a deacon in the water helping the one being baptized. The person is submersed three times, each time following their affirmation of faith in one member of the Trinity.

Following the baptism, the person comes out of the water and is **anointed again**, this time with oil of thanksgiving by a presbyter, dries off, is **clothed**, and is brought back into the community. Only then does the bishop **lay hands** on the person and offer her or him the **kiss of fellowship**. This kiss is a passing of the peace that is offered before one participates in the Table. So this is the first time that the person has received the kiss and will be the first time the person receives the **Eucharist**.

One interesting thing not seen in our excerpts was that during this period of the Church, catechumens were not taught everything before they were ritually initiated into the community of faith. Some things, especially the meaning of the "mysteries" of baptism and Eucharist, were reserved for the eight days from Easter Sunday to the next Sunday. This teaching was called **mystagogy**, or mystagogical instruction or preaching.

Fourth and Fifth Centuries. In the fourth and fifth centuries, the Church maintained the basic pattern we find in ***The Apostolic Tradition***, although different regions developed the individual ritual parts of baptism in different and more elaborate ways.

There were changes in the political and theological climate that were beginning to influence the later evolution of baptism. Christianity had become popular enough that Constantine legalized it in 312 and Theodosius outlawed paganism in the latter part of that century. The Empire became officially Christian. This would mean that over time there would be fewer and fewer adults to baptize, because everyone had already converted to Christianity. **Infant baptism** was slowly becoming the norm.

This shift caused some theological problems because it separated instruction and preparation from baptism. You cannot teach a newborn about the faith. All catechism follows baptism.

Augustine stepped into this situation and asked why the Church baptizes infants:

And this is the meaning of the great sacrament of baptism which is solemnized among us, that all who attain to this grace should die to sin, as [Christ] is said to have died to sin, because He died in the flesh, which is the likeness of sin; and rising from the font regenerate, as He arose alive from the grave, should begin a new life in the Spirit, whatever may be the age of the body? For from the infant newly born to

145

the old man bent with age, as there is none shut out from baptism, so there is none who in baptism does not die to sin. But infants die only to original sin; those who are older die also to all the sins which their evil lives have added to the sin which they brought with them. (**Enchiridion** 42–43)

His answer begins with liturgical practice and moves to theology, not the reverse. The question is, specifically, if baptism is for the forgiveness of sin, what kind of sin is forgiven in infants (since it is common practice for them to be baptized)? His answer is that infants have obviously committed no sin by their own actions, so (through his reading of Paul), he concludes that the sin forgiven is the sin of Adam, or **original sin**.

MEDIEVAL CHURCH

There are a number of sources we could consult from the church of the Middle Ages to look at baptism in those times. A good example of the point to which baptismal theology evolved comes from late in the period and is found in the **Decree for the Armenians**, which is from the Council of Florence (1439). The decree was issued in hopes of bringing about the union of the Armenian Church in the East with the Catholic Church in the West. It includes a lengthy section on the sacraments that is drawn heavily from the thought of Thomas Aquinas.

Three of the sacraments, namely baptism, confirmation and orders [ordination], imprint indelibly on the soul a character, that is a kind of stamp which distinguishes it from the rest. Hence they are not repeated in the same person. The other four, however, do not imprint a character and can be repeated.

Holy baptism holds the first place among all the sacraments, for it is the gate of the spiritual life; through it we become members of Christ and of the body of the church. Since death came into the world through one person, unless we are born again of water and the spirit, we cannot, as Truth says, enter the kingdom of heaven. The matter of this sacrament is true and natural water, either hot or cold. The form is: I baptize you in the name of the Father and of the Son and of the holy Spirit.

What we find here is that Augustine's logic has been reversed. Instead of working from infant baptism to original sin, the theological thought moves from original sin to baptism.

Fear of a child dying unbaptized and being eternally condemned because of original sin led to infant baptism being absolutely the norm. Baptism is assumed to be effective *ex opere operato* in making an **ontological change** in the baptizand, and therefore is **unrepeatable**.

In fact, the fear of dying while in a state of original sin was so great that many newborns were taken from their mothers while they were still lying in the birthing bed. The priest met the father, child, godparents, and any witnesses at the door of the church or baptistery and asked a series of questions including what the child was to be named. (This is why some people incorrectly refer to infant baptism as **christen-**

ing. The christening is simply the part of the ritual in which the child being baptized is given a Christian name.) After the examination, the priest exorcised demons from the child, anointed it, and put salt in the child's mouth before it was brought inside to symbolize that it "should be delivered from the corruption of sin, experience a relish for good works, and be delighted with the food of divine wisdom."

While priests were those ordained to administer the sacraments, any layperson could perform an **emergency baptism**. The Decree for the Armenians speaks to this:

> The minister of this sacrament is a priest, who is empowered to baptize in virtue of his office. But in case of necessity not only a priest or a deacon, but even a lay man or a woman, even a pagan and a heretic, can baptize provided he or she uses the form of the church and intends to do what the church does. The effect of this sacrament is the remission of all original and actual guilt, also of all penalty that is owed for that guilt. Hence no satisfaction for past sins is to be imposed on the baptized, but those who die before they incur any guilt go straight to the kingdom of heaven and the vision of God.

Given the high infant mortality rates during the Middle Ages, some have asserted that midwives did more baptisms than priests in this period.

Whether a midwife or a priest officiated, it is clear that baptism was not part of Sunday morning worship in the presence of the community. This partly explains why **baptisteries** were often separate buildings from the regular worship space.

Because infant baptism was the norm, three immersions gave way to pouring (**affusion**) as the standard mode of baptism in the West.

But if infant baptism addresses original sin, what is to be done about sin that occurs after baptism? A couple of practices evolved in relation to this problem.

First, since infants were baptized right after birth, it was usually private, not part of worship service and not on Easter, and the anointing that immediately followed baptism in the ancient church evolved into **confirmation** as a separate ritual/sacrament from baptism. This was partly due to the fact that while priests administered baptism, only bishops confirmed people. Bishops' responsibilities covered larger geographical areas than a priest's parish. Thus he would only come to individual parishes every so often, and confirmation had to be delayed. But this delay also allowed for instruction and preparation, for public testimony of the confirmand, and for encouragement in dealing with human sinfulness.

The second major development was the practice of **penance**. This sacrament was called the "second plank of the Church." If the Church, as a ship, was built with baptism, penance was used to repair holes in the hull.

PROTESTANT REFORMATION(S)

Protestants argued that we are justified by faith alone, not by works of the Church. For **Martin Luther** faith does not make baptism, but receives it. So he rejected the idea of *ex opere operato* in relation to baptism. One might think that this would mean that he would also reject the practice of infant baptism because it would seem that a child cannot receive baptism by faith. Luther, though, saw baptism as the covenant-making seal of **God's promise of forgiveness received in faith**. This eschatological emphasis on promise (as God's initiative) continues to make infant baptism appropriate. It is not that we are saved through baptism, but that God is the primary speaker in baptism promising us salvation to be received and experienced fully with mature faith.

We should note, moreover, that for Luther faith is not a work; it is not something we do so much as something we are given by a graceful God. So Luther was willing to claim tentatively that there may well be nascent faith in infants, given to them by God.

Luther returned baptism to the context of **communal worship**, emphasizing the rite of passage as **initiation into the Church**. Over time, he simplified the ritual of the sacrament a great deal, for instance, removing the placing of salt in the infant's mouth. Since there is no biblical language supporting the element, it was removed.

While Luther rejected confirmation as a sacrament, he did hold onto it as a second stage of initiation involving instruction and laying on of hands.

Ulrich Zwingli argued that the sacraments are *signs* of faith, not instruments of God's grace. So, in his theology, God in no way brings about salvation through baptism. Instead **the Church signifies the covenant** God has made with us through baptism. Even more than with Luther, this would seem to indicate that infants should not be baptized. Indeed, early on Zwingli lamented the practice of baptizing infants, but later he changed his mind (some argue due more to political pressure than theological reflection).

He did, however, offer a theological justification for continuing to baptize infants by drawing an analogy between infant baptism as a sign of the new covenant and the sign of the old covenant—the **circumcision** of Jewish male infants on the eighth day after their birth. So, Zwingli argues, it is not simply the faith of the individual being baptized that is at stake; baptism is a sign of the *Church's* faith and fulfilling its side of the covenant with God.

The **Anabaptists** asserted that since there is no evidence for infant baptism in the New Testament, it should be rejected as invalid. Justification is by faith, and thus baptism requires repentance and belief (as was true of those converted and baptized in the New Testament).

This group was accused of **re-baptizing** (thus the name Anabaptists), but of course their argument was that what happened to them as infants was not a real baptism at all since they were not yet believers. It was just a cold bath. Real baptism requires real faith. This rationale is why the Anabaptists claimed that the true church is made up only of those who consciously make the decision to **enact the testimony of faith** commanded by Christ and not by those baptized indiscriminately and unconsciously as infants.

One can imagine how other groups reacted to being told they were not part of the true Church. Luther and Zwingli both approved of persecution against the Anabaptists. Since the Anabaptists had chosen to live by a second baptism, persecutors said, they should die by a third baptism. **Felix Manz** was the first Anabaptist martyr in Zurich. In 1527, his hands were bound to his knees with a stick thrust between his arms and legs and he was thrown into the icy waters of the Limmat River. This was not one of the Church's finest hours.

Most of the Anabaptists continued practicing baptism by pouring. Baptism by **immersion** that came to influence the Baptist and Stone-Campbell movements in North America was inherited more from the Separatist movement in England that developed into various British Baptist movements than the Anabaptist movement described above. In addition to the claim that baptism in the New Testament was by immersion and thus should continue to be practiced that way, these groups claimed that the symbolic nature of immersion better fit the theology of burial and rising with Christ than does pouring or sprinkling.

John Calvin rejected both Luther's speculations about an infant's sleeping faith and Anabaptist emphasis on subjective experience of Christ as a requirement for baptism. Instead, he emphasized the **priority of grace** in his theology of baptism. Because God is sovereign, God's grace *precedes* both faith and the sign of faith (baptism). Therefore, infant baptism best proclaims **God's initiative in making covenant** with us. Put differently, infant baptism exemplifies predestination in the sense that it represents God's prevenient grace.

This does not mean that Calvin had no requirements for baptism. Only children of **baptized, Christian parents** could be baptized. Similar to Luther's emphasis on promise, Calvin argued that baptizing a child of Christian parents is for *future* repentance and faith. So even though Calvin simplified the ritual of baptism even more than Luther, he added **exhortations** to the parents emphasizing their role in raising the child in the ways of the faith.

When it comes to mode of baptism, Calvin recognized that the ancient church practiced immersion, but he did not see this as prescriptive for the Church. He argued that the mode was insignificant for admission into the Church.

CONTEMPORARY SITUATION

By the end of the Reformation(s), all the basic theologies of baptism around today were already in place. Developments in baptismal theology in Protestantism since the sixteenth century are all variations on the themes introduced during this time period. Although the above survey oversimplifies the positions we have examined, readers should be able to locate the theologies of their traditions as growing out of one of these foundational views.

That said, it should be noted that the **liturgical renewal movements** of the twentieth century have led to some blurring of the lines between these different positions. The significant reforms of the **Second Vatican Council** (1962–65) blurred the lines dividing Roman Catholic and Protestant sacramental theology and practice. Further blurring of the baptismal lines (especially among Protestant denominations) occurred due to one of the great achievements of the ecumenical movement: the

1982 adoption and publication of the highly influential document **Baptism, Eucharist, and Ministry (BEM)** by the Faith and Order division of the World Council of Churches. Traditions that accepted multiple modes of the ritual came to see immersion as especially representative of the theological emphases related to initiation into the church body. Traditions that once rejected baptisms of other communions (for instance, because the person was baptized as an infant or was not baptized by immersion) grew to accept persons into membership from these other communions without requiring re-baptizing. And baptismal liturgies and practices across denominations grew closer to each other in structure and language.

Blurring the lines between different denominational baptismal theologies and practices, however, is not the same as erasing those lines. The core theological and liturgical distinctions established during the Reformation(s) are still present in Mainline Protestantism. For instance, the question concerning who is the primary actor in the ritual—God or the one being baptized—is a central one. Is the ritual a means of grace (sacrament) or a mode of human witness to God's grace (ordinance)?

Moreover, even within traditions, different congregations, pastors, and individual Christians emphasize different theological aspects of baptism. Is the ritual primarily about initiation into the body of Christ, or regeneration, or the gift of the Holy Spirit, or what? How are these different elements to be weighed and prioritized, theologically speaking?

Worship leaders' responsibility extends beyond holding and sharing personal views. They must represent the tradition that ordains or commissions them and interpret that tradition for their congregations. Such representation of denominational theology by the clergy does not dictate congregants' personal theology of baptism but does serve to inform their theology and expand their experience of the sacrament or ordinance when it is administered in worship. The historical sketch above identifies a range of key theological questions with which one must deal when developing a full-blown theology of the ritual of baptism in relation to one's tradition. When considered cumulatively, answers to these questions build a case for determining the meaning of the ritual for a church and what counts as valid, authentic, and acceptable baptism practice and why. The list below draws together those questions:

A. What role should scripture and tradition play in defining the understanding and practice of baptism?

B. Who is the primary actor/voice in baptism: God, the Church, or the baptizand?

   1. Is baptism a means of grace or an act of faith only?

C. What is required for baptism: faith, repentance, faith of parents?

   1. Who is eligible to be baptized? (Why?)

D. How is baptism initiation into the Church?

1. Initiation into what church (congregation, denomination, universal Church)?

2. Is baptism required for church membership?

3. What does baptism say about the nature of the Church?

E. Is, and if so how is, the gift of the Holy Spirit related to baptism?

F. What is the relation of baptism and forgiveness of sin(s)?

1. What about sin that follows baptism? (Does, and if so how does, baptism affect our sinfulness given that we sin after being baptized? How does/should the church ritually deal with post-baptismal sin?)

G. What is required ritually for baptism?

1. What mode is acceptable/required: immersion, pouring, sprinkling?

2. What baptism formula should be used (and why):

   i.   . . . in the name of Jesus
   ii.   . . . in the name of the Father, Son, and Holy Spirit
   iii. . . . other trinitarian formula (e.g., Creator, Redeemer, Sustainer)?

3. What vows, affirmations of faith, or other promises are required of the baptizand or representatives?

4. Who is authorized to baptize?

5. What is the relation of baptism and confirmation?

6. Is baptism required for participation in the Table ritual? Why or why not?

H. How do you (and your tradition) rank (in terms of importance) these different descriptions of what baptism does:

1. Initiation into the Church

2. Incorporation into Christ

3. Participation in Christ's death and resurrection

4. Cleansing (remission of sins)

5. Testimony/profession of faith

I. Given your responses above, name the ways your personal theology of baptism coheres with your denominational/theological tradition and its historical precedents in the Medieval Church and the Protestant Reformation(s) and ways your theology is at odds with that heritage.

BAPTISMAL PRACTICES

At the opening of the last chapter, we noted that there are two ways to reflect on the meaning of Christian initiation (specifically baptism). The first, which was the focus of the previous chapter, is to locate oneself and one's tradition in the historical debates about baptism. The second is to examine actual practices and liturgies and locate oneself and one's tradition in relation to them and how they construct meaning. In this chapter, we gather the tools to accomplish this second mode of reflection. We will, respectively, reflect on appropriate times for Christian initiation and analyze the basic elements found in most rituals of Christian initiation (baptism and confirmation).

For our example liturgy concerning baptism, we will explore the primary baptismal liturgy found in *Evangelical Lutheran Worship* (Augsburg Fortress, 2006), the service book/hymnal of the Evangelical Lutheran Church in America (ELCA), with permission. Readers should compare this liturgy with those dealing with Christian initiation found in their own denominational service books. To assist with such comparison, the chapter includes videos of baptisms from different traditions.

THE TIMING OF BAPTISM

Baptism in the Liturgical Calendar. **Easter Sunday** and **Pentecost Sunday** are especially appropriate times for baptism and confirmation. As holy days, these are occasions when classes of persons seeking to join or be confirmed by the church are often baptized or confirmed. Lent is a time of preparation and catechism leading up to baptism on the Day of Resurrection. Baptisms can be performed at an Easter Vigil or any other Easter Day service. Because Pentecost is celebrated as the birth of the Church, when three thousand persons were baptized following Peter's sermon, this day is also used for baptism of groups in some congregations (Acts 2:37-42).

Of course, while Easter and Pentecost are traditional days associated with baptisms, *any* time the community of faith gathers for worship is an appropriate time for someone to be initiated into the community through baptism. Especially in traditions in which infants are baptized, baptisms occur throughout the year, whenever parents and pastors agree that the time is appropriate.

Baptism in the Ordo. As described earlier, the fourfold movement of most Christian worship is Gathering, Proclamation, Response, and Sending Forth. Baptism most properly falls in the **Response** movement, where the Table is also observed. Sacraments or ordinances follow word. As invitations to join the Church follow the sermon, we submit to baptism, having heard God's good news.

In truth, though, many churches perform baptisms early in the service. This is usually done for practical reasons more than theological ones. If it is an infant being baptized, pastors do not want to make the baby sit through two-thirds of the service before getting to the nursery. If believer's baptism by immersion is practiced, the pastor and those being baptized need a chance to dry off and return to the service before too much gets underway.

While practical considerations may have led to placing baptisms early in the service, theological rationales have been developed to demonstrate the appropriateness of the placement. Because baptism is initiation into the community of faith, it is appropriate that it be done during the **Gathering**. This can be seen as a temporal analogy to the spatial practice of congregations placing the baptismal font near the entrance to the nave (discussed in the chapter on worship space).

Infant baptism preceding the proclamation signifies the fact that the child will be nurtured into the faith in the same way that baptism following proclamation signifies a response to God's good news. Moreover, some congregations that practice believer's baptism invite baptizands to respond to the invitation to discipleship and make a confession of faith on one Sunday following the sermon, and then baptize them during the Gathering the following Sunday.

THE CORE BAPTISMAL PATTERN

While different denominations, congregations, and even clergy can have significantly different baptismal practices, underneath these differences is a basic shared ritual pattern. This pattern involves

- an introduction to the ritual,

- the presentation of the candidate to be baptized,

- examination of the candidate,

- blessing of the water,

- the bath itself,

- a blessing,

- and a communal affirmation of the one baptized.

Not all baptismal rituals include all elements listed in a formal fashion, but the basic flow they represent can usually be identified.

Introduction to the Ritual. The baptism ritual begins with the officiant explaining to the participants and reminding the congregation of the meaning, purpose, and importance of this rite of passage. This often involves references to the kinds of scripture passages and traditional language we examined in the previous chapter as well as references to the tradition's particular understanding of the import of the sacrament or ordinance. The introduction may be only a few short formal lines spoken while people are gathered at the baptistery or standing around the font, or it may involve the whole sermon as a full exposition of some aspect of the meaning of baptism.

Presentation of the Candidate. Next comes the presentation of the candidate. In the case of an infant baptism, the parents or godparents usually present the child formally for baptism. In traditions that practice believer's baptism, often a sponsor from the congregation or even the pastor presents the person to the congregation. In some traditions this is a short formal statement that is the same at every baptism; in others it may involve a biographical statement introducing the individual to the congregation. In the latter case, often there is a mention of what has brought the person to baptism at this point in his or her life.

Examination of the Candidate. Given that we call those to be baptized "candidates," we should not be surprised to find that after the candidates have been presented to the congregation, the presider asks them questions concerning their faith, their readiness for the new life of being a Christian, and/or their commitment to the Church. Often congregations are invited to reaffirm their own baptismal vows along with the candidates.

In some churches at the ordinance end of the theological spectrum, this part of the ritual actually occurs in a service prior to baptism (e.g., the week before). A candidate responds to the invitation to discipleship one week, gives a testimony, and/or makes the "Good Confession"—that is, affirms Peter's confession that Jesus is the Christ (Matt 16:13-19)—and then is baptized the next week.

In creedal traditions, the questions usually follow the historic, trinitarian pattern of the Apostles' Creed. Other traditional questions are sometimes asked, such as those relating to the renunciation of the devil (i.e., turning one's back on his or her old ways of life).

In the case of infant baptism, the questions are asked of parents and sponsors until the children reach the age of confirmation and can answer them for themselves.

Blessing the Water. In traditions that are at the sacramental end of the spectrum, the ritual next includes a prayer over the water. For those who think of the water as holy after being blessed, the prayer may include actions such as lowering the Christ candle into the water on the Easter Vigil or signing the water with the sign of the cross.

For traditions more in the middle of the theological spectrum, the ritual may simply involve a prayer, although water may be poured into the font during the prayer to enliven the symbolism for all gathered. The prayer itself usually includes a litany of biblical references to water—for example, the waters of creation, the flood, the exodus, and Jesus's baptism.

In traditions at the ordinance end of the spectrum, it is rare to find a prayer like this. Since the ritual is not viewed as a means of grace, the emphasis is not on the

157

elements (as symbolic) through which God acts but on the actions of the ones being baptized as a testimony (sign) to the baptizands' dedication to God and to the faith of the Church.

The Bath. Once the candidate has been approved for baptism and the baptismal waters have been prepared, the baptism proper, that is, the bath, is performed. In sacramental traditions only ordained clergy can baptize, whereas in some ordinance traditions clergy usually do, but any baptized Christian can.

The presider usually pronounces to the candidate and to the worshiping community, "I baptize you . . ." but sometimes the passive voice is used to indicate that the one officiating is simply a representative of the church: "You are baptized . . ."

Some evangelical and penetcostal traditions baptize in the name of Jesus alone (following the tradition in Acts 2:38), but most churches argue that legitimate baptism involves the trinitarian formula found in Matthew 28:18-20. Many who are committed to just language in worship strive to make the language inclusive here, with phrasing such as "in the name of God the Creator, Redeemer, and Sustainer." However, this ritual has been one of the most controversial situations for changing the traditional male terminology for the Trinity.

The candidate is baptized either by immersion (being submerged in water), affusion (having water poured over the head), or aspersion (sprinkling water on the head).

When **affusion** is the mode of baptism, the clergyperson pours from a pitcher or dips a shell into the font and uses it to pour water on the head of the candidate.

When **aspersion** is the mode, the clergy person dips his or her hand in the font and allows water to drip from it on the head of the one being baptized. This mode often blends the baptism with laying on of hands as the wet hand is placed on the candidate's head.

Most congregations that require **immersion** have a baptistery/pool in the sanctuary, but some evangelical traditions argue for the preference of flowing water such as lakes or streams. Traditions that allow immersion but usually baptize by affusion or aspersion (and thus have only an font and not a baptistery installed in the worship space) often fulfill a baptizand's desire to be baptized by immersion by performing the baptism outside of regular Sunday worship at a neighboring church with a baptistery. Representatives of the worshiping congregation are invited to attend, and the affirmation of the baptizand (see below) occurs on the following Sunday in regular worship.

Immersion is usually performed by laying the candidate back in the water, but some traditions lay the person forward.

You can find any of these modes done once or done three times in relation to each person of the Trinity.

Blessing the Baptized. After the washing, a blessing is often pronounced over the newly baptized member of the Church. This echoes the ancient practice of anointing the baptizand immediately following the baptism. In different traditions, this can involve prayer, laying on hands, anointing, and sometimes exhortation to live the Christian life.

Affirming the New Member. Finally, the congregation affirms the baptized as a sign that they are now their brothers and sisters in the faith. As one pastor reminds his congregation at this point every time a baptism is performed, "For the Church, water is thicker than blood."

In some traditions that are less formal, the affirmation can occur in the form of applause as the person comes up out of the water. In traditions practicing infant baptism, the pastor may carry the child through the congregation so all can see her or him. Sometimes the congregation speaks a word of support and commitment to the person in unison voice. Often when older children or adults are baptized, they join the pastor at the door after the service to be greeted by all members of the congregation.

Baptism liturgies of denominations other than the ELCA can be found in the following:

AMEC Book of Worship, 41–52

Book of Common Prayer (Episcopal Church, USA), 297–308

Book of Common Worship (Presbyterian Church (USA), 403–20

Book of Worship: United Church of Christ, 129–44

Book of Ritual (CME), 13–17

Celebrate God's Presence (United Church of Canada), 319–57

Chalice Worship (DOC), 26–32

The United Methodist Book of Worship, 81–114

CONFIRMATION

Confirmation is a practice that, in Protestant traditions, is lacking a clear, ecumenical theology. That said, the ritual is an extension of infant baptism, if you will. This means that it is not generally found in traditions that practice believer's baptism. The exception to this rejection of confirmation is that some believer's baptism congregations will confirm children who were baptized as infants in other traditions and then transferred their membership to this community of faith.

The word *extension* in the previous paragraph is meant to indicate that confirmation is not a completion of infant baptism. In traditions that practice infant baptism, God is viewed as the primary actor in the ritual. Thus it is complete in and of itself. God does not do a partial job and then complete it later in confirmation. In baptism, one is initiated into full membership in the Church. Confirmation, therefore, is not required of people baptized as infants, but is instead a gift to them. Confirmation does just what the title indicates: it is a ritual *confirming* what occurred during baptism given that the one baptized as an infant was a completely passive recipient of the rite.

As noted in the previous chapter, confirmation was originally an anointing by the bishop that followed immediately on the heels of a baptism. As the church grew across the centuries, bishops' geographic responsibilities expanded as well (meaning that they could not be present at every baptism); and as infant baptism became the norm (instead of the baptism of adult converts), confirmation evolved into a ritual separated from baptism and a rite of passage for adolescents. The Anglican tradition follows the historic Roman Catholic practice of having the bishop officiate at confirmations. In most Protestant traditions, by contrast, the pastor of the congregation officiates.

As a coming of age rite, confirmation usually follows a period of **catechism** (often occurring during Lent) that includes instruction in the core tenets and practices of the Christian faith leading to a mature faith. Theologically speaking, then, the act of confirming moves in both directions during the ritual: the church confirms the person's baptismal identity and the confirmand confirms the baptismal faith and vocation given to her or him during baptism.

The way this mutual confirmation is ritualized is that the confirmation ritual in most Protestant traditions follows the core pattern of the baptismal ritual (and indeed is often performed in conjunction with others being baptized). Following this pattern does not include re-baptizing the confirmands, but serves as a remembrance of the baptism.

First, the one officiating *introduces the ritual*. This introduction may be prescribed in the denomination's book of worship; but given the misunderstanding that many laity have concerning confirmation, this is an important moment for the officiant to interpret the ritual for the congregation.

Next is the *presentation* of the confirmand. Usually this is done by a sponsor but in some congregations the confirmands introduce themselves as part of a testimony to their faith.

The confirmand is then *examined*. The questions asked usually parallel the questions asked during baptism. When the confirmands were baptized, their parents answered for them. Now they answer for themselves—they confirm their commitment to the Christian faith and to the Church.

The officiant then *blesses* the confirmand. This act can involve praying for the confirmand, laying on hands, and/or anointing the confirmand, and the words spoken usually include a reference to remembering one's baptism.

Finally, the congregation as a whole **reaffirms** the confirmands, recognizing their gifts for baptismal vocation and promising to help them to continue to grow in their faith.

160

Confirmation liturgies in different denominational service books are sometimes distinct liturgies and sometimes they are part and parcel of the baptism liturgy or a affirmation/reaffirmation liturgy (see below). Examples are as follows:

AMEC Book of Worship, 52–55

Book of Common Prayer (Episcopal Church, USA), 309–11

Book of Common Worship (Presbyterian Church (USA), 421–23

Book of Worship: United Church of Christ, 145–56

Book of Ritual (CME), 18–19

Celebrate God's Presence (United Church of Canada), 358–68

Chalice Worship (DOC), 32–3

Evangelical Lutheran Worship, 234–37

The United Methodist Book of Worship, 86–94

RE-AFFIRMATION OF BAPTISM

Historically, many ordinance traditions have allowed re-baptisms. Since in the theology of these denominations, the primary actor/voice in the ritual is the baptizand, re-baptizing was seen as an appropriate expression of the need to renew one's commitment to and belief in Christ. Ordinance traditions that have been influenced by the ecumenical conversation, however, have greatly moved away from this practice in order to be in closer communion with sacramental traditions that affirm baptism as once-only rite of passage. Indeed, from either an ordinance or sacramental perspective, one need not be initiated into the universal Church more than once.

The perspective that led to re-baptizing, however, has merit: we humans are a flawed and sinful species. While God can always be trusted to live up to God's side of the baptismal covenant, we cannot. Thus, while rejecting the practice of re-baptizing, many traditions, including high sacramental ones, are now recognizing the need for individuals and communities of faith to reclaim their baptismal identity and calling.

Different traditions label such practices differently—renewal of baptismal vows, remembrance of baptism, or reaffirmation of the baptismal covenant.

In some sense, every time there is a baptism or confirmation during worship, those who are baptized are invited to reaffirm their own baptism. Specific times, however, can be set when individuals desire to recommit their lives to Christ and the Church using this ritual, and times can be set for entire congregations to reaffirm their baptism. Liturgical occasions such as Baptism of the Lord on the Sunday after

Epiphany, or an Easter Sunday when no one is being baptized, are especially appropriate times for a communal reaffirmation of baptism.

This ritual closely follows the structure and content of the baptism and confirmation liturgies. A difference is that when water is used, it must be used in a way that makes it clear that baptism is not occurring.

THE HISTORY AND THEOLOGY OF TABLE

There are two primary ways to reflect on the meaning of the Christian Meal, as there were with baptism. The first is to locate ourselves and our tradition in the historical debates concerning the theology and practice of the Table. The second is to examine actual practices/liturgies and locate ourselves (and our tradition) in relation to them and the way the rituals construct meaning. (A reminder is needed at this point, however. In the historical sketch provided, much of the complexity and diversity of practices in different historical periods and geographical regions is ignored for the sake of getting view of significant developments found in representative texts and movements that have shaped contemporary eucharistic thought and practices.) In this chapter, we will examine resources that allow us to do the first approach. In the next chapter, we will attend to the second.

Before we begin surveying the history of the Table, however, we need to name an issue—that is, the issue of naming. Different Christian traditions use and have used different terms to refer to the Christian Meal: Eucharist, Communion, Holy Communion, Love Feast, Lord's Supper, and Mass. These terms are not mutually exclusive, but neither are they are exact synonyms. They emphasize different understandings or experiences of the Meal, and show some of the problems with ecumenical conversations about Table practice.

When we discuss a specific tradition, we will use the terms it uses. When we are speaking more broadly, we will also use the awkward terms of Table and Meal (capitalized) because they are neutral, even if undescriptive.

BACKGROUND

As with baptism, the history of the Christian Meal begins with the context of the ancient Mediterranean world in which the Church was given birth. While food was eaten for physical nourishment, communal meals, especially banquets and feasts, also had social and religious significance. Religious identity and economic level determined what was eaten. Social hierarchy determined who ate with whom. Meals often began and/or ended with a blessing related to drinking wine. ***Collegia***, or associations, had regular (e.g., monthly) meals as times of fellowship and networking. While *collegia* of the wealthy might be formed around trade or a specific (foreign) cult, those for the poor were formed for the primary purpose of providing proper funerals for their members. When these groups met for meals, then, freeborn members, freedmen, and slaves would eat and fellowship together.

Our **Jewish** forebears were very much a part of this mix. In the diaspora, a synagogue would have looked very much like a *collegium* related to a specific foreign cult. There is some archaeological evidence that communal meals/feasts were held in synagogues, but be it in the diaspora or Palestine, there were two Jewish meals in the home that were key to Jewish identity and are a significant part of the Table's background.

The first is the weekly **Sabbath meal**. As part of honoring the Sabbath, each week Jewish families gathered in their homes for meals at which traditional blessings were offered. The prayer included thanksgiving for creation—especially for the gift of food as a sign of God's mercy and goodness—thanksgiving for the exodus as the paradigm of God's salvific acts in history, and a request that God act salvifically in the present and in the future as God has acted in the past. This last element might include a petition that God send the Messiah.

The second Jewish meal in the background of Christian worship is the Passover meal, the ***Seder***. The annual meal included symbolic food, prayers, and stories (*Haggadah*) remembering the events of the exodus. The way the ritual was rehearsed collapsed the distance between Israel's ancient past and the Jews of the contemporaneous generation by enacting the story.

EARLY CHURCH

New Testament. We'll follow the same pattern looking at the historical development of the Table in the Church as we did with baptism. So we start with the early church and again look at some New Testament texts that have shaped the history of the conversation.

We begin with the earliest New Testament reference to the Meal, found in **1 Corinthians**. In this letter from the mid-fifties, Paul is addressing significant divisions in the house churches in the city. The divisions included those based on socioeconomic differences, which showed up in the sharing of the Lord's Supper. Paul thought the Meal should represent the ***koinonia*** (fellowship) of the community, but that was not the case. Because of the influence Paul's discussion of this matter has had on the church's Table theology and practice across its history, it is worth citing at length:

> Now in the following instructions I do not commend you, because when you come together it is not for the better but for the worse. For, to begin with, when you come together as a church, I hear that there are divisions among you; and to some

extent I believe it. Indeed, there have to be factions among you, for only so will it become clear who among you are genuine. When you come together, it is not really to eat the Lord's supper. For when the time comes to eat, each of you goes ahead with your own supper, and one goes hungry and another becomes drunk. What! Do you not have homes to eat and drink in? Or do you show contempt for the church of God and humiliate those who have nothing? What should I say to you? Should I commend you? In this matter I do not commend you!

For I received from the Lord what I also handed on to you, that the Lord Jesus on the night when he was betrayed took a loaf of bread, and when he had given thanks, he broke it and said, "This is my body that is for you. Do this in remembrance of me." In the same way he took the cup also, after supper, saying, "This cup is the new covenant in my blood. Do this, as often as you drink it, in remembrance of me." For as often as you eat this bread and drink the cup, you proclaim the Lord's death until he comes.

Whoever, therefore, eats the bread or drinks the cup of the Lord in an unworthy manner will be answerable for the body and blood of the Lord. Examine yourselves, and only then eat of the bread and drink of the cup. For all who eat and drink without discerning the body, eat and drink judgment against themselves. For this reason many of you are weak and ill, and some have died. But if we judged ourselves, we would not be judged. But when we are judged by the Lord, we are disciplined so that we may not be condemned along with the world.

So then, my brothers and sisters, when you come together to eat, wait for one another. If you are hungry, eat at home, so that when you come together, it will not be for your condemnation. About the other things I will give instructions when I come. (1 Cor 11:17-34)

Apart from Paul's attempt to address conflict in Corinth, we can note several elements of Table practice in the Corinthian Church, or at least practices Paul wants the church to observe. First, the Lord's Supper is part of bigger meal, what is later called an **agape feast**. That is part of the problem here. The church is dividing up what is eaten and with whom it is eaten on the basis of other social meal practices, and that division is bleeding over from one meal to another.

Second, when Paul reminds his readers about how the Meal is to be observed, he quotes a tradition passed down to him ("For I received from the Lord what I also handed on to you . . ." v. 23). The **words of institution** (vv. 23-26), then, should not be viewed as language he invented, but liturgical language he inherited; and Paul (writing in the mid-fifties) is reminding the readers of what he taught them (in person in the early fifties). This means that within twenty years after the crucifixion, specific liturgical language had begun to be developed for celebrating the Table. (We cannot assume on the basis of the scant evidence we have that the language Paul uses was shared by all Christian communities. Table practices were likely quite diverse in the early church. But given that Paul inherited these words of institution, we can assume they were used beyond the Pauline churches.)

165

Third, Paul argues that if it is eaten unworthily, the Lord's Supper will result in illness or even death. While Paul's language here has a superstitious, almost magical sound to it that fits with an ancient but not a modern worldview, the weight he places on receiving the Meal appropriately should not be dismissed. Paul sees the Meal, or God acting through the Meal, as being a moment in which divine power is or can be exerted.

Next we turn from Paul to the stories of Jesus's last supper in the **Synoptic Gospels**, written fifteen to twenty-five years after 1 Corinthians (Mark 14:22-25; Matt 26:26-28; Luke 22:17-20). When we compare these three versions, we find some similarities of language. They share references to body and blood and the expression of remembrance and covenant in the words of institution. They all present the meal as occurring in the context of the Passover, even though none of them provide details of the meal that match practices of ancient Passover meals. The Passover context, nevertheless, defines the meal as having to do with salvation.

Mark was written first, and Matthew and Luke used Mark as a primary source for writing their narratives. Changes the later two make to Mark's version of the Lord's Supper, then, likely signal differences in theology and/or liturgical practices in the communities of faith for which they were writing than was the case for Mark's community. Note the major differences:

- Mark and Matthew name the Meal as pointing out that Jesus shed his blood and established the covenant "for many" but Luke changes the language to say "for you."

- Matthew adds to Mark's account that the meal relates to Jesus's work concerning the remission of sins.

- Luke has two cups—one at the beginning of the supper and one at the end.

In John's version of the Last Supper (**13:1-20**), Jesus washes the disciples' feet. There is no institution of the Meal in the scene parallel to that found in the Synoptics. While this would seem to indicate that John's community did not view the Meal as instituted by Jesus just before his death, it does not mean the community did not celebrate the meal.

In **John 6:30-58**, Jesus miraculously feeds a crowd, and in his speech, we find language that likely represents John's community's interpretation of the Meal (or the interpretation he wants the community to adopt):

So they said to him, "What sign are you going to give us then, so that we may see it and believe you? What work are you performing? Our ancestors ate the manna in the wilderness; as it is written, 'He gave them bread from heaven to eat.'"

Then Jesus said to them, "Very truly, I tell you, it was not Moses who gave you the bread from heaven, but it is my Father who gives you the true bread from

166

heaven. For the bread of God is that which comes down from heaven and gives life to the world."

They said to him, "Sir, give us this bread always."

Jesus said to them, "I am the bread of life. Whoever comes to me will never be hungry, and whoever believes in me will never be thirsty. But I said to you that you have seen me and yet do not believe. Everything that the Father gives me will come to me, and anyone who comes to me I will never drive away; for I have come down from heaven, not to do my own will, but the will of him who sent me. And this is the will of him who sent me, that I should lose nothing of all that he has given me, but raise it up on the last day. This is indeed the will of my Father, that all who see the Son and believe in him may have eternal life; and I will raise them up on the last day."

Then the Jews began to complain about him because he said, "I am the bread that came down from heaven." They were saying, "Is not this Jesus, the son of Joseph, whose father and mother we know? How can he now say, 'I have come down from heaven'?"

Jesus answered them, "Do not complain among yourselves. No one can come to me unless drawn by the Father who sent me; and I will raise that person up on the last day. It is written in the prophets, 'And they shall all be taught by God.' Everyone who has heard and learned from the Father comes to me. Not that anyone has seen the Father except the one who is from God; he has seen the Father. Very truly, I tell you, whoever believes has eternal life. I am the bread of life. Your ancestors ate the manna in the wilderness, and they died. This is the bread that comes down from heaven, so that one may eat of it and not die. I am the living bread that came down from heaven. Whoever eats of this bread will live forever; and the bread that I will give for the life of the world is my flesh."

The Jews then disputed among themselves, saying, "How can this man give us his flesh to eat?"

So Jesus said to them, "Very truly, I tell you, unless you eat the flesh of the Son of Man and drink his blood, you have no life in you. Those who eat my flesh and drink my blood have eternal life, and I will raise them up on the last day; for my flesh is true food and my blood is true drink. Those who eat my flesh and drink my blood abide in me, and I in them. Just as the living Father sent me, and I live because of the Father, so whoever eats me will live because of me. This is the bread that came down from heaven, not like that which your ancestors ate, and they died. But the one who eats this bread will live forever."

Notice the repeated "I am" statements in which Jesus refers to himself as the bread. John presents Jesus as going on to say that eating the bread results in eternal life. Indeed, John uses the more explicit language of "eating flesh," even "eating me," than the formulaic language of "take, eat, this is my body" found in Paul and the Synoptics. This close identification of the bread with Jesus's flesh and the salvation wrought by eating it is certainly metaphorical, but they are weighty metaphors. The language here will be quite influential later in church history for interpreting the Eucharist in high sacramental traditions.

In the **Acts of the Apostles**, we do not find an explicit description of Table practice in the early church nor an exposition of theology of the Meal. But there are two important references to the Meal that seem to assume the Table practice instituted in the Gospel of Luke. First, following Peter's sermon on Pentecost, the narrator mentions breaking bread following baptism (Acts 2:41-47). Second, a passing reference later in the book (20:7-8) similarly mentions that the church met for the breaking of bread on the Lord's Day. This implies that the Table was observed weekly on Sunday.

Notice that in none of the New Testament texts is there any mention of issues concerning who presides or how the meal is shared physically. This does not necessarily mean that these were not concerns of the New Testament churches, but simply that no need had arisen to call for addressing them in writings that have been preserved.

Second Century. Near the end of the first or beginning of the second century, *The Didache*, an early church order, prescribes how the readers are to observe the "Eucharist":

> And concerning the Eucharist, hold Eucharist thus: First concerning the Cup, "We give thanks to thee, our Father, for the Holy Vine of David thy child, which, thou didst make known to us through Jesus thy child; to thee be glory for ever."
>
> And concerning the broken Bread: "We give thee thanks, our Father, for the life and knowledge which thou didst make known to us through Jesus thy Child. To thee be glory for ever. As this broken bread was scattered upon the mountains, but was brought together and became one, so let thy Church be gathered together from the ends of the earth into thy Kingdom, for thine is the glory and the power through Jesus Christ for ever."
>
> But let none eat or drink of your Eucharist except those who have been baptised in the Lord's Name. For concerning this also did the Lord say, "Give not that which is holy to the dogs."
>
> But after you are satisfied with food, thus give thanks: "We give thanks to thee, O Holy Father, for thy Holy Name which thou didst make to tabernacle in our hearts, and for the knowledge and faith and immortality which thou didst make known to us through Jesus thy Child. To thee be glory for ever. Thou, Lord Almighty, didst create all things for thy Name's sake, and didst give food and drink to men for their enjoyment, that they might give thanks to thee, but us hast thou blessed with spiritual food and drink and eternal light through thy Child. Above all we give thanks to thee for that thou art mighty. To thee be glory for ever. Remember, Lord, thy Church, to deliver it from all evil and to make it perfect in thy love, and gather it together in its holiness from the four winds to thy kingdom which thou hast prepared for it. For thine is the power and the glory for ever. Let grace come and let this world pass away. Hosannah to the God of David. If any man be holy, let him come! If any man be not, let him repent: Maranatha, Amen."
>
> But suffer the prophets to hold Eucharist as they will.

The text describes a prayer of thanksgiving (*eucharist*), the use of the cup and bread, and a prayer to be said once partakers are full. Scholars debate whether the meal referenced here is the Lord's Supper or more of a full communal meal because, on the one hand, no words of institution are spoken but, on the other, only the baptized are allowed to partake. (In other words, there is debate as to whether the *Didache*'s use of *eucharist* is a technical label for the meal, as clearly came to be the practice later, or is simply a reference to giving thanks.)

Whether the *Didache* refers to a full meal or the Lord's Supper, it foreshadows the standard practice of excluding the non-baptized from the Eucharist by the mid-second century, at least as represented in **Justin Martyr's** *First Apology* (written in the mid-150s). While there are a number of other writers in this time period that speak of the Meal in exegetical and theological fashion, no one else this early describes liturgical practice as clearly as does Justin. As an apologetic defense of the Christian faith, *First Apology* is not prescribing practice for the Church so much as explaining it to those outside the faith. Justin actually describes the Meal twice, which he says Christians call "Eucharist." In the first description, he presents the Table as a ritual following one's baptism:

> But we, after we have thus washed him who has been convinced and has assented to our teaching, bring him to the place where those who are called brethren are assembled, in order that we may offer hearty prayers in common for ourselves and for the baptized [illuminated] person, and for all others in every place, that we may be counted worthy, now that we have learned the truth, by our works also to be found good citizens and keepers of the commandments, so that we may be saved with an everlasting salvation. Having ended the prayers, we salute one another with a kiss. There is then brought to the president of the brethren bread and a cup of wine mixed with water; and he taking them, gives praise and glory to the Father of the universe, through the name of the Son and of the Holy Ghost, and offers thanks at considerable length for our being counted worthy to receive these things at His hands. And when he has concluded the prayers and thanksgivings, all the people present express their assent by saying Amen. . . . And when the president has given thanks, and all the people have expressed their assent, those who are called by us deacons give to each of those present to partake of the bread and wine mixed with water over which the thanksgiving was pronounced, and to those who are absent they carry away a portion.
>
> And this food is called among us the Eucharist, of which no one is allowed to partake but the man who believes that the things which we teach are true, and who has been washed with the washing that is for the remission of sins, and unto regeneration, and who is so living as Christ has enjoined. For not as common bread and common drink do we receive these; but in like manner as Jesus Christ our Saviour, having been made flesh by the Word of God, had both flesh and blood for our salvation, so likewise have we been taught that the food which is blessed by the prayer of His word, and from which our blood and flesh by transmutation are nourished, is the flesh and blood of that Jesus who was made flesh. For the apostles, in the memoirs composed by them, which are called Gospels, have thus delivered unto us what

169

was enjoined upon them; that Jesus took bread, and when He had given thanks, said, "This do ye in remembrance of Me, this is My body"; and that, after the same manner, having taken the cup and given thanks, He said, "This is My blood"; and gave it to them alone. Which the wicked devils have imitated in the mysteries of Mithras, commanding the same thing to be done. For, that bread and a cup of water are placed with certain incantations in the mystic rites of one who is being initiated, you either know or can learn. (65-66)

In the second description, the Eucharist takes place after the service of the word, so the earliest core structure of the ordo—that of word and Table—is seen here:

And on the day called Sunday, all who live in cities or in the country gather together to one place, and the memoirs of the apostles or the writings of the prophets are read, as long as time permits; then, when the reader has ceased, the president verbally instructs, and exhorts to the imitation of these good things. Then we all rise together and pray, and, as we before said, when our prayer is ended, bread and wine and water are brought, and the president in like manner offers prayers and thanksgivings, according to his ability, and the people assent, saying Amen; and there is a distribution to each, and a participation of that over which thanks have been given, and to those who are absent a portion is sent by the deacons. And they who are well to do, and willing, give what each thinks fit; and what is collected is deposited with the president, who succours the orphans and widows and those who, through sickness or any other cause, are in want, and those who are in bonds and the strangers sojourning among us, and in a word takes care of all who are in need. But Sunday is the day on which we all hold our common assembly, because it is the first day on which God, having wrought a change in the darkness and matter, made the world; and Jesus Christ our Saviour on the same day rose from the dead. For He was crucified on the day before that of Saturn (Saturday); and on the day after that of Saturn, which is the day of the Sun, having appeared to His apostles and disciples, He taught them these things, which we have submitted to you also for your consideration. (67)

It is unclear whether Justin is really describing two different eucharistic practices related to different liturgical occasions or he intends for the two accounts to be harmonized. Compare the elements of the two descriptions below:

FIRST APOLOGY, 65-66	FIRST APOLOGY, 67
• Baptism • Prayers for the community and the newly baptized Kiss of peace • Bring to presider elements of bread and wine mixed with water • Presider offers prayer of praise and thanksgiving • People assent with "Amen" • Deacons distribute the elements to those gathered • Deacons carry elements to those absent	• Gather on Sunday • Scripture reading • Presider preaches • Prayer • Bring elements of bread, wine, and water • Presider offers prayers and thanksgiving • People assent with "Amen" • Elements are distributed to those gathered • Deacons carry elements to those absent • Offering

Neither of these descriptions explicitly mentions use of the words of institution as part of the liturgy, but Justin does refer to them in the theological exposition that follows the first decription. It is unclear, then, whether the words of institution were used only theologically or also liturgically.

In this exposition, Justin also apologetically explains that Christians believe the blessed bread and wine to be the body and blood of Christ. While it is clear that he means this very seriously, it is harder to determine whether he understands this language literally or metaphorically. Either way, the language here (similar to mystical yet ambiguous language found in other writers of the early centuries of the Church) prefigures the development of the doctrine of transubstantiation and debates about the real presence of Christ in the meal in centuries to follow.

Third Century. Less than a century later, at least some Christian communities began moving in the direction of using formal, normative liturgical texts at the Table. The detailed example we will use as our example is **The Apostolic Tradition** (ca. 215) that we discussed in the chapter on the history of baptism. Because we know so little about the origin of the text, it is unclear whether the author is describing actual practice or attempting to prescribe practices. Nevertheless, after its discovery in the nineteenth century, the text was very influential on liturgical reform in the twentieth century that is still a part of Table rituals today.

After describing the ordination of a bishop, *The Apostolic Tradition* describes the role of the bishop in presiding at the Eucharist. The part of the service described flows in the following manner:

- Ordination on the Lord's Day
- Kiss of peace offered to the bishop

- Deacons bring oblation to bishop
- Bishop offers prayer of thanksgiving
- Bishop also gives thanks if oil or cheese and olives are offered

The reference to the possibility that oil, cheese, and olives might be offered seems to imply that the Eucharist might or might not be shared as part of a larger meal. In contrast to the use of extemporaneous prayer at the Table as described by Justin, the author here prescribes formal prayers of thanksgiving for each offering. The prayer of thanksgiving following the offering is as follows:

> And when he is made bishop, all shall offer him the kiss of peace, for he has been made worthy. To him then the deacons shall bring the offering, and he, laying his hand upon it, with all the presbytery, shall say as the thanksgiving:
>
> > The Lord be with you.
> >
> > And all shall say, And with thy spirit.
> >
> > Lift up your hearts.
> >
> > We lift them up unto the Lord.
> >
> > Let us give thanks to the Lord.
> >
> > It is meet and right.
> >
> > And then he shall proceed immediately:

We give thee thanks, O God, through thy beloved Servant Jesus Christ, whom at the end of time thou didst send to us a Saviour and Redeemer and the Messenger of thy counsel. Who is thy Word, inseparable from thee; through whom thou didst make all things and in whom thou art well pleased. Whom thou didst send from heaven into the womb of the Virgin, and who, dwelling within her, was made flesh, and was manifested as thy Son, being born of [the] Holy Spirit and the Virgin. Who, fulfilling thy will, and winning for himself a holy people, spread out his hands when he came to suffer, that by his death he might set free them who believed on thee. Who, when he was betrayed to his willing death, that he might bring to nought death, and break the bonds of the devil, and tread hell under foot, and give light to the righteous, and set up a boundary post, and manifest his resurrection, taking bread and giving thanks to thee said:

> Take, eat: this is my body, which is broken for you.
>
> And likewise also the cup, saying:
>
> This is my blood, which is shed for you. As often as ye perform this, perform my memorial.

Having in memory, therefore, his death and resurrection, we offer to thee the bread and the cup, yielding thee thanks, because thou hast counted us worthy to stand before thee and to minister to thee.

And we pray thee that thou wouldest send thy Holy Spirit upon the offerings of thy holy church; that thou, gathering them into one, wouldest grant to all thy saints who partake to be filled with [the] Holy Spirit, that their faith may be confirmed in truth, that we may praise and glorify thee. Through thy Servant Jesus Christ, through whom be to thee glory and honour, with [the] Holy Spirit in the holy church, both now and always and world without end. Amen. (4.1-13)

A fair amount of this prayer likely sounds familiar to modern readers, demonstrating the conservative nature of ritual and the influence of this text on the liturgical renewal movement of the twentieth century. Note the structure of the prayer, for it is even more influential on later developments than some of the specific language that is used:

- Preface (opening dialogue)

- Thanksgiving for redemption in Christ, rehearsing/remembering the story of Christ

- Words of institution indicating the Meal commemorates Christ's death

- Epiclesis (invocation of the Holy Spirit)

- Doxology to the Trinity concluding with Amen

These elements are the basic building blocks (albeit the order often varies) of what becomes the primary eucharistic prayers in both the East (**Anaphora** in the Divine Liturgy—the word *anaphora* is also used in liturgical scholarship for a eucharistic prayer more generally speaking) and West (**Canon** of the Mass). This fact does not necessitate a direct influence. We do not have enough evidence to claim that *The Apostolic Tradition* was the origin of these basic elements in the eucharistic tradition. It is simply the earliest extant example we have of the tradition that evolves into a somewhat standard Table practice. We have numerous extant examples of such practice from the fourth century. In these later examples, the elements listed above are present and the prayers continue to move from **anamnesis** (remembering) to epiclesis, usually following a **trinitarian schema**—praise for the creator and thanksgiving for the works of Christ leading to the invocation of the Holy Spirit.

MEDIEVAL CHURCH

It is centuries before we have another liturgical document that includes this level of detail concerning the Eucharist that we find above. For our purposes, however, it is more important to note *theological developments* that led to and evolved throughout the medieval period than to examine specific liturgies. In the Middle Ages, the theology of the Eucharist developed significantly, and revolved around two related ideas.

The first theological issue was the development of a **sacrificial understanding** of the Meal. The medieval Church came to understand the Mass not simply as an occasion for commemoration of the death of Christ, but as a ritual moment in which Christ acts on our behalf again and again. In other words, every time the Mass is said, Christ sacrifices himself for us once again. Thus the piece of furniture at which the meal takes place is not properly a table; it is an **altar**. This is partly why in the Middle Ages, church buildings more and more took on the character of temples—places where sacrifices are offered. Similarly the number of masses multiplied because the Eucharist was thought to make the atoning sacrifice present *ex opere operato* every time it was performed.

Mention of this doctrine raises the second theological issue: **the real presence of Christ** in the Meal. As noted earlier, as early as from the Gospel of John (chapter 6), the Church had inherited weighty and provocative metaphorical language that identified the bread with Christ's flesh. In the medieval church, this idea became so strongly emphasized that more and more the consecrated bread and wine were *identified* with the body and blood of Christ in a real and literal way. After all, if Christ is sacrificed in the Mass, Christ must be present in the Meal. While the idea had been around for a few centuries, it was the Fourth Lateran Council in 1215 that officially sanctioned and dogmatized the term **transubstantiation** to name this experience of Christ's real presence in the Eucharist:

> There is one Universal Church of the faithful, outside of which there is absolutely no salvation. In which there is the same priest and sacrifice, Jesus Christ, whose body and blood are truly contained in the sacrament of the altar under the forms of bread and wine; the bread being changed (*transsubstantiatio*) by divine power into the body, and the wine into the blood, so that to realize the mystery of unity we may receive of Him what He has received of us. And this sacrament no one can effect except the priest who has been duly ordained in accordance with the keys of the Church, which Jesus Christ Himself gave to the Apostles and their successors. (**The Canons of the Fourth Lateran Council**, Canon 1)

It was later in the thirteenth century that **Thomas Aquinas** (1225–74) gave the doctrine of transubstantiation its lasting, solid theological foundation. He did so by drawing on the newly rediscovered thought of Aristotle. Aristotle made a distinction between the *substantial* and *accidental* nature of things. The **substance** of something is its inner, true reality—its essence. This substance is imperceptible to the human senses. **Accidents** refers to the elements of that thing that are perceptible to the senses—its appearance, taste, smell, feel, sound. Usually there is a correspondence between the accidental and substantial nature of something. If one changes, so does the other. If a tree dies (the loss of substance), its appearance withers (the accidents change). Aquinas, however, argues that in the Eucharist the substance of the bread and wine are transformed into the substance of the body and blood of Christ

174

while the accidental nature of the bread and wine remain constant—the elements still smell, taste, and feel like bread and wine.

In relation to the sacrificial interpretation of the Eucharist and the developing doctrine of transubstantiation, during the late Middle Ages leading up to the thirteenth century that we have been discussing, the **Veneration of the Sacrament** developed. Worshipers began to genuflect and kneel during the moments of consecration and elevation. Similarly, when persons entered the nave or approached the altar, they genuflected before reserved elements in the **tabernacle** or on the altar because they are the body and blood of Christ—Christ truly present in the temple, in the elements.

Part of this veneration contributed to turning the liturgy of the Mass into a visual ritual more than the work of the people. The laity watched the clergy perform the Eucharist on their behalf. Of special importance was observing the **Elevation of the Host** in order to come into closer communion with God. So reluctant were laity to partake of the sacrament that the Fourth Lateran Council in 1215 declared that all should receive Communion at least once a year on Easter (Canon 21). Even then, to avoid spilling Christ, the clergy placed the bread directly on the tongues of the laity and the cup was reserved for the clergy.

PROTESTANT REFORMATION(S)

The Protestant Reformation(s) were, to a great extent, a liturgical reformation. And as such, the reformers radically rethought sacramental theology and practice.

As we have already seen, in 1520, **Martin Luther** started the sacramental reformation ball rolling with the ***Babylonian Captivity of the Church***. Luther said that the Roman Catholic hierarchy was holding the Church captive within three walls: the withholding of wine from the laity, transubstantiation, and view of the Eucharist as an atoning sacrifice.

He broke down the walls in the following way. First, he argued that Christ gave both elements—bread *and* wine—to the disciples, so all the baptized should receive both elements. Along with this, by changing the eucharistic liturgy from Latin to German Luther transformed the Meal from something observed with emphasis on objects to an *event* in which it is the birthright of the baptized to participate.

Second, Luther rejected the doctrine of transubstantiation but not the idea of real presence. He rejected the idea that the priest effects the change in the elements *ex opere operato*, but he interpreted the biblical language of "This is my body/blood" literally. Instead of bread and wine *becoming* body and blood, elements are both bread/wine and body/blood. Christ is present in the bread and wine in the same way fire is present in a heated bar of iron—"every part is iron and fire." This is sometimes mislabeled "consubstantiation." Better terms are **sacramental unity** or **sacramental ubiquity**.

Finally, based on his soteriology, Luther rejected the claim that the Eucharist was a repetitive sacrifice. According to Paul, we are justified by faith alone: Christ died

175

once for all. Luther argued, then, that there is no need for any other work (such as a sacrament) to save us.

Ulrich Zwingli thought Luther did not go far enough in rejecting transubstantiation. He argued that holding on to some sense of real presence still leaves room for idolatry of the eucharistic elements. Thus Zwingli viewed the sacraments (or better, ordinances) as "signs" of faith, as a **memorial** and not as means of grace.

Whereas Luther continued to proffer a literal understanding of "This is my body," Zwingli emphasized a literal reading of the exaltation/ascension of the resurrected Jesus to the right hand of God. The resurrected Christ cannot be *physically* present in two places at one time (ubiquity, as opposed to omnipresence). The ascension means that Christ is (physically) in heaven to stay until the **parousia**. Thus Jesus's words, "This is my body," must be metaphorical and mean, "This *signifies* my body." The emphasis for Zwingli, then, is on the action of the community instead of on God acting through the elements.

In 1529, political supporters of the Reformation(s) brought Luther and Zwingli together (against their wishes) for the **Marburg Colloquy**. As seen in the **Marburg Articles**, it was a unifying meeting on almost every issue but the Eucharist. Zwingli argued that the bread and wine *signify* the body and blood. The Latin for this is *hoc significat corpus meum*. The story goes that Luther wrote on the negotiating table the words *hoc est corpus meum*, "This *is* my body." Every time Zwingli tried to argue otherwise and use the word *significat*, Luther just pointed to the words on the table indicating that they had to be taken at their plain sense (*sola scriptura*).

This break with Luther was the second major rift among the Protestants we have noted (the first being over baptism of infants with the Anabaptists; see the earlier discussion). Indeed, whereas Luther reshaped the service of the Mass to better reflect his Protestant theology, Zwingli's understanding of the Lord's Supper led to a whole new liturgy that diminished the importance of the Table. The proclamation of the word takes central importance, and thus the Eucharist need only be celebrated occasionally (e.g., quarterly).

As with baptism, **John Calvin** less brought some new innovation to the debate concerning the Eucharist and more offered a position that lies between Luther and Zwingli. Calvin asserted (like Zwingli) that Christ's physical body is indeed in heaven. He continued, though, to assert that by virtue of his justifying death, Christ's real presence is mediated to those receiving the sacrament *by the Holy Spirit*. Beyond this broad claim that in the Eucharist we experience a mystical union with Christ, Calvin refused to speculate about the specific mode or location of Christ's presence. He claimed that we may not be able to understand Christ's presence in the Meal, but we *can* experience it.

In place of the mode of Christ's presence, Calvin emphasized that whatever benefit there is to receiving the Lord's Supper (that is, as a means of grace) is received *by faith*. This was a major break with Lutheranism that claimed Christ was present regardless of faith.

Calvin's synthesis was influential theologically, but his liturgical push was not. He called for weekly communion, but the laity (and the Geneva Council) had been conditioned by the medieval practice of yearly communion and were focused on the word and thus celebrated the table only quarterly.

CONTEMPORARY SITUATION

By the end of the Reformation(s), all the basic theologies of the Table held and practiced today were already in place. Developments in eucharistic theology since the sixteenth century are really all variations on the themes introduced during this time period. Although this survey oversimplifies the positions we have examined, readers should be able to locate their own theologies and the theologies of their traditions as growing out of one of these foundational views.

That said, we should note that the liturgical renewal movements of the twentieth century have led to some blurring of the lines between these different positions. The significant and influential reforms of the **Second Vatican Council** (1962–65) blurred the lines dividing Roman Catholic and Protestant sacramental theology and practice. The Catholic Mass became more participatory on the part of the laity: priests began to stand behind the altar, to pray the **Eucharistic Prayer** (as with all of the liturgy) in the vernacular of the congregation instead of Latin, and to serve the cup to all who partook in the Meal. These changes both brought Roman Catholic eucharistic practice closer to that of some Protestant communions and influenced the practices of some Protestant communions.

Following Vatican II, further blurring of the eucharistic dividing lines (especially among Protestant denominations) occurred due to one of the great achievements of the ecumenical movement: the 1982 adoption and publication of the highly influential document ***Baptism, Eucharist, and Ministry*** (BEM) by the Faith and Order division of the World Council of Churches. This document (and the ecumenical process out of which it grew) pushed some traditions and individual congregations to celebrate the Meal more frequently, adopt new Eucharistic Prayer forms, enter into communion with other traditions, alter the mode of distribution of the elements, and/or embrace new vocabulary to describe the Meal.

Blurring the lines between different denominational eucharistic theologies and practices, however, is not the same as erasing those lines. Even while denominations have grown closer in this arena, the core theological and liturgical distinctions established during the Reformation(s) are still present in Mainline Protestantism. For instance, one way for readers to identify where they stand in relation to the issue of Christ's real presence in the Meal is to reflect on what is done with the elements left over after everyone has been served and worship has been concluded. Traditions that emphasize divine action in the ritual and locate Christ's presence in the physical elements—that is, those who believe that in some way the bread and cup have become the body and blood of Christ—either consume the remaining elements or are very deliberate in ways they dispose of them (e.g., pouring the wine into a sink with a drain that goes straight into the earth instead of one that goes into the sewer, or spreading breadcrumbs for birds to consume instead of throwing them in the garbage). On the other hand, those who reject the idea that the Lord's Supper involves a unique access to Christ's presence and instead interpret the ritual as an expression of human action or those who emphasize divine action in the sacrament but locate Christ's presence in the liturgical act of communing with God and with one another—that is, those who believe the bread and cup remain simply bread and wine/juice—feel no compunction about simply throwing the leftover bread into the trash and pouring leftover wine/ juice down the kitchen sink.

The question concerning disposal of leftover bread and cup can be a significant clue to one's theology of the Table, but only a clue. As our historical sketch points out, there are many facets to a theology of this ritual.

Moreover, even within the same tradition, different congregations, pastors, and individual Christians emphasize different theological aspects of the Table. Worship leaders' responsibility, however, extends beyond holding and sharing personal views. They must represent the tradition that ordains or commissions them and interpret that tradition for their congregations. This representation of denominational theology by the clergy does not dictate congregants' personal theology of the Meal but does serve to inform their theology and expand their experience of the sacrament or ordinance when it is administered in worship. The historical sketch above identifies a range of key theological questions with which one must deal when developing a full-blown theology of the Table in relation to one's tradition. When considered cumulatively, answers to these questions build a case for determining the meaning of the ritual for a church and what counts as valid, authentic, and acceptable baptism practice and why. The list below draws together those questions:

A. What is the best name for the sacred meal in Christian worship and why?

B. What role should...

    1. scripture play in defining the understanding and practice of the Table, and

    2. tradition play in defining the understanding and practice of the Table?

C. Who is the primary actor in the Meal: God or those gathered to share in the Meal?

    1. Is the Meal primarily a means of grace or an act of faith?

D. In what way is the Meal *anamnesis*, re-membrance?

    1. What is "re-membered"?

    2. How does this "re-membering" occur?

E.   Who is eligible to receive the Meal (and why)? Anyone, only the baptized, only the baptized and confirmed, only those who are members of the specific denomination?

   1.   What level of understanding of the Meal is required for participation in the Meal?

   2.   Is repentance needed?

F.   Is Christ present in the Meal in a manner that is different from God's/Christ's presence with us always?

   1.   If yes, how is Christ present?

      i.   Where is Christ present in the Meal: in the elements, in the fellowship/communion, elsewhere?

   2.   If no, how does the Meal function in worship? What is its purpose in the life of faith?

G.   How is the Meal related to Christ's

   1.   ministry?

   2.   death?

   3.   resurrection?

H.   What is the relation of the Meal and baptism?

I.   What is required ritually for the Meal to be valid?

    1.   What language should be used at the table, in terms of

        i.   prayers?
        ii.   narrative of institution?
        iii.   epiclesis?
        iv.   distribution of the elements?

    2.   What modes of distribution are acceptable?

        i.   What mode is theologically best and why?

    3.   Who is authorized to officiate at the table and why?

        i.   Ordained clergy
        ii.   Elders among the laity
        iii.   Anyone

    4.   How often and when should the Meal be celebrated? Why?

TABLE PRACTICES

At the opening of the last chapter, we noted that there are two ways to reflect on the meaning of the Table. The first is to locate oneself and one's tradition in the historical debates about the Meal. This approach was the focus of the previous chapter. The second is to examine actual ritual practices and liturgies and locate oneself (and one's tradition) in relation to them and how they construct meaning.

In this chapter, we gather the tools to accomplish this second mode of reflection. First, we reflect on appropriate times for the Meal in the ordo. Second, we analyze the basic elements found in most Table rituals. For our example Table liturgy, we will explore the primary Great Thanksgiving found on pages 35–40 in *The United Methodist Book of Worship* (A Service of Word and Table I © 1972 The United Methodist Publishing House; © 1980, 1985, 1989, 1992 UMPH. Used by permission. All rights reserved). Readers should compare this liturgy with the Meal rituals in their own denominational service books.

THE TIMING OF THE MEAL

First of all, we need to recall where the Meal comes in the standard flow of the worship service, or the *ordo*. As we have seen in the chapter on the ordo, one of the earliest structures of Christian worship is the movement from **word to Table**. This developed into the fourfold movement of most Christian worship: Gathering, Proclamation, Response, and Sending Forth.

The Meal, then, most properly follows the proclamation in the Response movement as the *primary* response of the gathered assembly to the word proclaimed. (Indeed, in traditions that celebrate the Table most Sundays—that is, ones that practice services of word and table as opposed to services of the word—the third movement of the ordo is considered that of Table: Gathering, Proclamation, Table, Sending Forth.) Having heard God's good news in the scripture and sermon, the congregation next communes with God-in-Christ and and with sisters and brothers in Christ at the Table.

While in the minority, there are some congregations where the Table is part of the Gathering. The order of the service moves from **Table to word**. In the nineteenth century, many frontier congregations in North America were without pastors. They gathered weekly for worship, for singing and prayer and a sermon offered by a lay minister. They only had the sacraments administered when a circuit rider came around. (Along with trends passed on from the Reformation(s), this situation partly explains why the Table continues to be celebrated monthly or quarterly in some congregations instead of weekly.) However, in some ordinance traditions, such as in the Stone-Campbell tradition, the pattern was opposite. These frontier congregations gathered weekly for singing, prayer, and the Lord's Supper, which as an ordinance was administered by lay elders in the congregation. They only had preaching when the circuit rider came around. The movement from Table to word in some churches grows out of this history.

Another factor of this ordering has been an evangelical approach to the sermon. Such preaching aims for a decision by the hearers, so the sermon ends with an invitation to discipleship at the close of the service. Such purpose and flow was seen by some as disrupted by placing the Table after the sermon. Placing it before the sermon keeps the sermon/invitation at the climax of the liturgical plot.

THE CORE PATTERN OF THE MEAL

As we turn to the liturgy of the Table ritual itself, we can see that we have inherited the basic pattern of celebrating the Meal from the New Testament:

Jesus **took** bread, **blessed** it (eucharisted it), **broke** it, and **gave** it to the disciples.

Then he **took** the cup, **blessed** it (eucharisted it), and **gave** it to the disciples.

The seven action verbs highlighted above shaped a **sevenfold pattern** of officiating at the Table. This pattern is not found in Mainline worship practices often anymore, but it is still maintained in some traditions influenced by Zwingli. The pattern unfolds in the following manner: a clergyperson or a lay elder takes the bread and prays over it, deacons distribute the bread to the congregation seated in the pews, and everyone eats it at the same time. Then the pattern is repeated with the cup—someone prays, the deacons distribute the wine or juice in individual cups, and everyone drinks at the same time.

Given the repetitive nature of these actions, however, most Eastern, Catholic, Anglican, and Protestant traditions condense the pattern into a **fourfold pattern** in which the bread and cup are dealt with together.

First, the elements are brought to the table or, if they are there throughout the service, they are uncovered. In other words, they are **taken**.

Second, the one or ones who are officiating offer the prayer of thanksgiving. In most denominations, this is some form of a **Eucharistic Prayer** or **Great Thanksgiving** similar to what we discovered in **The Apostolic Tradition** in the previous chapter. In such traditions, the words of institution are usually part of the prayer. In other denominations, the prayer is referred to simply as the **prayer for the bread and cup** and the words of institution are spoken separately. In either case, the elements are **blessed**. Often this prayer is followed by the congregation offering the Lord's Prayer in unison.

Third, after the prayer, the bread is **broken**. Most traditions parallel this by **elevating the cup**. These actions may be done in silence, or with words such as those in *The United Methodist Book of Worship* (39), "Because there is one loaf, we, who are many, are one body, for we all partake of the one loaf. The bread which we break is a sharing in the body of Christ" and "The cup over which we give thanks is a sharing in the blood of Christ." Or in traditions that do not include the words of institution in the blessing, they can be said as the bread is broken and the cup is lifted. Sometimes this pattern is condensed so that the bread is broken and the cup is elevated as part of the prayer instead of following it.

Finally, the elements are distributed (**given**) by those officiating and/or by servers to the congregation. Distribution in this form may involve passing the elements through the pews as noted above (in which case members of the gathered assembly essentially serve each other) or, as is more often the case, involves worshipers coming forward to be given the elements while standing or kneeling before the altar or table (often at an **altar rail**).

THE WIDER LITURGICAL PATTERN

Most traditions place this core fourfold pattern of the Table in a particular liturgical context. Beforehand, there is usually some form of an **invitation to the Table**. Often this is a brief, standard, formal invitation that names who is able to participate in the ritual and describes something of the purpose of the meal. In some traditions, where this invitation is less formal, it is tailored to fit the specific liturgical occasion and theme of the service. (Too often, though, informal invitations expand into communion meditations that compete with the sermon. Even though the purpose of the invitation is to focus the experience of the Meal, an extended invitation often draws more attention to itself or to the person extending it than to the meal. A good rule of thumb is that the invitation to participants should always be shorter than the table prayer offered to God.)

In some traditions, participants, having heard the invitation, prepare to receive the Meal by offering to God a **prayer of confession** and/or offering each other signs of reconciliation and forgiveness by **passing the peace** of Christ to one another.

Finally, for many traditions, the presentation of the elements is combined with the presentation of the **monetary offering** for the morning.

After the meal has been served and the elements have been returned to the table, many traditions close the ritual with a short **prayer after communion**, a prayer of gratitude for what was received in the Meal. This prayer usually draws the Response movement of the Ordo to a close and leads into the Sending Forth.

185

THE TABLE PRAYER

Let us narrow our focus from the ritual of the Meal as a whole to the structure and language of the Table prayers that are central to this ritual. The primary Table prayer has various names:

- **Anaphora** (Greek, "offering"),

- **Eucharistic Prayer**,

- **Great Thanksgiving**, and

- **Great Prayer of Thanksgiving**.

If we were to survey such prayers in Protestant denominations before the liturgical renewal movement, the ecumenical movement, and Vatican II took place in the mid-twentieth century, we would find a wide variety of prayers and prayer structures in use. The liturgical convergence that formed in the latter part of the twentieth century resulted in bringing Table prayers in different traditions much closer to one another. While there is still variation across denominational lines (and certainly different interpretations of the content of the Table prayer), the core pattern and much of the specific language of Table prayers is held in common by traditions that use formal texts of prayers as opposed to extemporaneous table prayers. As mentioned in the previous chapter, this result is due to a great extent to scholarly study of and ecclesial claiming the importance of the heritage of Jewish Sabbath meal prayers of blessing, Justin Martyr's description of Table practice in the second century, and the Table prayer included in the ritual of the ordination of a bishop in *The Apostolic Tradition* of the third century.

The basic prayer of Great Thanksgiving is **trinitarian** in perspective and structure. It has three broad movements:

- thanksgiving focused on the creative and providential care of God;

- commemoration of the redemptive works made manifest in the person and works of Christ; and

- an invocation of the Holy Spirit to make the Meal an effective communion and to extend the work of the Church from the Table out into the world.

These three movements are framed by an opening dialogue between the person presiding and the congregation and a concluding doxology offered in praise of the Triune God.

Thanksgiving. The prayer begins with an **opening dialogue** often called the **Sursum Corda** (from the Latin for "lift up your hearts"). A form of this dialogue stretches back at least to *The Apostolic Tradition*. Most Protestant denominations that use some form of an anaphora use the exact form of the opening dialogue represented in our example liturgy. The reason for this is that the **English Language Liturgical Consultation** published an influential revision and commentary on English translations of ancient Greek and Latin expressions of **ordinary** elements of the liturgy such as the Lord's Prayer, *Kyrie Eleison*, and creeds. The Sursum Corda is one of these texts. At times, congregations will use "God" in the place of "the Lord" to avoid patriarchal language.

The opening dialogue unfolds in three responsive movements. In the first exchange, the officiant and people greet one another. In the second, the presider invites the people to offer their hearts to God and the people assent. In the third, the officiant invites the people to join in the prayer of thanksgiving, and the people agree.

The next section of the prayer of the Great Thanksgiving is called the **preface**, in the sense that it serves as the first or introductory part of the prayer proper. Thus, following the opening dialogue, the presider leads the people in speaking to God. The first words offered to God then are words of thanksgiving for acts usually associated with the first person of the Trinity, especially divine activity recorded in the Hebrew Bible leading up to the Christ event: creation, acts of providence, covenants between God and God's people, the gift of the law, and the proclamation of the prophets. With such a sketching of salvation history, some versions of Table prayers might extend the preface into the Christ event, but usually that turn is reserved for after the next element.

Most denominations offer a general eucharistic prayer in their service book, like the one represented here. But many also provide alternatives, either in the service book itself or in denominational supplementary materials. The preface is a place where such a **proper** is included. Language related to the liturgical season or specific day on which the Eucharist is being celebrated can be substituted for or added to the general sketch of salvation history.

The presider concludes the preface by transitioning to the congregation offering the **sanctus** (Latin for "holy"), which is spoken or sung in unison. It is appropriate to offer such an acclamation of praise following the thanksgiving for God's care of the world as given witness by ancient Israel. The language for praise signals the transition from the focus on salvation history before Christ to the Christ event itself, in that it joins worshipers with the angels singing "Holy, holy, holy" to God in the vision of the heavenly court in Isaiah 6:3 and then shifts to join the worshipers' voices with those shouting hosannas in eschatological expectation of the one coming in the name of God at the point at which Christ entered Jerusalem (e.g., Mark 11:9-10; language adapted from Ps 118:26). This second part of the congregational acclamation is technically called the **benedictus** (Latin for "blessed") but often the whole response is simply called the Sanctus.

The wording of the Sanctus/Benedictus is fairly standard across Protestant traditions, again due to the work of the English Language Liturgical Consultation discussed above in relation to the opening dialogue.

Commemoration. The next section of the prayer, often referred to simply as the **post-sanctus prayer**, shifts to focusing on the Christ event and the redemption wrought through it. The focus may stretch from the incarnation to Christ's death and resurrection. In some traditions, this section of the prayer takes the form of a Proper and thus the emphasis changes to reflect the liturgical season or the Gospel lection for the day.

The Post Sanctus section, in which thanks is given for the Christ event, usually leads up to the **words of institution**. Christ's words naming the bread and the cup as his body and blood are recited. In some congregations, the bread is broken and the cup is elevated as the words of institution are prayed. In others, the bread is broken and the cup is lifted after the prayer (sometimes with words and sometimes in silence).

Not all versions of Prayers of Great Thanksgiving include the words of institution. Instead of part of the prayer offered to God, they are addressed to the congregation to recall the meaning of the Meal. This naming can take place as part of the invitation to the Table before the prayer, the breaking of the bread and the elevation of the cup following the prayer, or even following distribution of the elements through the pews in congregations where all wait to eat the bread and drink the cup at the same time.

Reciting Christ's words of institution includes Christ's command to celebrate this meal in remembrance of Christ. The section following the words of institution continues this theme of remembrance and is thus called the **anamnesis** (Greek, "remembrance").

Paralleling the anamnesis is an **offering** or **oblation** of those gathered at the Table. As the community remembers Christ's sacrificial act, it dedicates itself as a sacrifice to God. The celebration of Christ's saving acts in the anamnesis culminates in the congregation making a spoken or sung **acclamation**, celebrating Christ's death (expressed in past tense), resurrection (present tense), and *parousia* (future tense) as the center of salvation history remembered in the Meal.

Invocation. Following the congregational acclamation, the one presiding invokes the Holy Spirit in the **epiclesis** (Greek, "calling upon"). The language in the epiclesis and/or its interpretation can vary from tradition to tradition based on their theology of real presence. Protestants who argue that Christ is uniquely present in the elements will pray with a different kind of specificity from those locate Christ's sacramental presence in the community or who argue against any unique divine presence in the Meal.

In some traditions the invocation of the Holy Spirit in the Meal leads to a time of offering **intercessions**, that is, prayer on behalf of others. In other denominations or congregations, intercessions are part of the prayers of the people that occupy a different moment of the liturgy than the Great Thanksgiving.

Finally, the prayer concludes with a **doxology** offered by the presider. As the prayer is structured in relation to the Trinity, so the doxology at the end is explicitly

Trinitarian in nature. The doxology itself is complete when the congregation offers its assent by speaking or singing **Amen** in unison.

Primary Table liturgies of denominations other than the UMC can be found in the following service books:

AMEC Book of Worship, 26–37

Book of Common Prayer (Episcopal Church, USA), 333–39

Book of Common Worship (Presbyterian Church (USA), 25–29

Book of Worship: United Church of Christ, 42–52

Book of Ritual (CME), 20–27

Celebrate God's Presence (United Church of Canada), 239–67

Chalice Worship (DOC), 8-10, 13–14

Evangelical Lutheran Worship, 106–14

Liturgy of the Reformed Church of America, 11–15

PART FIVE
ENERGY

In popular idiom, *energy* refers to the source that allows something to perform work. It takes energy to run an automobile, light a lamp, and push a sailboat across the surface of the sea. In physics, however, *energy* is a technical term for that property of objects and systems that can be transferred to other objects or systems and can be converted into different forms (e.g., mechanical, thermal, and kinetic forms of energy). Wind hits sails, causing a ship to overcome the friction of water and cross oceans. Gasoline's energy can be transferred to an automobile engine through combustion. The water of a river pulled toward sea level by the force of gravity can be used to propel turbines, creating electricity used to turn on lights.

Therefore, in our use of categories of physics as metaphors for different elements of Mainline Protestant worship, energy refers to those actions of worship that are the public works of the people (*leiturgia*), those elements that transfer meaning and experience from one partner of the sacred conversation to another. Specifically, in this section of the book, we examine liturgical speech, congregational song, and physical embodiment of liturgical acts.

THEOLOGY OF SPOKEN LITURGY

It is an obvious statement to say that worship is filled with speech, but familiarity should not lead us to take such speech for granted. There are three questions concerning speech in worship that need to be considered by worship planners and leaders:

- *Why* do we speak as part of our liturgy?

- *What words* should we choose to speak in worship?

- *How* should such words be spoken?

We will deal with the first question—theological considerations—in this chapter and turn to the other two questions related to worship planning and liturgical performance in the next.

SPEECH IN THE SACRED CONVERSATION

Humans, by definition, are a linguistic species of animals. However we answer the question of what distinguishes *homo sapiens* from other living beings on this planet, the way we communicate and the abstract ideas and values that we are able to communicate must surely play a part in the answer. God spoke the world into being, and we are made in the *imago Dei*. We humans make meaning of the world by speaking.

It is no wonder, then, that at the center of worship, at the center of naming and praising God-in-Christ's worth-ship as our Ultimate Concern, as the Meaning in all meanings, the Church speaks. Worship can (and should) involve silence, visual art, instrumental music, meditation, and the like, but it must also involve a lot of talking.

Our practical theology of worship as a whole, the model to which we return repeatedly across the chapters of this book, proposes that we consider Christian worship as a type of **sacred conversation**. With our focus on speech, a quick review is called for.

193

In this conversation are four primary voices. With worship primarily being adoration of God, the **congregation's voice** dominates worship most in the sense of speaking. That is, worship is prayer, and is thus at its core the congregation speaking to God. Because the congregation speaks as a community, the congregation also talks amongst itself in liturgy.

Even though the congregation is the primary voice in worship, **God's voice** initiates the conversation, because all interaction between the divine and human is initiated by God. God calls the congregation into worship, proclaims good news to us, and sends us forth into the world.

The sacred conversation is more complex than a two-way dialogue, however. One does not make meaning of the world without conversing with the world. Thus the **world's voice** is heard in worship as well. The world offers various forms of reason (in the sense of scripture, tradition, *reason*, and experience) for the congregation to consider as it constructs a Christian worldview. And the world calls the congregation to meets the needs of the world and its inhabitants. In liturgy, the world speaks to call the congregation to accountability for its mission of service to all God's creation.

Also complicating the conversation is the fact that the congregation, God, and the world do not talk to each other for the first time in any particular worship service. The congregation is part of the communion of saints, which liturgically speaking is a way of saying that our worship continues a conversation that began long before we gathered on Sunday, will continue long after we have returned to the dust of the earth, and extends far across the globe beyond the boundaries of our local community. In other words, the **Church's voice**—that is, the voice of the "holy, catholic Church"—echoes throughout the sacred conversation of liturgy.

Worship planners, to a significant degree, script the way these different voices speak in the liturgy. Therefore, it is important that they think through a range of theological issues concerning this speech so that the conversations can be as fruitful, effective, and faithful as possible.

LEX ORANDI, LEX CREDENDI

"The law of prayer is the law of belief." As we noted earlier, the relationship between theology and liturgy is circular in nature. Each informs and is shaped by the other. Worship gives voice to a community's faith *and* at the same time shapes the faith of the community.

When shaping the liturgical speech that will occur on any given Sunday, therefore, the worship planner must take seriously three layers of theology at play in this circular process.

First, is the **theology of the congregation's denomination**. Worship leaders, by virtue of their ordination, commission, and/or call, represent the denomination to the congregation and have a responsibility to bring the theology of the denomination into the liturgy. A congregation's liturgy should be an expression of its denomination's faith.

This does not mean that elements of a denomination's theology should not at times be challenged in congregational worship. Only God is perfect. Thus no theology is. Protestants hold strongly that the Church is reformed and always reforming. Planning worship involves both representing denominational theology faithfully and at times challenging that denominational theology prophetically.

The second layer of theology to be considered is the **theology of the congregation** itself. While a congregation does not represent a homogeneous collection of believers who share the exact same theology, there is a basic theological core or leaning that binds the community together and distinguishes it from other congregations, even other congregations in the same denomination. Worship leaders step out of the pew and into the chancel in the sense that they are appointed, called, and hired to represent the congregation. Liturgy should be an expression of a congregation's faith. Indeed, failing to attend to the theology of the local congregation conscientiously while planning liturgical speech can result in forcing the congregation into a conversation in which they are not true participants.

As with denominational theology, however, this responsibility does not mean that a congregation's theology should never be challenged in worship. Worship leaders are, after all, called to *lead*. A congregation, and its individual members, cannot grow in their faith if preachers and liturgists just pat them on the back during worship. Planning worship involves representing congregational theology faithfully and at times challenging it prophetically and pastorally.

Finally, the third layer of theology at play in planning for liturgical talk is the **theology of the worship planner(s)**. We have already hinted at this layer in calling the worship leader both to represent and challenge denominational and congregational theologies above. A worship planner should not propose that one of the voices in the sacred conversation say something that fundamentally goes against her or his own theology. Liturgists, preachers, and the like have a responsibility to bring their unique theological perspective to bear on the life and worship of a congregation.

That said, this responsibility is not license to force one's theology on a congregation. While worship leaders must be true to their theological worldview and are called to lead the community theologically, they are also representatives of the denomination and congregation. For the liturgy to be a true conversation and not a worship leader's monologue delivered by different people, the tension between leadership and representation must be carefully maintained.

These layers of theology are seen most clearly in the two primary forms of speech in worship: preaching and prayer.

PREACHING

Homiletics, the critical study of preaching, is a discipline distinct from liturgical studies. Indeed, in most seminaries, preaching is taught separately from worship. This division makes sense given that learning to preach involves study of the art of or a set of skills related to communicating the gospel that is quite different from the knowledge base and skill set required to plan and lead worship more broadly speaking.

Nevertheless, preaching should be studied in the context of worship. Preaching does not occur in a vacuum but as part of the Proclamation movement of the ordo, following the Gathering and leading toward the Response. The reading of scripture and the preaching of the sermon compose a significant percentage of words spoken in most Protestant worship services. Therefore, a theology of the liturgical conversation must take the sermon into consideration.

Different traditions and, indeed, different preachers hold different views of the task of preaching. Indeed, the **theology of preaching** is a sub-discipline of homiletics that generates much debate. How one views the task of preaching theologically is related to one's broader theology. In this short section, then, a single theology of preaching will not be proposed. Instead, we will name a few of the primary questions to consider in developing a theology of preaching as a significant element of liturgical speech.

The first question to consider is: **What is the relation of preaching to the whole of worship?** Worship planners strive to create a service that is unified to some degree in theme and tone. Does the sermon determine what that unity will look like or does a sense of the unity determine what the sermon will look like? This is a question concerning a liturgical hierarchy of priorities. In evangelically oriented traditions, the sermon usually is the driving force behind liturgical design. In traditions emphasizing the liturgical calendar, the liturgical occasion and associated themes may drive liturgical (and homiletical) design. In sacramentally oriented traditions, the table anchors the service, and considerations of liturgy and sermon are subordinate to it.

A different element of this question concerns the unique role of the sermon in the liturgy. Protestants have long lifted up Paul's comment that faith comes by hearing (Rom 10:17) as justification for the centrality of the sermon in liturgy. The sermon, however, is only one form of **proclamation** in the service. For instance, a praise band song based on a psalm, a personal testimony, a choral anthem celebrating creation, and the recitation of a creed are all forms of proclamation. What is, or what should be, distinct about the sermon so that it complements these other liturgical forms of proclamation and they complement it?

A second question is: **Where is God in the sermon?** In other words, what role does God play in the preparing, preaching, and/or reception of the sermon—is God speaking in the sermon, or is the preacher speaking about God in the sermon? The answer to these questions is related to one's view of how **divine revelation** occurs, especially in the context of worship. We have said that in the conversational model of worship, proclamation represents God's voice. That is, obviously, a metaphorical statement. The preacher is clearly the one literally speaking. But different traditions and theologies will give different weight to the role of the preacher as God's representative. Even if a preacher wants to hold on to God as *both* speaker and that about which is spoken in the sermon, the sermon will be designed differently if the emphasis is more on God as subject or more on God as the object of the liturgical speech.

To better see the difference between these two options, consider the difference between two common prayers before the sermon. Those who pray some form of Psalm 19:14 ("Let the words of my mouth and the meditations of my heart be pleasing to you, Lord, my rock and my redeemer") are naming their sermon as an offering to God, implying the preacher is the primary voice in the sermon. Those who pray a form of John the Baptist's words in John 3:30 ("He must increase and I must decrease") are asking that the preacher's voice and ego be diminished in the sermon so that God's voice might be primary.

The question of God's role in the sermon leads to a third question concerning the word of God: **What is or should be the relation between the sermon and scripture?** Most preaching in Mainline Protestant traditions (with Protestantism's historical emphasis on *sola scriptura*) is **biblical preaching**. This means that the sermon serves the biblical reading(s) for the day through exposition in some form. Yet preaching is different than biblical commentary. Preachers do not simply repeat a biblical text; they proclaim the gospel in relation to an interpretation of a specific text. Thus preachers' fuller sense of God's good news influences the way they approach and interpret any particular text as well as the way they use a text in sermons.

Moreover, in addition to interpreting scripture, preachers are tasked to meet the **needs of the congregation** as she or he understands them. How does the preacher bring these needs and the scripture lesson together in the sermon? This question is related to one's understanding of the nature and authority of scripture. One who attempts to read scripture literally because it is God's timeless, inerrant word will answer differently than one who views a vast gulf between contemporary experiences and worldview and scripture as a historically conditioned product representing the experiences and theological reflections of ancient human authors.

PUBLIC PRAYER

Complementing preaching, prayer is the second primary form of liturgical speech we need to consider.

We do not, or should not, pray simply because God demands it of us or because we have needs we desire for God to address. Prayer is lifting up everything that concerns us to the One who concerns ultimately. We believe all of existence is connected with our relationship to God through Christ. Therefore, we name in prayer those things about which we are joyful, anxious, and sad. We name those things for which we feel blessed and about which we feel righteous anger. We offer praise to God, give thanks for God's providence and salvation, confess our sins, raise existential questions, offer petitions for our needs, and raise up supplication that God address the needs of others.

We do this differently in private than we do in community. In private prayer, an individual speaks one-on-one with God. Leading a community in prayer, on the other hand, is a representative role. A lone person may be the only one speaking aloud, but all are praying.

A straightforward example of the difference between praying alone and praying in community is that one leading public prayer should avoid the first-person singular (e.g., "I ask you, O God . . ."). To use the first person implies that "I" pray for the community while they listen. In a sense this view holds that the worship leader speaks to God on behalf of the community. The worship leader funnels the community's prayer to God.

A better way to think about public prayer is related to Søren Kierkegaard's analogy of worship as a play that we reviewed in the chapter on ritual and worship. The leaders feed the lines to the congregation, who are the actors, so that they can perform for the real audience of worship: God. Thus the person vocalizing the prayer that is addressed to God chooses words, images, and thoughts (including first person plural pronouns) that engage heart and minds of the individuals in the gathering so that they can become the unified body of Christ offering one prayer in unison through Christ to God.

Pastors spend a lot of time writing sermons. Leading a congregation in prayer is no less important than proclaiming the good news to them. Composing and finding words to which the whole community can say "Amen" is no easy task. It takes skill, heart, and insight into the human condition, imagination, faith, sound theology, and practice.

Being familiar with a range of communal prayers will help worship leaders do this and allow them to plan liturgies in ways that invite congregations to have different experiences of praying together to God. The following list (organized alphabetically as opposed to an attempt to rank their importance) presents a few of the more common and useful forms of public prayers used in worship.

A **bidding prayer** is a liturgical form in which a leader invites (bids) the congregation to meditate on and/or speak aloud concerns related to different topics offered to God in some logical sequence (e.g., world, country, Church, congregation). The form allows the leader to express broad concerns of the community and then for individuals to express more specific concerns related to the broad themes. Thus bidding prayers are longer prayers often functioning in the liturgy as prayers of the people.

A **collect** (pronounced COL-lect instead of col-LECT) is a short prayer form that usually expresses a narrow concern. It has set parts that can be expressed in a single sentence or can be expanded as needed for the occasion. The five movements of the prayer are the *address* to the divine; adoration of the divine expressed by naming an *attribute* that foreshadows the next movement of the prayer; the *petition* in which the people ask for something that the attribution implies God can give; a stated *purpose* for the petition usually begun with the words "so that"; and a *closing* ending with the affirmation "Amen." Coming from the Latin *collecta* in the sense of collecting the people together for worship, collects are usually found in the Gathering functioning as an invocation, but the short form can be used in other places as well, such as a prayer of illumination.

A **corporate confession** is a prayer in which the congregation prays in unison to confess sins to God. While the prayer itself may be of different structures, there is a fairly standard liturgy for confession: usually a worship leader opens with a *call to confession*; the congregation prays the *prayer of confession* in unison; and finally the worship leader offers *words of assurance/absolution* to the congregation naming the forgiveness God gives through Christ. Because people from different walks of life pray the confession together, it must name sin in broad ways that all gathered can confess. Often then, the corporate confession is followed by a time of *silence* in which congregants can make individual confession before the words of assurance are offered.

A **litany** (from the Greek root *lite* meaning "supplication") is prayer in which a worship leader offers a series of petitions, with the congregation responding to each petition using a recurring formula. Petitions can be ordered in a logical sequence as described under the entry for a bidding prayer above, and, similarly, allows the leader to express broad and varied concerns of the community, functioning as the prayers of the people. The content of both the petitions and responses can vary widely based on the liturgical occasion, but the structure of individual petitions is fairly regular: the *petition* is offered by the leader; at the end of the petition the leader offers a *prompt* (such as "God, in your mercy . . ."); the congregation then offers a *response* in unison (such as "hear our prayer").

A **pastoral prayer** is an approach to the prayers of the people in which a worship leader in a single voice offers a prayer representing the gathered community. It is called a "pastoral" prayer because traditionally the one who offers it is a pastor of the congregation lifting up their pastoral concerns. While the structure of the prayer can vary based on the liturgical occasion and the range of concerns raised, a common form is signaled by the acronym ACTS. The prayer begins with *adoration* of God; next comes a *confession* of sin followed by *thanksgiving* for forgiveness and other gifts of God; finally the prayer ends with *supplications*.

BEAUTIFUL LANGUAGE

In addition to worship planners needing to think through issues related to representing the different voices in worship and having facility with a number of types of prayers, they need to attend to two other theological issues related to the language of worship.

The first is related to **aesthetics**, specifically, the concern that liturgical language be appealing, indeed beautiful. Like liturgical architecture, visual art, and music, liturgical speech should evoke wonder and a sense of the deep import of the community's worship. This means liturgical talk should be poetic without striving to be poetry for the sake of being beautiful. Beauty, in terms of liturgical language, is a means toward an end. By attending to the beauty of language, worship planners are working to make the congregation's liturgical talk an appropriate and worthy offering to God and to evoke the imaginations of members of the worshiping community that they might experience a richer engagement with the whole of the sacred conversation and especially closer communion with God.

Beauty is, as they say, in the eye of the beholder. This means that what counts as beautiful liturgical talk is not universally so, but is contextually determined. The sacred conversation should take place in the idiom of the community while raising that idiom to its highest level. It should use common vocabulary that congregants can speak and understand readily but that at the same time lifts their thoughts and hearts to sacred heights. In other words, liturgical language must be poetic without forfeiting the quality of being practical.

To plan and compose liturgical speech, then, worship planners need to love language—to love playing with words, dancing with grammar, and painting God's world with lines that make the congregation pause to catch their breath. This love must include a sensitivity to the fact that liturgy is not a written word. There may be text on the page, but it only becomes liturgy when it is spoken by the mouth for the ear. Language means something different in the ear than in the eye. Shaping liturgy, then, for the multitude of voices that participate in the sacred conversation, requires worship planners to attend to how the liturgy *sounds*. An element of this involves variety in speech: planning for speaking in unison requires sensitivity to the length, rhythm, and pace. In designing worship, planners must write the way people talk instead of forcing people to talk the way they write.

All of this is to say that worship planners must attend to both what is said (content) and how it is said (rhetoric) to offer worshipers a liturgy that not only touches the mind but also the heart (and ear).

JUST LANGUAGE

The second theological issue worship planners need to consider in relation to liturgical speech is **ethics**. When designing the liturgy for a particular occasion, worship planners need to choose liturgical language that is just and inclusive. This concern should not be dismissed as the latest fad of "political correctness." As we discussed above, the law of prayer is the law of faith. The vocabulary we use in worship shapes what congregations and its individual members believe in deep, significant, and sometimes unconscious ways. There are three categories worship planners need to consider in relation to justice and inclusivity: liturgical language for people, for God, and for Jesus/Christ.

First, liturgical **vocabulary for people**. The question is: In our liturgical labeling of people, are we appropriately loving our neighbors with our speech? Are we doing unto others with our speech as we would have them do unto us? Are we naming others in ways that value them equally as made in the image of God, or are we naming them in relation to a status related to a cultural hierarchy of power?

Use of *man* or *mankind* for the whole of humanity is an example of an unjust practice invading worship. To assume *man* is an inclusive term for all humanity is to see women as derivative of men. Consider the difference between a minister saying to a couple at the conclusion of a heterosexual wedding "I now pronounce you, husband and wife" versus "I now pronounce you man and wife." The first names each in relation to the other while the second names only the woman in terms of her relation to the man, implying her identity is subordinate to his. Whenever we use male language for the whole of humanity or use language that consistently puts the male first ("men and women," "he and she"), it grows out of and reinforces patriarchy in which male is the norm or ideal and female is derivative. The Church cannot construct faith in a liberating gospel in which half the population is presented as less than the other half. We are faithful to God's command to love others as ourselves when instead of "mankind" we say "humanity" or "humankind."

Of course, use of patriarchal language is not the only way the Church speaks unjustly and exclusively about humans in its liturgy. We can (intentionally or unintentionally) denigrate people in relation to race; age; sexual orientation; sexual identity; living situations; economic status; educational level; political leaning; whether they are single, dating, partnered, married, divorced, or widowed; and their relationship with God and/or the Church. Consider the following examples of vocabulary that is degrading to some segment of the population:

- "black list"

- "blind faith"

- to "Jew" someone down (financial negotiations)

- using "Mother" as the only feminine term used for God (implying all women should be mothers)

- to "gyp" someone

- "crazy" (for mental illness)

- such a "blonde"

- that was so "gay"

- "redneck"

- "Mexican" as a label for all Latino/a people

- Someone "went off the reservation"

- Modifiers to terms that otherwise would be acceptable can also be hurtful. The words *just* and *only* are prime examples: "She is just a housewife." "He is only a high school graduate."

If worship is to invite all into God's grace and love and into the Church's embrace, our language must be inviting *to all*.

201

Second, worship planners need to attend to **vocabulary for God** when choosing liturgical language. As with the concern about language for people, this concern is an *ethical issue*. The way we describe God implies the values we place on those whom God has created. A pastor was once leading a women's Bible study on Genesis 1 and came to verses 26-27, which claim that humans are made in God's image. The pastor asked the women in what ways they were made in God's image but got no answer. The group was silent. After a pause, the pastor asked the question again, and finally a woman spoke up, "We are not made in God's image. Our husbands are made in God's image, and we are made in our husband's image." Through hearing all of their lives (remember faith comes by hearing; *lex orandi, lex credendi*) that God is "Father" and "King" (and even in the text that God is "he") and that Eve came from Adam's rib, these women had been denied the identity of ones created in the *imago Dei*. Our language for God has ethical side effects.

In addition to being an ethical issue, however, use of limiting language for God is an act of *idolatry*. To present God in white male terms (as has dominated the Western Church) is to limit God by race and gender—categories that do not apply to God. In other words, we present God as being finite, made in the image of the finite humans who have throughout history had the most power to name God—"man" creating God in "his" image. It is idolatrous to worship anything less than God as God.

Patriarchal terminology is not the only problem with language for God, however. Other language can demean God in relation to our broader theology of the gospel. For instance, militaristic or vengeful descriptions of God had a place in ancient worldviews that are inappropriate today.

Of course, all language is finite, especially all language for God, who is utter mystery. All theological language for God is metaphorical. Thus any and every label or description of God limits and is unworthy of God. In liturgy, therefore, we should try to use as wide a range of the most appropriate metaphors we can find for the divine as possible—to expand and not contract our congregation's theological views and personal experiences of God.

Finally, worship leaders need to attend to **vocabulary for Jesus/Christ** when choosing liturgical language. The terms *Jesus* and *Christ* are meant to signal both a connection to and a distinction between the historical Jesus and the Christ of contemporary faith. Obviously for the Church, Jesus of Nazareth is the Christ, but our trinitarian theology claims the second person of the Trinity is not limited to the incarnational expression of the Christ. The historical Jesus was clearly a Jewish, Mediterranean, first-century male. The second person of the Trinity transcends maleness.

When referring to Jesus of Nazareth or Jesus as a character in the Gospel narratives in the past tense, it is obviously appropriate to use masculine pronouns and the like. The question is whether it is appropriate to use those same terms when referring to the Christ of faith, the second person of the Trinity in the present tense. There are different views on this question, and it is beyond the scope of this chapter to try to catalogue the various approaches and push for a specific solution. Mainly it needs to be asserted that the question is worthy of significant reflection to shape intentional liturgical use.

There are two other complications to **trinitarian terminology** as used in liturgical speech to be considered that relate to both of the last two discussions above concerning language for God and Jesus/Christ. The first concerns the use of the label *Lord*, which is commonly applied to both the first and second persons of the Trinity. Lord is, historically speaking, a term for a male. A woman would not be called a "lord." This would seem to imply that the term is exclusive and should be rejected for liturgical use. Yet, in North American culture, Lord is almost exclusively used for the divine in religious contexts. For many, this fact, along with its dominant use throughout the two testaments of the canon (e.g., in the Hebrew Bible as a substitute for the divine name YHWH) justifies its continued use. For others, though, it represents a deep patriarchal bias in our theological language, and thus they reject its continued use.

The second complication concerns the trinitarian formula *Father, Son, and Holy Spirit*. Some reject the patriarchal exclusivity in naming the first and second persons in male terms and prefer a formula such as "Creator, Redeemer, and Sustainer" even though it loses the relational character of the familial metaphors and instead emphasizes a primary functional role assigned to each person. Others try to retain the relational quality by expanding the formula with language such as "God who is Mother and Father, only begotten Child, and Holy Spirit." One of the complicating factors of this issue is that some individuals, congregations, and denominations argue that the traditional male language in the formula must be used at baptism for it to be a legitimate baptism (following Matt 28:19). Again, some use this as justification for continued use of the traditional formula in worship, others see it as a bygone exclusive tradition and disregard the traditional formula in baptisms, and still others seek a middle ground by using alternate formulae at different times when invoking the Trinity in liturgy but retaining the traditional formula for baptisms.

Adapting worship practices to use just language is a complex and potentially conflictual process. Worship planners and leaders should act and speak in ways that congregations experience as an invitation to embrace and experience new, inclusive, and expansive expressions for the divine and the human instead of a move toward which they respond defensively.

CHOOSING AND PERFORMING WORDS FOR WORSHIP

In the previous chapter, we discussed a range of theological considerations concerning worship speech. We will not repeat those theological concerns here but instead turn to the more practical approaches to choosing and performing liturgical speech.

BEGINNING WITH SCRIPTURE

The centrality of scripture for Protestant theology translates into its centrality for Protestant worship. Congregations gather to pray over God's word, to hear the word read, to hear it interpreted and proclaimed, and to be sent forth to live it out in the world. Thus regular Sunday Protestant worship planning often begins with scripture.

Indeed, the words of the scripture reading(s) for the day should be the primary locus for determining the rest of the words used in worship. In other words, the scripture lesson(s) set the tone and direction of the sacred conversation on most Sundays. Moreover, scriptural words and images getting used, adapted, and countered in other parts of the liturgy is as much an interpretation of scripture as is the sermon. Thus critical exegesis is just as important for planning the liturgy as a whole as it is for sermon preparation.

There are three primary methods for choosing scripture readings for a particular service. The first is a lectionary, classically referred to as *lectio selecta* (Latin, "selected readings"). We discussed the history of the lectionary resulting in the **Revised Common Lectionary** (RCL) in the chapter on the liturgical calendar and need not repeat it here. Instead a few comments on the use of the RCL in planning worship are appropriate.

The RCL was designed as a *liturgical* set of readings while many Mainline Protestant preachers use it primarily as a *homiletical* resource. When used as a homiletic resource, the preacher chooses one or more of the lections for the day as the text on which to base the sermon and the others are ignored, perhaps even to the point of not being read in worship. When used as a liturgical resource, all four readings are read in

205

worship and used to plan the service, including one or more being emphasized for the sermon. When used only as a homiletical resource, the cumulative power of reading across the canon Sunday to Sunday is lost and congregants may be unaware of any connection between the readings (especially if the preacher jumps from the Gospel lection to the Epistle to the Gospel to the Hebrew Bible from week to week). When used as a liturgical resource, the worship service has a flow related to the progression of the lectionary instead of being reliant solely on the preacher.

The second approach to choosing scripture for worship common among Protestants (at least historically speaking) is **lectio continua** (Latin, "continuous reading"). In this mode, a congregation reads through a biblical work passage by passage, week by week, with the preacher offering exposition of the texts.

A modified form of this approach is to work through representative passages of a biblical writing, reading *semicontinuously*. Thus instead of spending four months on Philippians, a congregation might devote four weeks to it. (The RCL prescribes semicontinuous readings during Ordinary Time.)

The third approach to choosing scripture for worship is **thematic** in nature. The worship planner, preacher, or worship team chooses a theme for the worship service and then finds a scripture text to fit that theme. Themes may be chosen for individual Sundays or for a series of weeks.

This topical approach is pastoral in nature in the sense that it often begins with worship planners perceiving needs in the congregation and shaping worship (including choosing scripture readings) to address those needs—in contrast to the above two approaches that begin with scripture and then move toward the congregation's needs.

Whichever of the three methods is used, once a text or texts are chosen, worship planners should use them as a basic guide for all other liturgical and homiletical decisions made in planning the service. The word "guide" here does not imply that all other liturgical language in a service must flow directly from the text(s) for the day or must directly engage the themes of the text(s). It is not a matter of the text(s) controlling the whole of the service (since a worship service does *many* things) so much as influencing the whole. At times worship planners may want to employ language in other parts of the liturgy that counters or balances the biblical language. For example, if a text focuses graphically on God as judge, there may be a need to emphasize God's grace in other parts of the service.

Similarly, worship planners must balance the specifics of the biblical text(s) with the themes of the liturgical season and the flow of the ordo. There may be themes and issues that have risen as part of the ongoing sacred conversation that need to kept in the mix of the liturgy. Or, finally, there may be immediate congregational, contextual, social, or pastoral concerns that need to be raised in the service that do not relate directly to the text(s) for the day.

One way to think of the *limited centrality* of scripture for planning worship is to imagine the liturgical talk throughout a service as resonating with the text(s) for the day more than being tightly controlled by the text(s). In physics, **resonance** is defined in terms of energy that vibrates one system causing another system to vibrate at the same frequency. Various liturgical actions throughout the worship service need not use specific vocabulary and themes drawn from the text(s) to be in proper relation to the scripture for the day (although this is at times appropriate). But for the service to be a unified whole instead of simply disparate acts on a liturgical to-do list, all of the various liturgical actions should vibrate back and forth in a way that all are related. For Protestants, at the center of this unifying resonance, without strictly dictating its content, is scripture.

OTHER POINTS OF RESONANCE

We have already mentioned that in addition to scripture, we shape liturgical language in relation the church calendar, the flow of the ordo, and congregational needs. We should also name four other sources of liturgical language to which worship planners should attend regularly.

The first is **traditional liturgical language**. Historical liturgy is a gift from our forebears to the contemporary church, and as we noted early in this book, ritual is conservative in nature and slow to change. When a twenty-first-century congregation gathers to offer praise and prayer, to hear proclamation of God's good news, and to celebrate the sacraments/ordinances, it does so with congregations stretching over the last twenty centuries.

We should not assume that praying a eucharistic prayer based on *The Apostolic Tradition*, reciting a creed from the fourth century, singing a hymn text penned during the Reformation(s), or referring to a nineteenth-century theologian in a sermon is dredging up relics of antiquity with no relevance for the present. Lifting up the voices of the historic Church in the sacred assembly is key to making the contemporary sacred conversation as relevant as possible. The human condition that is addressed by God's good news is the same today as it has always been. Indeed, the God we worship is an eternal God. We lose our identity as part of the **communion of the saints** worshiping that same God across the millennia if we relegate the past to the past in our liturgy.

This does not mean, however, that all historical worship language can be used without revision. We are, after all, the Church reformed and always reforming. Liturgical language of the past can be patriarchal or anti-Semitic, represent the relationship between the Church and government in ways no longer seen as appropriate, or express theology that is rejected in today's congregations. Thus at times, we may have to adapt historical liturgy to be able to use it or to write new liturgical language inspired by elements of a historical piece we find valuable.

The second source of liturgical language on which worship planners need to regularly draw is **denominational liturgical language**. Some denominations that have a hierarchical form of polity require congregations to use a significant amount of fixed liturgical language, while others with a congregational form of polity might have no authority to make such an assertion. Most traditions lie somewhere between these two poles fixed forms/language and flexibility. Regardless, a local congregation should value using the language of its wider denominational communion in its regular worship as it claims a particular identity and theology in today's ecumenical landscape.

In addition to a primary worship book, most Mainline denominations produce a myriad of liturgical resources. These are published by the denomination's press, posted on the denomination's web resources, produced in the denomination's seminaries and theological schools, and the like. Worship planners can cast their nets wide to get diverse voices from within a denomination to be part of an individual congregation's worship talk.

A third source of liturgical language to add to scripture, historical liturgies, and denominational liturgies is **contemporary ecumenical liturgical language**. One of the great gifts of the ecumenical movement is that different denominations have drawn closer and closer together in much of their liturgical speech. United Methodist, Presbyterian, and American Baptist worship planners might all use the same call to worship drawn from the same ecumenical resource related to the RCL on a given Sunday.

Good worship planners, therefore, have **worship books from diverse denominations** on their bookshelves and links from various denominational and ecumenical liturgical sites in a bookmark folder on their internet browsers. As with much of historical liturgical language, and even with some denominational liturgical language, worship planners will at times find the need to revise ecumenical liturgical texts in order to make them appropriate for a specific congregation. This is a good practice as long as copyright regulations related to a liturgical document (printed or digital) allows for such adaptation.

Finally, there are **anthologies of prayers and worship elements** by different authors that that can be useful in expanding the sacred conversation to include voices neglected in the history of Western worship: voices from diverse races, ethnicities, genders, geographical locations, historical periods, and so forth. Collections of prayers and liturgical resources can be organized by liturgical occasion, theological themes, or pastoral and social topics. Worship planners should build a library that contains numerous such anthologies. Again, worship planners may need to adapt, instead of simply adopt, language from such resources, if copyright allows it.

We discuss copyright issues in more detail in relation to congregation song, so we need not go into a detailed discussion of the matter here. Suffice it to say that worship planners should not steal (plagiarize) others' property. We cannot speak of ethical concerns in our worship and at the same time be unethical in our worship practices. Most liturgical resources are published for the very purpose that they be used by congregations and thus be reprinted or projected on screen. Fewer are open to their language being changed. But nearly all expect their work to be cited when used. A note in small print at the end of the bulletin or at the bottom of the screen is enough to show that this liturgical speech is drawn from a specific source. And this is a good liturgical practice in that it reminds the congregation of the breadth of voices that are part of its sacred conversation.

In the earlier chapter on the church year, we noted the kinds of liturgical resources available that are related to different seasons available in *Chalice Worship*. Denominational service books (and other ecumenical liturgical resources) also include liturgical texts that are organized thematically. A good example is found in *Celebrate God's Presence: A Book of Services* of the United Church of Canada (United Church Publishing House, 2000, used by permission).

COMPOSING LITURGICAL LANGUAGE

In addition to *finding* liturgical language to use in a specific service, worship planners should also develop skills at *composing* liturgical language. One of the benefits of composing liturgical language is that it can be tailor-made for a specific worship service and a particular congregation whereas all of the resources above are intended for broader use.

When worship planners set themselves to the task of writing a liturgical piece, there are some things to consider before setting pen to paper (or fingertips to keyboard).

They should begin, as mentioned above, with the scripture reading(s) for the day. **Prayerful exegesis** of the text(s) will allow the worship planner—both consciously and intuitively—to develop vocabulary, themes, figurative language, and flow of ideas that resonate with the scripture.

At the same time, worship planners should meditate on the **function of the liturgical element** to be composed. Is it intended to call the congregation together to worship, invoke God's presence, invite worshipers to acts of renewed discipleship in response to the proclamation, or send the people forth to continue their service to God in the world? The tone and force of the language will be different depending on the function of the speech.

Finally, the worship planner should reflect on **who will be speaking** the liturgical element to be composed. Will these be words spoken by a lay reader standing at the lectern? Will the piece be a responsive reading between a clergyperson and the congregation? Will it be a prayer spoken in unison by the congregation as a whole? Will five different children speak lines in succession? Different kinds of speakers, especially the difference between a single voice and unison speech, requires different kinds of vocabulary, sentence structures, and rhythm.

When worship planners begin writing, they should **speak the lines aloud**. Most of our education trains us to write for the eye, but liturgical writing (like homiletical writing) is for the mouth and ear. So one composing liturgical speech needs to attend not to the content alone but also to the sound of the piece and how easily or smoothly it can be spoken. In fact, a good practice is to have someone else read the piece to the worship planner, and then she or he can edit on the basis of how it sounds.

Taking time away from the piece and returning to it fresh will also invite a new hearing and may lead to further edits. While this process should not be rushed, at some point we have to trust God and hit the "print" button.

209

PERFORMING LITURGICAL SPEECH

Some shy away from the term *performance* in relation to worship because the word can have a derogatory sense to it. To say someone "performed" the liturgy sounds like we are accusing individuals of feigning sincerity. But let us recall the definition of ritual we used in the first chapter of the book: *Rituals are the patterned, symbolic enactment of a community's historically rooted identity and values.*

The term **enactment** in the definition implies performance (i.e., acting) in the sense of **speech act theory**, which we also discussed earlier. Some language does not simply *refer* to something that is external to the speech (e.g., "tree") but instead *acts* (e.g., "I order you to . . ."). Thus, when we say that rituals enact meaning, we mean that they do not simply refer to meaning external to the ritual, but they also "perform" meaning within the community. Rituals do not only refer to the values and identity from a community's past, they make meaning of and for the community in the present.

Our interest in this section is specifically in the role worship leaders have in performing the liturgy when they preside over some element of worship. Later in the Energy section, we will deal with issues related to embodiment, so our more narrow concern here is the **vocal performance** of liturgical speech.

In presiding over worship, the worship leaders' performance sets the tone for the sacred liturgical conversation. The performance in the chancel or on the dais enables the congregation to perform the ritual in a certain way in any given worship service. Put differently, worship leaders are never up front during worship for themselves. They serve God and the congregation. Whether standing in the pulpit, at the lectern, behind the table, or with the praise band, those leading worship work to make the conversation between the congregation, God, the Church, and the world as appropriate and meaningful as possible for all conversation partners. Whenever a worship leader becomes concerned about what is owed her or him—for instance, attention, appreciation, or agreement—a liturgical performance is distorted into a theatrical performance. When we lead a congregation in offering worship to God, and engaging the world and the Church as part of that offering, we must make sure that we do all we can to ensure that our words and the way we speak them are the best we have to offer.

We often claim that some people are "naturals" at things such as public speaking or leading worship, and, indeed, some people do have a natural charisma for these sorts of tasks that others must cultivate. That said, there is little that is natural about the task of leading liturgy. In what other natural (or ordinary) settings do we ask people to speak in unison or alternate every other line? When else do we use phrases such as "Let us" instead of "Let's" or "O God" instead of just "God"? Even in worship that strives to be informal, there is a **formality** to presiding in the liturgy required to demonstrate the significance and seriousness of what is being performed. Still, in this formality, worship leaders need to foster in themselves the ability to appear to be at ease in a way that draws attention to the liturgical action and content instead of drawing it toward themselves. We must preside in a manner that constantly reminds all in the assembly that this worship is sacred while also making the experience accessible and welcoming.

To lead worship in a manner that is formal yet natural requires **practice**. On the one hand, practice means that liturgical leadership should be rehearsed. Worshipers can always tell and are usually distracted when someone leads a call to worship or reads scripture in worship without being prepared. Stumbling over an awkward phrase or mispronouncing name after name in a long genealogy in Genesis gets in the way of those in the pews making meaning of that element of the liturgy. Rehearsal is required for responsible liturgical speech.

On the other hand, practice means that worship leaders get better at this conversational formality over time. Many reading this book have never or rarely led worship at this point in their vocational development. We should not be too critical of ourselves at this point in our experience. The more we do something, the better we get at it. That said, at this stage of learning to be a worship leader, we should seek honest, supportive, critical feedback on our liturgical performance. Otherwise, we will develop some bad habits that we are not even aware we are creating.

There are a number of broad goals for which the worship leader should aim in terms of liturgical speech. First, and most obvious, liturgists must speak so that **everyone in the congregation can hear**. We make a mistake when we assume that the amplification system will do all the work for us. We need to attend to our projection, the pace at which we speak, our use of emphasis, and the crispness of our words.

Second, worship leaders should speak in a way that **leads the congregation**. Our performance, the manner in which we preside, sets the tone for how the whole of the worship service is experienced and enacted by the congregation. We do not simply lead by telling the congregation what to do—"Stand and turn to hymn number 437"—but by modeling liturgical speech that all can enact. When we call invite others to praise, our voices should sound like we are full of praise.

Third, we should speak in ways **appropriate to the particular liturgical context**. Different liturgical settings call for different styles of worship. A liturgist in a two-hundred-year-old congregation that assembles in a Neo-Gothic sanctuary will lead a liturgical action differently than one standing before a start-up congregation in storefront church. Worship leaders use different vocabulary depending on the educational levels of their congregations. Presiders use a different tone at a wedding than at a funeral. And depending on the themes and scripture(s) for the day, liturgical speech may need to sound quite different in different parts of the ordo.

Finally, worship leaders should speak in ways that **serve the content** of the liturgical speech. *Performance is interpretation.* A lector's performance of a biblical text informs the congregation's interpretation, intellectual understanding, and emotional experience of that passage. And the same is true of all readings and prayers in a service.

HISTORY OF CONGREGATIONAL SONG

One of the most "energetic" elements of Christian worship is music. Pastors do not have to be music majors to lead worship faithfully and effectively, but one cannot talk about worship in the West and worship planning and leadership in Mainline Protestantism without having some basic historical, theological, and practical knowledge of congregational song.

In the next two chapters, we will deal with **theological** and **practical** issues related to choosing songs for worship. In this chapter, readers will gain a basic orientation to the history of the practices of communal singing in worship that any non-musically trained pastor or liturgical planner ought to know. Put differently, we are not going to approach worship music musically so much as we are going to approach it liturgically in terms of liturgical theology and liturgical function. In our overview of the evolution of musical practices and theology across church history, we will use the same basic historical schema that we have used in earlier chapters, so the periodization should be familiar.

A great deal of the history of music in the West *is* the history of music in the Church, but we are not going to be able to deal with subtleties in this brief chapter. Indeed, we will not focus on instrumental or choral music in and of themselves. Our focus is a broad understanding of our heritage of **congregational singing** in worship and how that heritage continues to impact liturgical practice today. In other words, this chapter is composed of a collection of historical glimpses to offer context for using music in worship today, not an exhaustive survey of church music.

BACKGROUND

As with every historical topic in liturgics, the history of church music begins in the cultures in which the early church began.

Roman culture inherited its use of music from Greek and Etruscan cultures. The **Greeks**, especially, valued music and categorized different musical modes and different types of songs. The **Romans** inherited these modes and types and certainly music was widespread in the Roman Empire, but musical talent and performance was not valued as highly in Roman culture as in Greece. Still, **hymns** of different types were written and sung to various gods. Religious music could be performed at cultural processions, weddings, funerals, and sacrifices. The line between social and religious use of music was blurry. Such music was usually **instrumental or singing accompanied by instruments**. Early church music likely drew on some of these musical practices and styles but, as we shall see below, also formed musical practices that intentionally stood over against Roman practices.

A closer and more direct influence on the use of music in early church worship was the rich musical tradition in the **Hebrew Bible and in late Judaism**. The fact that Moses, Miriam, and Deborah and Barak (Exod 15:1-18, 20-21; Deut 31:16-22; 31:30–32:43; Judg 5:1-3), and the like are presented in narratives as singing canticles shows how central music was to Hebraic life and worship. Even more significant are the psalms. Read Psalm 150 aloud:

> Praise the LORD!
>
> Praise God in his sanctuary;
>
> > praise him in his mighty firmament!
>
> Praise him for his mighty deeds;
>
> > praise him according to
> >
> > his surpassing greatness!
>
> Praise him with trumpet sound;
>
> > praise him with lute and harp!
>
> Praise him with tambourine and dance;
>
> > praise him with strings and pipe!
>
> Praise him with clanging cymbals;
>
> > praise him with loud clashing cymbals!
>
> Let everything that breathes praise the LORD!
>
> Praise the LORD!

Even when read in English instead of the original Hebrew, this text has a musical feel to it. If this hymn is paradigmatic, **temple worship** was at its core **praise**. Notice how much instrumental music, movement, and singing is a part of that praise. In contrast to the full historical record about Greek music, there is no such record of Hebraic musical theory. Thus we have little idea what music in the temple sounded like—we simply know it was an integral part of communal religious experience.

Not only does Psalm 150 remind us of the importance of music in ancient Israelite and Jewish worship, it also foreshadows the influential role the **Psalms** would play throughout Christianity.

Music continued to be an important element of **Second Temple Judaism** into the first century. By this time, however, **unaccompanied singing** was the primary form of music used in synagogue and familial worship. An example of this is the Gospels' presentation of Jesus and his disciples singing a hymn to conclude their worship after celebrating Passover at Jesus's Last Supper (Mark 14:26).

EARLY CHURCH

Early Jewish Christians extended unaccompanied singing into their Christian worship in **house churches**. Indeed, Paul speaks of hymns as a common element of worship in the fifties (1 Cor 14:26). Later in the century, the author of Colossians is more explicit:

> Let the word of Christ dwell in you richly; teach and admonish one another in all wisdom; and with gratitude in your hearts sing *psalms*, *hymns*, and *spiritual songs* to God. (3:16, italics added)

Given that ancient Greeks made technical distinctions between different types of religious songs, it is likely the author's mention of psalms, hymns, and spiritual songs here is making similar distinctions. **Psalms** likely refers to singing of the Psalter from the Hebrew Bible. **Hymns** (like their Greek counterpart) are likely metered songs sung to God and to Christ. What is meant by **spiritual songs** is less clear, but some scholars conjecture that the reference is to extemporaneous forms of musical expression.

Unaccompanied singing continued to be a part of Christian worship throughout the next few centuries while instrumental music in worship was frowned upon because in the Roman Empire it was an integral part of war, shows, and circuses, among other things. The Church saw the use of instrumental music, then, as promoting pagan idolatry and immorality. The early church sang in **unison**, which the early church fathers interpreted as a sign of the unity of the Church.

PLAINCHANT

As the Church grew and entered more into mainstream society, some Christians felt the need to withdraw from the world. These **monastic movements** took on an ascetic form of existence and developed a detailed regiment of worship. These practices began in the third and fourth centuries, but in the early Middle Ages they evolved into lasting forms.

Instead of weekly worship alone, monks divided the day into hours of prayer, with certain liturgical structures specified for each time. The **daily office**, as this practice came to be called, included praying the entire Psalter every week.

Plainchant, or plainsong, was developed for singing different parts of the liturgy and for singing the Psalms. As a musical form, plainchant involves a single melody without accompaniment. One syllable of a word could be given dozens of different notes in succession, and multiple syllables could be sung at the same note. These chants would be sung in unison, responsively with a soloist singing a main part and the choir or congregation repeating a response throughout it, or antiphonally with two groups singing alternate verses.

The later and more lasting form of chant known as **Gregorian chant** is more familiar today. In the sixth century, Pope Gregory worked to standardize liturgical practices across different regions and this process affected church music as well, even though Gregory probably had no direct hand in reforming chant. But legend has it that Gregory dictated the chants himself.

The influence of chant is still found in Protestant worship today. Chant evolved in various ways in different denominational traditions, for example, in the Anglican Church, and continues to be used in higher liturgical traditions, especially for the reading of the psalm as part of weekly worship. But even in Protestant churches where chant is not used, the act of **reading psalms responsively** is an evolution from plainchant. Most Protestant hymnals of the past century have included a responsive Psalter in the back. In the last half century, these have intentionally included a **refrain** that can be sung as a response during the reading. These refrains may come from common hymns or praise songs, or may have been written for that specific psalm. They are rarely chants, but they continue the influence of chant from the third to the twenty-first century.

In addition to chanting the Psalms, the heritage of chanting is found in some hymns in Protestant hymnals that use lyrics (sometimes ancient, sometime newer) set to ancient modes/melodies—scales from which the melodies of plainsong come.

AUGUSTINE

By the time Christianity was legalized in 313, and certainly after it became the official religion of the Roman Empire in 380, the Church had become more of an institution than a countercultural movement. With this shift came changes in worship—use of public buildings such as the basilica and using Latin instead of Greek in worship. But this also meant Christian worship music could become more mainstream, if you will, and play a more integral role in worship. This shift had both positive and negative potential.

No one knew the paradoxical potential of congregational singing better than Augustine. Augustine was a trained musician who loved music, but he was also suspicious of its power to manipulate emotions and draw attention away from the meaning of the words. What he wrote in **Confessions**, Book 10, Chapter 33, on the cusp of the Church transitioning from its early to its medieval period is worth reading at length because his basic stance has been influential ever since.

> Sometimes, I seem to myself to give them more respect than is fitting, when I see that our minds are more devoutly and earnestly inflamed in piety by the holy words when they are sung than when they are not. And I recognize that all the diverse affections of our spirits have their appropriate measures in the voice and song, to which they are stimulated by I know not what secret correlation. But the pleasures of my flesh—to which the mind ought never to be surrendered nor by them enervated—often beguile me while physical sense does not attend on reason. . . .

> On the other hand, when I avoid very earnestly this kind of deception, I err out of too great austerity. Sometimes I go to the point of wishing that all the melodies of the pleasant songs to which David's Psalter is adapted should be banished both from my ears and from those of the Church itself. . . .

> However, when I call to mind the tears I shed at the songs of thy Church at the outset of my recovered faith, and how even now I am moved, not by the singing but by what is sung (when they are sung with a clear and skillfully modulated voice), I then come to acknowledge the great utility of this custom.

Augustine names the Early Church's concern that music in worship **stirs the emotions** in contrast to a **rational lifting of the mind**, and wonders if the Church should exclude music from worship altogether. This makes sense: at times it is difficult to know whether music in a worship service is particularly moving because the Holy Spirit is at work in the message it conveys or the melody, harmony, and beat simply move hearers the way, say, any song at a secular musical concert might.

Instead of opting for the exclusion of music in worship, Augustine argues for a mediating position that influences the theology and use of music in Christian worship for the rest of church history. The principle he proposes is that **music in worship should be valued as long as it supports the words of the faith**. In other words, when it comes to choosing church music, content always trumps aesthetics, but never to the point of ignoring aesthetics.

MEDIEVAL CHURCH

In addition to the earlier mention of the standardization of Gregorian chant in the medieval church, there were some other major developments in church music during the Middle Ages.

First, the liturgy in the medieval period shifted from something in which the laity actively participated into something they watched being performed by professional clergy on their behalf. The liturgy was spoken in Latin, which over time became unintelligible to the laity. Eucharist was celebrated in the sanctuary but the elements were often not received by the laity gathered to watch devotionally from the nave. Similarly, music shifted more and more from being sung by the congregation to being sung by **choirs** that were usually composed of clergy, and certainly always composed of men and boys, excluding women and girls.

Second, there were some general innovations in music that affected church music. Music began to be written down in the latter part of this period. **Musical notation** allowed for musical pieces to be more complex than memory could hold.

Written music meant that in addition to plainchant (with the emphasis on "plain"), new forms of complex singing were brought into worship. Single melody lines gave way to **polyphony** in which different tunes and texts would be sung simultaneously. Although a long way from it yet, this was the precursor to **harmony** as we know it today. Part of this shift included a move toward each syllable of a word or line in a song being given its own note, much as we do today.

Another advance in music in the medieval period that may have been the most dramatic and influential development in church music of all time was the inclusion of the **organ** in worship. While there were surely occasions when instrumental music appeared in Christian worship in the form of a flute or a harp or such, the standard since the time of the early church was unaccompanied singing.

The organ itself was not a new invention. Small portable organs had been around in the Mediterranean world long before the birth of Christ. But probably around the 900s, they started becoming fashionable in churches. The shift from a cappella to accompanied singing marks a dramatic change in the way music functions in worship. The organ grew and evolved to a point where basically every church could have its own orchestra in one instrument.

PROTESTANT REFORMATION(S)

The Protestant Reformation(s) involved radical liturgical changes from medieval worship. Worship was led in the vernacular of the congregation, shifting the worship experience of the laity from visual to aural. Emphasis on watching the Eucharist was replaced with the centrality of proclamation. This emphasis on proclamation had implications for how music was viewed by the different reformers.

Martin Luther basically adapted the Catholic Mass to make it palatable to Protestant sensitivities. Luther loved music, was raised on music, and as an Augustinian monk was well versed in Gregorian chant. He recognized the emotional power in music of which Augustine spoke and thus valued its effectiveness in developing devotion among the laity. So he encouraged the singing of the liturgy of the Lutheran Mass. He also encouraged **congregational song in the vernacular** to aid in the clearer understanding of the word of God and to engage all the people in worship:

- He translated traditional Latin chants into German to be sung by the whole congregation, not just a clergy choir.

- And he wrote a number of hymns himself, composing tunes in styles popular in German culture of the day and borrowing well-known tunes from the Latin Mass.

Luther's most famous hymn, which is still found in almost all Protestant hymnals, is "A Mighty Fortress Is Our God." Notice that even in the midst of the Reformation(s), Luther draws the text for his hymn from the traditional source of the Psalms (this hymn is based on Psalm 46). The Church has been singing this hymn since ca. 1527.

Like Luther, **Ulrich Zwingli** was a trained musician and loved music. In contrast to Luther, however, Zwingli saw no place for it in worship. He argued that all profane art should be banished from the worship space as idolatrous and distracting. He leaned on the side of Augustine that distrusted religious experience associated with music. The focus in worship, he argued, should be on the word of God alone. So in Zwingli's arm of the Reformation(s) there was no singing in worship. Moreover, while art was being dismantled from worship spaces taken over from the Roman Catholic Church, so also were organs were dismantled and burned.

John Calvin often took a middle road between Luther and Zwingli in terms of liturgical theology and practice. This is true also in terms of music in worship. He did allow music in worship but not to the extent Luther did. Like the early church, Calvin only allowed unaccompanied, unison singing. He thought singing should be offered as praise to God by the whole congregation, not simply a choir. And with the focus in Protestant worship on the word of God, he thought the only proper content for singing was scripture itself. Thus Calvin primarily had his congregation sing metrical versions of the Psalms collected in what came to be called the **Genevan Psalter** (first edition, 1539).

Many of the tunes for the versified Psalms in the *Genevan Psalter* were written by **Louis Bourgeois**. Perhaps the most familiar of his tunes today is "The Old Hundredth." It is the tune most commonly associated with the "Doxology," but the name of the tune refers to the fact that early on it was associated with Psalm 100 in English, even though it had originally been composed for Psalm 134 in French. The English metrical version of Psalm 100 is "All People That on Earth Do Dwell," and the Church has been singing it since 1561.

ENGLISH HYMNODY

The next major advancement in Protestant congregational song comes two centuries later in the eighteenth century. A new tradition of hymn-singing in the church arose in England, and it started with **Isaac Watts**. In terms of music, Watts did for English worship what Luther did for German worship. He is considered the father of English hymnody, and it would be difficult to exaggerate his influence on the evolution of worship.

The story goes that when he was about sixteen years old, Watts complained to his father about the psalmody being sung in worship. As with many teenagers in worship today (perhaps in every era!), traditional church music bored him. His father responded, "Then write something better." So Watts did.

As a Puritan pastor, Watts broke with the Calvinist practice of having his congregation only sing psalms. Theologically, he found it problematic that Christians were singing only from the Old Testament and never singing about Christ. So he filled his hymns with imagery and phrases taken from across the biblical canon. For a given Sunday, he would write a hymn that fit with the message of his sermon, connecting the music for the day with the theme of the proclamation for the day. Many of his hymns follow the tradition of focusing on the Psalms but integrate into them other biblical, especially christological, language—in a sense Christianizing them.

We should also recognize that in a very new fashion, Watts did not at all limit his poetry to the language of scripture. He mixed ancient language with contemporary expressions and images to create hymns that were, in his words, suited to "the present case and experience of Christians." Most of the Reformers had been suspicious of

219

religious experience created through music. Watts moves the pendulum back toward an appreciation of the way singing relevant content invites appropriate religious experience.

Watts wrote around seven hundred hymns—seven hundred!—and published four books of hymns. His hymns remain greatly influential long after his death, and many are still sung today, 250 years after his death. Most Protestant hymnals will have numerous examples of his work, such as "O God Our Help in Ages Past," "Jesus Shall Reign Where'er the Sun," "When I Survey the Wondrous Cross," and "Come, We, That Love the Lord."

Perhaps his best-known hymn is "Joy to the World." While we think of this song today as a Christmas hymn, that was not Watts's original intent. He wrote it as an "imitation" of Psalm 98 in New Testament language. The Church has been singing this christological imitation of Psalm 98 hymn since 1719.

John and Charles Wesley represent the second generation of English hymnody in the eighteenth century. They took Watts's approach to hymn writing and applied it to their evangelical movement that grew out of the Anglican church (both were ordained priests in the Church of England). While John was the organizer of the Methodist movement in England, Charles was its poet. Both roles were extremely important for the way music would shape the Methodist movement and all of English-speaking hymnody to follow.

Let's begin with **Charles.** He wrote somewhere between five and nine thousand hymns and poems (approximately ten times as many as Watts!). The principles behind his lyrics are very similar to Watts. One cannot study early Methodist theology without studying Wesleyan hymns. The hymns were a central element of the evangelical mission of the movement:

- Charles employed heavy use of biblical language.

- He wanted to express the experience of Christians in their day (specifically the pious experience of the assurance of God's grace).

- He wrote hymns for special occasions and holidays. He especially had more hymns reflecting the Christian year than had been the case for Watts.

- Also, in comparison to Watts, Charles included a strong sacramental (especially eucharistic) emphasis in many hymns, reflecting the early movement's emphasis on the Table.

Most Protestant hymnals today still include numerous hymns by Charles. Some of the most familiar are "O, For a Thousand Tongues to Sing," "Come, Thou Long Expected Jesus," "Hark! The Herald Angel Sings," and "Christ the Lord Is Risen Today."

A great example of Charles's hymn-writing sensitivities is "Love Divine, All Loves Excelling." We can see in this hymn how far hymnody has evolved in the fact that instead of using the Bible as the primary source of language and imagery for the hymn, Charles Christianizes language from John Dryden's opera *King Arthur*. Notice how the language Charles uses is corporate but speaks of salvation and sanctification in intensely personal terms.

Shifting our attention from Charles to his brother, we can begin by noting that John wrote a few hymns himself. Some of these are still found in Methodist hymnals, but rarely elsewhere. He was not the poet Charles was. In terms of producing hymns, he focused more on translating hymns by German pietists into English (e.g., "Give to the Winds Thy Fears" by Paul Gerhardt).

More than a writer or translator of hymns, however, John Wesley served as the **hymnal** editor and publisher for the Methodist movement. He edited the hymns he collected (including his brother's hymns!), changing language to match the theology he wanted laity to learn as they sang (remember: *Lex orandi, lex credendi*). Then he published and sold the hymnals to be used in Methodist society meetings. Indeed, he and Charles pioneered the publication of inexpensive hymn collections focused on particular theological themes so that common people could afford them.

At this point in history, hymnals printed only words, no music. They were pocket-sized and bought by individuals, not kept in church pews. Those leading the singing would choose tunes familiar to the congregation to which to sing the songs. They used **tunebooks** to help them make their choices. John changed this practice. In his hymnals, he indicated specific tunes to be used with specific hymns, so that all Methodists would be singing the same tunes from group to group across the land. (It is interesting to note that every Methodist hymnal since the movement's earliest days has followed John's editorial choice of having Charles's "O For a Thousand Tongue to Sing" as the first hymn in the collection.)

Something else included in Methodist hymnals since those early days were instructions John compiled for congregational singing. They are worth reading in their entirety, especially thinking about them in relation to the history of congregation song and how they relate to Augustine's tension between emotion and content in the experience of singing in worship:

John Wesley's Instructions

I. Learn these tunes before you learn any others; afterwards learn as many as you please.

II. Sing them exactly as they are printed here, without altering or mending them at all; and if you have learned to sing them otherwise, unlearn it as soon as you can.

III. Sing all. See that you join with the congregation as frequently as you can. Let not a single degree of weakness or weariness hinder you. If it is a cross to you, take it up, and you will find it a blessing.

221

IV. Sing lustily and with good courage. Beware of singing as if you were half dead, or half asleep; but lift up your voice with strength. Be no more afraid of your voice now, nor more ashamed of its being heard, than when you sung the songs of Satan.

V. Sing modestly. Do not bawl, so as to be heard above or distinct from the rest of the congregation, that you may not destroy the harmony; but strive to unite your voices together, so as to make one clear melodious sound.

VI. Sing in time. Whatever time is sung be sure to keep with it. Do not run before nor stay behind it; but attend close to the leading voices, and move therewith as exactly as you can; and take care not to sing too slow. This drawling way naturally steals on all who are lazy; and it is high time to drive it out from us, and sing all our tunes just as quick as we did at first.

VII. Above all sing spiritually. Have an eye to God in every word you sing. Aim at pleasing him more than yourself, or any other creature. In order to do this attend strictly to the sense of what you sing, and see that your heart is not carried away with the sound, but offered to God continually; so shall your singing be such as the Lord will approve here, and reward you when he cometh in the clouds of heaven.

AMERICAN REVIVALISM

The next major developments in congregational singing require us to jump the pond and land in America. In the early 1800s, the pietistic movements that emphasized religious experience as an indicator of conversion began to take hold in a way that would shape American Protestantism forever. (Remember, in this book we are using *pietistic* broadly to refer to movements focused on individual experience/emotion influencing the Christian life instead of the more narrow label for the Lutheran movement influenced by Philipp Spener.) With revivalistic worship came a need for new congregational music.

Significant elements of the Second Great Awakening grew up from Presbyterian roots, with Watts still being very popular among the revivalists. But for simplicity of singing, Americans often added **refrains** to Watts's hymns. While people might not know the verses, they could easily join in on the choruses.

Mainly, though, new music was written that had an evangelistic ring to it while being less theologically focused than the Wesleys' hymns and more experientially focused than Watts's. With the emphasis on a personal conversation experience, the corporate character of earlier church music often gave way to a more personal tone. Instead of *us*, *we*, and *our*, these songs are filled with *I*, *me*, and *my*. This was the beginning of what came to be known as **gospel music**.

Perhaps the most famous hymn writer of the movement (from the mid-nineteenth to early twentieth century) was **Fanny Crosby**. She was a Methodist with no formal theological training, who became blind soon after birth. While living in New York City and working for the education of the blind, she wrote hymns . . . lots of hymns. Remember Isaac Watts wrote over seven hundred hymns and Charles Wesley wrote over five thousand hymns and poems. Fanny Crosby wrote over 8,500 hymns! Many are still familiar in American Protestantism: "Jesus Is Tenderly Calling You Home," "Pass Me Not, O Gentle Savior," "Praise Him, Praise Him," "Rescue the Perishing," and "To God Be the Glory."

Gospel tune writers would set her texts to music, and then they would be published. A new reality set in at this point as well. Publishing sacred music had become a business seeking a profit. Crosby was paid two dollars a song while the publishing companies held the copyrights to her words and collected royalties from continued sales, perhaps as many as one hundred million copies.

Her most popular hymn is likely "Blessed Assurance." The words of the hymn invite the singers to embrace a personal, individualistic experience of Christ. The use of a refrain similar to those found in popular music of the day is easy to remember, allowing those singing the hymn to assimilate the message. The music has a beat different than that found in English hymnody, inviting the piano to bang out the gospel tune with a strong rhythm.

A significant element of the Pietistic movements involved professional revivalists who also influenced church music. One example is **Dwight L. Moody**. Moody was an evangelist and religious entrepreneur. He founded the Moody Bible Institute and Moody Publishers, which published gospel music along with many other kinds of writing. Moody's right-hand man in terms of music was **Ira Sankey**. Sankey was the song leader for Moody's revivals and was known as the "Sweet Singer of Methodism." In fact, even today in Great Britain and Australia, gospel songs are still sometimes called "Sankeys," as in "Sing me a Sankey." Moody and Sankey traveled the world, leading revivals in the mode that would later be adopted by the Billy Graham Crusades, with Sankey's role being filled by George Beverly Shea.

Sankey, a composer in his own right, worked with hymn writers (like Fanny Crosby) and other composers to develop music for the revivals and to publish the songs throughout the nineteenth century. This new business approach to church music (by Moody Publishers and many others) resulted in reams and reams of gospel music of varying quality being written and published.

This proliferation is why hymnals today are still filled with so many gospel hymns from the 1800s, and this business model was the precursor of the contemporary music movement in the late twentieth century.

SPIRITUALS

The next development in congregational singing in the American context is the **spiritual** that grew out of slave Christianity. The background for this musical tradition is quite complex. The Second Great Awakening certainly influenced slave worship, but slave worship in America also predated the revivalistic movement of the nineteenth century.

Some white slaveholders required their slaves to become Christian for both salvific and manipulative reasons. White or Black preachers hired by the masters told the slaves that Paul said to obey their masters and that their obedience would gain them admittance into heaven after death. In this context, with masters or overseers watching, the slaves were taught hymns of the white church and sung the likes of Isaac Watts and Charles Wesley.

The slaves who claimed the Christianity forced upon them, however, also found in biblical stories a different theology than that which they heard from white preachers. They would gather in secret in the dark of night in what has come to be called the **hush harbor** or the **invisible institution**. They would place large iron pots in the middle of gathering and hang damp quilts around the outer edges to catch the sound. In these clandestine worship services, the slaves would hear a different proclamation by one of their own, have a different experience of the Christian faith, and sing different music. The slave preacher would speak of the exodus and a God who would liberate them from slavery. The sermon itself would have musical quality, as would the responsive moaning and clapping during the sermon.

And as part of their worship, they would sing songs that melded elements from West African music, Protestant psalms, and American hymns—all of these reshaped by the experience of the oppression of slavery. They often sang spirituals in call (solo) and response (all) format, echoing the call and response of the sermon. In these songs there is a level of claiming experience in congregational singing that goes far beyond anything Isaac Watts, Charles Wesley, or even the white gospel hymn writers could have imagined. The songs involved sliding tones and syncopation and expressed emotions ranging from deep lament over their current situation to great, joyous eschatological hope in the God of freedom. Moreover, following in the traditions of Western Africa, the African American slaves used their whole body to sing—clapping, stomping, dancing.

Often the spirituals had a double or **coded meaning** that could be sung within the ear of the white master as well as in secret worship: celebrating the Bible stories of the faith while also teaching about escape from slavery. The "Kingdom of God" or "life after death" referred to the freedom in the north; "gospel train" or "chariot" referred to the Underground Railroad; the "Jordan River" referred to the Ohio River dividing the South and North. Some spirituals were considered "map songs" and gave directions for those who would try to escape. "Follow the Drinking Gourd," referring to the Big Dipper containing the North Star, is a prime example. Other spirituals were "signal songs" that communicated in code that a secret event was planned. For instance, "Swing Low, Sweet Chariot" indicated chariot drivers—Underground Railroad conductors—would be arriving soon, so that passengers would be alert and ready to leave. "Steal Away" and "Let Us Break Bread Together" indicated that there would be a secret meeting or secret worship that night. These coded messages did not distract from the surface-level religious significance of the songs; they deepened them and made religion real and practical.

After the Civil War, many (not all, but many) Black churches rejected spirituals as part of their desire to become more a part of mainstream white culture. But the spirituals continued to play a significant role in the Black community. African American choirs toured across the northern states and Europe singing spirituals for white audiences to raise money for the creation of Black colleges in the south. So a **concert tradition** of spirituals evolved.

Nearly a century later, these spirituals were reclaimed in the Black community as part of the civil rights movement, being sung in churches and in marches. This use also reintroduced white churches to the spirituals, and many of the spirituals have been reclaimed in Mainline denominational hymnals.

Let's look at one example in detail: "Wade in the Water."

The song alludes to water imagery in different places in the Bible.

- Moses crossing the Red Sea to escape from Pharaoh.

- Joshua crossing the Jordan River to lead the people into the promised land.

The phrase "God's gonna trouble the water" refers specifically to the healing story in John 5:4 where people come to the pool of Bethesda waiting for the angel of the Lord to stir the waters and whoever gets in first would be healed. This song was sung during baptisms because all of its water imagery is symbolic of God's salvation that continues to be remembered in the practice of baptism, in which the Holy Spirit is given.

Harriet Tubman, however, would also sing this song as she conducted people on the Underground Railroad to remind them to head north to cross the Ohio River to salvation and to instruct them *literally* to wade in creeks, ponds, and rivers along the way to throw bloodhounds off their scents.

GOSPEL MUSIC

Popular music styles in the nineteenth century began to shift from emphasizing harmony to emphasizing melody with a **beat**. We see this reflected in some spirituals and with the beginnings of gospel hymns of the nineteenth century. This emphasis on beat has shaped most of the history of popular music throughout the twentieth century; the twentieth century was the century of rhythm. With ragtime and swing as the beginnings of jazz, the early decades of the century banged out rhythms on the piano, had brass sections sounding the back-up beat, and the drum set was prominent in the center of the stage. They were, after all, dance bands. By the second half of the twentieth century, beat so dominated that harmony and horns mostly disappeared and rock-and-roll bands were reduced to instruments that could drive a rhythm: drums, keyboard, and guitars.

With the development of radio and affordable recordings, popular music would start influencing people's tastes in music far more than church music; and popular music would, in turn, start influencing church music. With broadcasting and recording as possibilities for distribution, church music began to mix with popular music. **Black Gospel Music** that could be heard in Black churches across the land could now be heard on the radio and was popular among African Americans and white

Americans alike, with men and women who sang in churches now becoming gospel music celebrities. There is no better example than the "Queen of Gospel" **Mahalia Jackson**. She recorded some thirty gospel albums with dozens of singles going gold and appeared on television often.

In a similar fashion, **Southern Gospel Music**, or white gospel music that evolved out of the evangelical gospel music of the nineteenth century, moved into the mainstream in the twentieth century, sharing more and more of the production qualities of popular music of the day, with emphasis on rhythm.

No one has been better at this than **Bill and Gloria Gaither** and the different groups with whom they have performed. They not only wrote and performed music but created recording companies and record labels, and they epitomized gospel music as an industry related to popular music more than music for congregational singing, especially as exhibited in their Homecoming concerts and television shows.

Both forms of gospel music have representative examples in recent Protestant hymnals, along with a similar development in the 1960s—**Christian folk music.** Influenced by the music of the civil rights movement and the popular folk movement including artists such as Bob Dylan and Joan Baez, guitar-led music (such as "Lord of the Dance " and "Pass It On") made its way into youth camps and mainstream worship in both post-Vatican II Catholic churches and Protestant churches.

PRAISE MUSIC

The gospel music industry and Christian folk music are the stepparents of the contemporary or praise music industry. They are "stepparents" in the sense that Christian contemporary music did not directly descend from gospel music so much as it grew out of the Charismatic movement of the 1970s and the related evolution of the megachurch.

As noted above, gospel music moved out from the Church into the mainstream entertainment industry. From its beginning, however, Christian Contemporary Music (CCM) was oriented toward the popular music market, not the Church. Christian singer-songwriters, bands, and recording labels were created to offer an entertainment alternative to popular music considered less wholesome. Creation of this music, draw to concerts, and the sale of records were tied to the creation of Christian radio stations. So, all-in-all, CCM aimed toward fame and money similar to the wider music industry. That is not to say that people writing and performing this music did not believe what they were singing and did not think of themselves as serving God. Naming the situation this way is to recognize, however, that CCM artists were trying to sell records—not equip the Church for singing.

Eventually, however, this music did start making its way into churches. Recordings were played in worship, or a soloist would sing with an instrumental cassette recording backup. Praise bands appeared in the chancel. Organs became dusty sitting behind the drum set. So while CCM originally had no real intention to reform worship in regard to congregational singing, it developed into praise music, which has indeed become a major influence in worship reform.

There are pros and cons to this movement in relation to congregational singing. The primary advantage is clear enough: if the music culture of America has been defined by rhythm for over a century, it is time for the Church also to sing music that is driven by a beat. The pipe organ can play an amazing range of music, but one thing it does not do well is pound out a beat. If one of the purposes of church music is to invite experience, it is important that the church use music related to contemporary experience outside the Church.

One problem with CCM in communal worship, on the other hand, is that most of it, especially early on, was not written for group singing. It was written for a solo voice or for a performance group. When used in worship, then, the congregation was placed in the role of singing along with the solo performer up front, just as a crowd might do at a pop concert. This is hardly liturgy as "the work of the people." As the market for praise music in worship grows, however, the publishing industry has developed and continues to develop more and more of music with congregations in mind. Megachurch movements have especially been responsible for some of this shift.

A theological problem with praise music in worship is that the lyrics in the music almost exclusively come from an evangelical perspective. This orientation does not fit the more moderate or progressive theological orientations of many Mainline denominations and congregations. Such Mainline churches that use commercially published praise music in worship often have to ignore Augustine's advice concerning the use of music to support words of faith and simply choose aesthetics or style over content. This music leads to an individualistic, devotional experience in worship as opposed to the unity of the community traditionally associated with congregational singing. But as we saw, this critique is really leveled at the direction congregational music began to travel as part of the revivalistic movement of the nineteenth century. This situation is starting to change as some artists with progressive tendencies are writing and performing in this style of music, but the change is still slow and very small at the moment.

RECENT DEVELOPMENTS

For the sake of an introduction, the history above is presented in a fairly linear fashion that makes the evolution of congregational singing seem simpler than it is. For example, the sort of hymns represented in Reformation(s) and English hymnody did not disappear as revivalistic and gospel music developed. Hymns from across the centuries have continued to be sung alongside newer forms and styles of congregational music. And often hymnal committees have altered the wording of these older hymns to fit the worldview and idioms of the contemporary church.

Traditional hymn writing has continued as well. Indeed, there have been a number of **new hymns** produced in recent decades that fit the traditional style but also embrace new language and often more contemporary theologies than found in "contemporary music." This development coincides with the process of liturgical renewal that is part of the Mainline consensus.

Another development that does not fit clearly on our historical chart is the recent interest in **global music** as part of congregational singing in American churches. With the rise of globalization and the recognition that Christianity is growing in the Global South and the East while it diminishes in the West, scholars and groups have introduced the Western church to music from other regions as part of becoming a worldwide body of Christ. The Iona Community (through GIA publications) and the Global Ministries of the United Methodist Church (with a series of *Global Praise* volumes) have especially helped in making musical resources from around the world available to European and North American congregations. Slowly, Mainline Protestants are beginning to include songs from Latin America, Africa, and Asia in their hymnals and in supplemental songbooks. The Spanish song "*Tù has venido a la orilla*" quickly gained popularity among North American congregations as it found its way into denominational hymnals.

CONCLUSION

There are a few overarching lessons this historical survey can teach those who plan Mainline Protestant worship today.

First, congregational singing has been constantly evolving since the beginning of the Church. Knowledge of this fact should put the current "worship wars" in context for us and lessen the anxiety some feel. The current struggle between traditional hymnody and praise music in many denominations and congregations is not a new dynamic in church life.

A second lesson worship planners and leaders should take from this historical survey is that songs written for congregational singing live a long life even in the midst of musical evolution. Indeed, the basic patterns and types of traditional church music continue on even as new ones are added. We still sing psalms. We still chant. We still weigh content of the lyrics against the emotions evoked by the music. We still use the organ. We still sing Watts and Wesley and Crosby. We still use hymnals. We still sing spirituals, gospel music, and Christian folk songs. In the distant future, when something new comes along, we will likely still be singing some exampels of praise music along with the new musical forms.

A final lesson is that we should recognize that there are always various trends at play in church music that at any time may grow to have more influence, changing and enhancing congregational singing in ways we cannot yet imagine.

The current state of congregational singing is perhaps the most complex the church has ever experienced. Although the current worship wars often lead us to think of two styles opposed to each other, in reality there is great diversity in terms of musical styles originating out of the great range of ethnic, ecclesial, geographical, and theological sources that are part of the body of Christ. Our approach to singing the Christian faith will both continue and continue to evolve.

A THEOLOGY OF CONGREGATIONAL SONG

We continue studying congregational singing from a liturgical perspective instead of a musical perspective, with the goal of gaining basic knowledge needed for designing and presiding at worship services. In this chapter, then, we turn from the historical background of current Mainline Protestant practices to a *theological* view of singing in Christian worship.

Distinctions between the historical and theological surveys should not be drawn too strongly. In the previous chapter, we reviewed not only musical practices as they evolved across church history but also the evolution of theologies of congregational song. In other words, what follows is an extension of and is informed by our historical survey. Although the Church is not limited to its past, tradition does and should inform our liturgical theology and practice—and this is certainly the case when it comes to music.

MUSIC IN THE LITURGICAL CONVERSATION

Throughout this book we have utilized a practical theological model of Christian worship rooted in conversation between God, the congregation, the historic and global Church, and the world. This conversation is mediated by Christ and moderated by those leading worship.

Music, like anything we consider including in worship, should help foster this sacred conversation or it should not be used. Nothing in worship is spoken, enacted, or sung for its own sake. While music should be beautiful, it is not beauty for beauty's sake. It is not entertainment or performance in the vein of a concert or even singing around the piano in the parlor. Whether we are talking about a hymn sung by all, an anthem sung by a choir, a pop Christian piece presented by a praise band, or a prelude offered by the organist, all music *must* be liturgy—works of the people—not just the work of the musicians, received by the people.

Worship music, therfore, can and should, relate to different voices in the sacred liturgical conversation at different times.

At times singing is prayerful, a word of praise or petition offered by the **congregation** to God. Historically the Church has seen praise as the primary liturgical role of music. That is why most hymnals start with songs of praise to God.

At times singing is proclamation, a word spoken metaphorically by **God** to the congregation, wider Church, or even the whole of creation. Consider "Here I am, Lord" by Daniel L. Schutte, based on the call narrative in Isaiah 6:8-10. Even though the title of the hymn represents the voice of the congregation, this hymn is actually a conversation initiated by God's voice (represented by singing in unison or a solo voice in the stanzas) with the congregation responding (with the diversity of responses represented by singing in harmony in the refrain).

At times, a song represents the voice of the **historic Church**, speaking from the past to the present, or from a distance to those gathered here. Sometimes these are hymns related to a denomination's particular history such as Lutheran use of hymns by Martin Luther or Methodist use of hymns by Charles Wesley. More often, we sing hymns that speak to the Church in the wider sense of its identity, songs stretching across the centuries. The contemporary hymn "I Believe in God the Father" is a lyrical version of the ancient, ecumenical Apostles' Creed by David Gambrell.

Similarly, consider a Euro-American congregation singing "Jesu, Tawa Pano," the Zimbabwean gathering song by Patrick Matsikenyiri. Singing it first in its original language and then in English connects the congregations with the **global Church**, with sisters and brothers of the faith around the world, claiming that we do not gather in this particular place in isolation.

And finally, at other times, a song lifts up the voice of the **world** beyond the Church. Most often these hymns offer a word of need for the world that the Church is called to address. Consider "O for a World." This is a recent hymn by a Roman Catholic woman, Miriam Therese Winter. The song invites the congregation to envision and hope for the reign of God to be manifest in the world.

PURPOSES FOR CONGREGATIONAL SINGING

In addition to thinking about congregational singing as representing and relating to the different voices in the conversation of worship, we can consider music theologically from the perspective of different *purposes* it has in worship. Describing these purposes overlaps with what we have just said about the conversational model, but unpacks some issues in new ways.

First and foremost, singing is **doxology**. We use this term not in a technical sense of a particular type of song but in its broader sense of adoration sung as an offering to God. Praise can certainly be, and is, spoken in worship. Music is not required for a community of faith to offer adoration to the divine. There is, however, a different quality to praise that is sung versus praise that is spoken by a representative voice or even spoken in unison. Consider Psalm 148:

Praise the LORD!
Praise the LORD from the heavens;
   praise him in the heights!
Praise him, all his angels;
   praise him, all his host!
Praise him, sun and moon;
   praise him, all you shining stars!
Praise him, you highest heavens,
   and you waters above the heavens!

Let them praise the name of the LORD,
   for he commanded and they were created.
He established them forever and ever;
   he fixed their bounds,
   which cannot be passed.
Praise the LORD from the earth,
   you sea monsters and all deeps,
fire and hail, snow and frost,
   stormy wind fulfilling his command!
Mountains and all hills,
   fruit trees and all cedars!
Wild animals and all cattle,
   creeping things and flying birds!
Kings of the earth and all peoples,
   princes and all rulers of the earth!
Young men and women alike,
   old and young together!

Let them praise the name of the LORD,
   for his name alone is exalted;
   his glory is above earth and heaven.
He has raised up a horn for his people,
   praise for all his faithful,
   for the people of Israel who are close to him.
Praise the LORD!

The psalm is a call to praise God as creator of all and is filled with lofty language and punctuated with exclamation points. When it is read responsively in worship, however, it is often performed in a monotone, deadpan fashion. Of course we do not have to (and should not) read it that poorly as an offering to God, but we often do. In contrast, a melody forces us to praise with fuller voice than we use when speaking. Go to **www.abingdonpress.com/protestantworship** online and listen to the familiar hymn by Francis of Assisi based on this psalm set to the seventeenth-century tune, Lasst uns Efreuen: "All Creatures of Our God and King."

While music (like other art in worship) is not beauty for beauty's sake, it should nevertheless be **beautiful**. To ignore aesthetics in evaluating elements of worship is to deny the gift of beauty God offers us. As recognized since at least the time of Augustine, the beauty of music well performed can offer worshipers a powerful emotional experience that connects them to God, the Church, and the gospel. Bad music, however, can detract from such an experience during the liturgy. While congregations and church musicians will have different levels of musical ability, we should only offer God our best. To offer music that is not our best (like offering any liturgical act that is not our best) is like offering pocket change instead of tithing when the plates are passed through the pews.

Jesus commands us to love God with our whole heart, soul, strength, and mind (Luke 10:27). Most of Protestant worship (with its emphasis on the word, specifically the spoken and heard word), primarily engages the mind. Well-performed music is one of the most significant ways that the Church has **engaged the emotions** in worship. Since Augustine, the Church has not only recognized the positive psychological aspects of using music in worship, but has been concerned about the power of music to *manipulate* emotions over rational thinking—singing eight hundred verses of "Just As I Am" manipulates emotions to get people to come down for an altar call instead of opening the door for worshipers to have a faithful response. We must be careful not to confuse being moved by music with being moved by the Spirit. On the other hand, to imagine the Spirit cannot or does not work through the beauty of music is limiting God.

Worship music with lyrics **rehearses the faith** in a way different than preaching or reciting a creed does. Congregations *enact* the doctrines, memories, stories, and hopes of the Church differently in song than in other forms of spoken discourse used in the liturgy because language functions differently in song. Poetry is not the normal use of language. Theological talk forced to follow specific metrical patterns and rhyming schemes leads congregations and individuals to experience and assimilate that theology in a different way than when listening to or speaking prose. Add falling and rising pitch and various rhythms to the mix and the impact is even stronger. We remember melodies differently than we remember texts. This music memory ability means worshipers assimilate lyrics we sing over and over again in ways they do not even realize. Think about how much harder it is to memorize a script of some sort versus how easily one can recall the words of a song she or he has not heard in years.

Because music manifests the truth of *Lex orandi, lex credendi, lex vivendi*—the law of prayer is the law of faith and the law of life—in a most powerful manner, worship planners must consider the power of lyrics set to music in terms of theological formation very carefully when choosing worship music. Messages in hymns and praise songs stick with people in unconscious but powerful ways—both positive and negative. A hymn with bad theology forms people's faith just as strongly as a praise song with good theology. This is why Augustine argued that content must always win over the choice of a good tune.

Consider, for instance, the practice of singing a doxology in the liturgy. The words used in many churches make up the final stanza of Thomas Ken's "Morning

Hymn" and is sung to the tune of the Old Hundredth, composed by Louis Bourgeois for the *Genevan Psalter*.

> Praise God, from whom all blessings flow;
> praise him, all creatures here below;
> praise him above, ye heavenly host;
> praise Father, Son, and Holy Gost. Amen.

If a congregation sings those words *every* Sunday year after year after year, how can they not think of God as male? A sermon or Sunday school lesson here or there cannot counter the way the masculine pronouns and metaphors are burned into congregants' memories and thus their world-view. They may say they don't think of God as literally being male, but their singing makes it hard to think of God otherwise.

How different would faith formation be if we sang alternate words Sunday after Sunday, year after year? Consider these lines from the contemporary doxology by Bryan Wren:

> Praise God, in Jesus fully known:
> Creator, Word, and Spirit one.

Another purpose of music on worship is seen in the fact that since the early centuries of church history, the Church has recognized that singing together **creates communion** in the assembly. Setting words to a melody and adding harmony offers an ideal for the way the Church is to live out the faith. Just consider the difference in the experiences of singing together as a community of faith and a board meeting arguing over the budget!

This sense of unity formed by singing together is perhaps stronger today than ever before because the way we experience music in today's world is so different than it was for our forebears. Before the technological advances of the twentieth century, one could not listen to music that was not performed live. And part of life was sing-ing together, not just religious songs in worship but secular songs in the parlor as Sister played the piano. Today, however, music is mainly consumed in private. We do not even listen on stereos anymore; we listen to our handpicked songs with ear-buds plugged into our smartphones so no one else can hear. We may sing along with recordings or even at live concerts, but it is rare to sing secular songs in unison any-more. Congregational singing, then, is a countercultural act that enacts something of our Christian identity and values. In a day when not only music but all of life is more and more individualized and privatized, the body of Christ stands and sings the faith together in a united voice.

Consider the communion hymn "One Bread, One Body" found at **www.abingdon press.com/protestantworship**. The first-century words and imagery of the table from **The Didache** (ch. 9) used in the hymn are not the only ways it emphasizes the unity of the community. John B. Foley, the Jesuit priest who wrote both the words and music of this hymn, intentionally composed the tune to be sung in unison.

The unity that our congregational singing symbolizes extends beyond the local community. We sing words and tunes that are not only from our own time. We sing as part of the **communion of saints**. By drawing on lyrics and musical styles from different periods of the Church's history, we profess that we stand in continuity with our forebears in the faith. We do not simply remember the Church's tradition, but we become part of that tradition when we sing words and tunes passed down for decades and centuries. We do not only sing our contemporary faith but the faith of Christians in all ages and places.

So while we definitely need music and lyrics that represent contemporary consciousness, we lose something vital when we institute a contemporary style of music in worship that completely replaces everything sung by our ancestors from the Second Great Awakening, and the invisible institution, and English hymnody, and the Reformation(s), and the Middle Ages, and the early church.

Consider a hymn that may not be very familiar: "The Glory of These Forty Days" (see link at **www.abingdonpress.com/protestantworship**).

The glory of these forty days
we celebrate with songs of praise;
for Christ, by whom all things were made,
himself has fasted and has prayed.

Alone and fasting Moses saw
the loving God who gave the law;
and to Elijah, fasting, came
the steeds and chariots of flame.

So Daniel trained his mystic sight,
delivered from the lions' might;
and John, the Bridegroom's friend, became
the herald of Messiah's name.

Then grant that we like them be true,
consumed in fast and prayer with you;
our spirits strenthen with your grace,
and give us joy to see your face.

The original Latin text attributed to Gregory the Great dates back to the sixth century in the early Middle Ages. If those planning worship cast this hymn into the mix of worship without plowing the field first, people unfamiliar with the tune might be frustrated and simply dislike it and not sing. But imagine that in this service, a worship leader introduces the hymn (or it is introduced in the bulletin) as a song the Church has been singing at the opening of Lent for fourteen centuries. This serves a great way to teach the congregation a little about the history of the practice(s) of Lent in order to inspire a holy Lent that draws us not only into closer communion with God but also with our forebears in the faith.

CONGREGATIONAL SONG IN THE ORDO

When the Church offers its best in worship, the prayers, proclamation, and singing for the day are all thematically connected and all parts of the liturgy resonate with each other. The worship service from beginning to end has a primary (although not exclusive) **theological focus** that is drawn from the scripture reading(s) for the day. Congregational songs are chosen to support, unpack, and celebrate that focus.

That theological focus, however, is expressed and experienced differently during the parts of the service. While a worship service focuses on a primary theological or existential theme, the liturgy is also marked by dramatic movement. A short story has a single plot, but that plot still unfolds across paragraphs, and the reader experiences that plot differently during the conflict and rising action than at the end when resolution has been achieved.

In worship, then, congregational singing not only explores the theological focus of the day, it also helps **set the tone** for the dramatic unfolding of that theme across the four movements of the ordo. The four parts of Christian worship, as discussed in an earlier chapter, are the Gathering, Proclamation, Response, and Sending Forth. Each movement functions differently, so a song appropriate for the Sending Forth will rarely be appropriate for the Gathering. Often the tone is different for music in each movement related to these different functions. Congregational singing is part of the musical score that moves the plot of worship along and gives it experiential depth.

Songs sung during the **Gathering** should foreshadow theological, scriptural, and experiential themes that will arise later in the service. They must also, however, relate to primary functions of the first movement of worship—gathering disparate individuals into the sacred assembly and invoking the presence of God. Therefore, opening songs are often celebratory songs offering praise to the God who promises to be with us in worship. And sometime they serve as explicit calls to worship, like "Uyai Mose," the gathering song from Zimbabwe.

Usually songs sung during the **Proclamation** movement focus closely on the theme of the biblical text(s) read or the sermon to be preached, but there are also hymns that celebrate scripture and proclamation of the word more broadly or that can serve as a prayer for illumination. Clara Scott's nineteenth-century gospel hymn, "Open My Eyes That I May See" can function this way in the ordo.

Songs for the **Response** movement of worship depend on what liturgical actions are being performed. There are many ways we respond to the proclamation of God's word during the liturgy. Response is usually where a congregation sings communion songs as they move toward the Table. Songs can be sung that are related to the prayers of the people or receiving the offering. Or since Proclamation calls for decision and action, it is in the Response section where invitations to discipleship fit. Singing is often a part of the invitation because the words and music combine with the sermon to bring an emotional element. Such is the case with "Take My Life."

Finally, songs during the **Sending Forth** often echo back to the theological theme of the day in a way that is especially fitting for believing and living out that theme beyond worship. But some songs appropriate for the close of worship serve as benedictions in their own right. These songs can be calm and peaceful since benedictions usually offer a blessing of peace, or they can have a beat to them that sends people marching out into the world as witnesses to the good news of Jesus Christ. In "God Be with You Till We Meet Again," members of the congregation bless each other as they depart to their different paths in life, but with the hope of worshiping together again next Sunday.

CONCLUSION

A good way to end this chapter, reflect on the theologiy and theological functions of congregational singing, and to come full circle with the previous chapter is to quote Thomas Dorsey. Dorsey is known as the father of black gospel music, and his compositions include the likes of "Take My Hand, Precious Lord," "Peace in the Valley," "Old Ship of Zion," and "God Be with You." In terms of a theology of music and the relation of singing and emotion, this twentieth-century composer is a descendent of Augustine from the fifth century and John Wesley from the eighteenth century. In the quote that follows, Dorsey is speaking about gospel choirs, but his words apply to the whole of congregational singing:

> As I go from town to town, I find some very good choirs and some very poor choirs. I find some who sing the music too slow and some who sing it too fast. I find some who do not possess enough spirit and others who have too many embellishments that may be mistaken for spirit. Loud vociferous singing, uninspired gesticulations or self-incurred spasms of the body is not spirit. I believe in shouting, running, and crying if the Holy Spirit comes upon one, but I don't believe in going to get the Spirit before it comes. (Source unknown)

CHOOSING CONGREGATIONAL SONGS FOR WORSHIP

In the previous two chapters we surveyed the history of congregational song and reflected on a theology of congregational singing in relation to different functions within a waorship service. We turn now to apply the insights gained in these chapters to the practical task of choosing congregational songs as part of the regular worship planning process.

We begin by looking at the tools for finding hymns and songs. This will include examination of how hymnals are constructed and online resources that help worship planners find hymns and contemporary praise songs.

Having found potential songs for worship, worship planners must decide which ones are appropriate for use in the liturgy of a particular worshiping community. In the second part of the chapter, then, we ask what principles should be used when picking music for worship to make sure they are the best songs to advance the sacred conversation on this particular liturgical occasion.

Finally, we close with a word concerning copyright issues related to printing songs in a bulletin or projecting them onscreen.

PARTS OF THE HYMNAL

Before we begin choosing the music for a worship service, we have to know how to use a hymnal. How to use a hymnal may seem obvious: open it up to a certain page and start singing. Using a hymnal to find hymns related to a particular scripture text or theological topic, however, can actually be quite complex. A hymnal offers a worship planner hundreds of options. How is one to narrow down to the three or four songs to be used on the Fourteenth Sunday after Pentecost? If worship planners just start flipping through the pages looking for something that "grabs" them, it will be like flipping through the whole of the Bible looking for a text on which to preach. We almost always pick something with which we are comfortable, that we would lean toward anyway, whether it is the best fit or not.

The way Mainline Protestant hymnals are organized and the tools they include to help worship planners are not identical by any means, but they are quite similar. As we discuss these elements of a hymnal we will continue to use as our example the Presbyterian Church (USA)'s hymnal, *Glory to God* (GTG). Readers of other denominations should have their hymnal available to compare as the discussion progresses.

Hymns, of course, take up the bulk of the hymnal, but that is not all that most denominational hymnals include.

They usually also include some **liturgical/ritual resources**. As we have noted, most Mainline denominations also have worship books that include many more worship resources. Hymnals, therefore, only include the liturgies to which the whole congregation needs access during worship. These usually include a complete worship service as a sample of the order of worship and sacramental liturgies, especially when congregational response is part of the standard liturgy. As seen in the table of contents GTG includes a standard service for the Lord's Day (that includes Eucharist), baptism and baptismal reaffrimation (including confirmation) liturgies, daily prayers, and some other standard liturgical elements (especially creeds). These liturgies reflect standard denominational theology, language, and practice. The higher the liturgical tradition, the more authoritative these services are.

Because of the ancient and continuing influence of the Psalms on Christian worship most hymnals have a **Psalter section** near the back of the hymnal providing responsive readings, chants, and/or musical responses. Instead of a distinct Psalter, the GTG has chosen to scatter the Psalms throughout the hymnal and includes a psalm index.

In the past, many Mainline Protestant hymnals contained only a portion of the biblical collection of Psalms and even chopped the individual psalms into short portions. There has been a revived interest in the use of psalms in worship in recent decades and thus hymnal committees have expanded Psalters in hymnals in the last several decades. Sometimes the expansion reflects the use of psalms in the Revised Common Lectionary and sometimes the entire psalter is included.

Finally, at the end of the denominational hymnal are a number of standard **indexes**. While the person in the pew may rarely glance at these, some of them become a worship planner's best friends when it comes time to choose hymns for the weekly services. We will look more closely at a few of these below.

With this quick overview in hand, for the remainder of the chapter we are going to focus on the parts of the hymnal related to congregational singing.

STRUCTURE OF THE HYMN COLLECTION

In most Mainline Protestant hymnals, hymns are arranged topically/doctrinally in some fairly standard ways, even though each hymnal has unique elements.

Most hymn collections begin with a **trinitarian structure**—starting with hymns of praise and hymns focused on theological themes related to the Creator, then the Redeemer, and finally the Spirit.

These hymnals gather hymns related to particular seasons of the **liturgical year**. These are usually placed under the major heading of the second person of the Trinity and finish under the Spirit. This makes sense, since the church calendar is organized around the Christ event and christological themes (Advent—preparation for the coming of Christ; Christmas—the nativity; Epiphany—the revelation of Jesus as the Christ; Lent—Christ's passion; Easter—Christ's resurrection), ending with the gift of the Spirit to the Church at Pentecost.

Most hymnals also have an **ecclesiological section**, songs celebrating the gift, character, and mission of the Church. This section often extends from the Holy Spirit.

Related to the ecclesiological section, hymnals also have a set of hymns that are related to **specific acts of worship**—gathering, offering, benediction, and especially baptism and Table. Also included are hymns collected for special rites of the Church such as weddings and funerals.

Finally, hymnals usually have an overarching structure that moves from creation and the beginning of life, through salvation history and the mission of the church, to the eschatological end of individual life and turning of the ages.

STRUCTURE OF THE HYMN PAGE

The pages where hymns appear are filled with important information that is helpful to the worship planner. Not all hymnals are laid out in exactly the same fashion, but most of this information can be found in any hymnal.

In the top corner of the pages are the **headings** we find in the table of contents. Sometimes the header on the left-hand page is the major section heading and the one on the right is the subheading. These are helpful when worship planners are searching for hymns related to a theme: find a heading that relates to the theme and flip through the section's pages.

The top line is the **hymn title**. It should be noted, however, that most hymns, especially older ones, do not have titles per se. Instead their first lines are simply listed as the title. In hymns and gospel songs with refrains, the first line of the refrain is sometimes used as the title. This means that worship planners scanning though the hymnal looking for a hymn related to a specific topic should not let the first line as a title shape their understanding of the content, any more than the first line of a novel tells us what we need to know about the plot of the book.

At the bottom of the page, we find **source information** on the left-hand side: author of the text, composer of the music, usually with dates for when the text and music were first published. This information is followed by copyright information. If there is no copyright information on the page, this means the hymn is in the *public domain*. While this information may not seem especially important for finding hymns for a specific service, it can be. In terms of cumulative worship practices, worship planners should desire to choose hymns that stretch across the Church's history and represent different voices within the Church.

On the right-hand side at the bottom of the page is the **tune name** followed by the **meter**. Multiple hymns may use the same tune. The more worship planners choose hymns, the more they start recognizing common tune names and meters.

As we will see below, meter can be very helpful in choosing hymns. Each number in the meter designation represents the number of syllables in a line. (Now by "line" we mean the lines of the lyrics; not a line of the music as laid out on the page.)

Underneath the tune name and meter, some hymnals will place other information such as a temp suggestion. Here we are told a place in the hymnal where we can find the same tune written in a lower key, which some may prefer for singing. Some, but far from all hymnals, include a few lines of **commentary** at the bottom of each hymn. These lines are not meant to serve as an exhaustive interpretation of the hymn but instead offer a key interpretive lens through which to study and experience it.

Many denominational hymnals have a **companion volume** that goes further in interpreting the hymns included in the collection. These can be very helpful to worship planners as they interpret and choose congregational songs.

HYMNAL INDEXES

Let's turn from the individual hymn page to the indexes at the back of the hymnal. Worship planners will use some of these often; others less so. For instance, rarely will one use a **copyright index** (acknowledgments) when searching for hymns. It can be helpful to note, however, that any given hymn can have multiple copyrights associated with it—for the text in the original language, the text in English translation, the tune (or melody), the harmonization, a descant, and so forth.

Perhaps more often but still infrequently will a worship planner look for a hymn by a specific person or movement, so a **source index** (authors, composers) will also be of little weekly use.

Also, worship planners will rarely use the **tune index** when searching for hymns. This index can be helpful, however, for worship planners who do not read music. If one comes across a hymn that is unfamiliar but the words make it worth considering for use in a worship service being planned, she or he can look up other hymns with the same tune. If there is one with which he or she is familiar, he or she can evaluate the music in terms of whether the congregation knows and can sing the tune and whether the tone is appropriate for the movement in the ordo for which a song is needed.

Imagine you have found the hymn, "Come Sing to God" (#805 in GTG), and think the lyrics fit well with the theological focus of the service you are planning, but it is a hymn neither you nor your congregation has ever sung. Unsure what it sounds like, you look at the bottom of the page and identify the tune name as ELLACOMBE. When you check the Tune Index, you find two familiar hymns set to the same tune: "I Sing the Mighty Power of God" (32) and "Hosanna, Loud Hosanna" (197). Now you can use the song with confidence of its singability.

Worship planners will use the index of **First Lines and Titles** more often. This index is helpful when worship planners know a hymn they want to consider choosing but are not sure where it is in the hymnal. Even if that hymn ends up being one that is not chosen, by looking it up one has found a section of the hymnal worth flipping through.

Following on the idea of thumbing through sections where a heading relates to the theme of the day, it is important to note that hymnal headings are imprecise because hymns are often not as focused we might like when we plan worship. An editorial committee must use organizing themes for a hymnal that are broad enough to gather in multiple songs. Moreover, many hymns could easily fit under multiple headings. That is why worship planners need to use a hymnal's **topical index**. Some of the topics indexed will match the headings used to organize the hymnal and then list other hymns that fit with that topic. The index will, however, also list a range of topics not identical with the headings, often narrower in focus. Still, no index is exhaustive, and it may not use the same vocabulary a worship planner is using in thinking about the liturgical theme for the day. Therefore, one needs to look for related terms, synonyms, and even antonyms for the theme to find a wide range of hymns that might fit the aim and focus of the liturgy.

Because worship planning usually starts with choosing scripture and the service focuses on that scripture, hymnals include a scripture index to help worship planners find hymns connected with a focal passage. GTG not only has a **scripture index**; it also includes **lectionary index** to suggest hymns related to scripture texts for specific days in the liturgical calendar.

Now suppose worship planners have used the above indexes to find a hymn whose text fits the scripture and theme for the day perfectly, but the congregation has never sung it and the tune is unfamiliar. Does that mean they must reject this hymn and find another? Maybe; but before discarding it, there may be another hymn tune, a familiar tune, that can be substituted to use with the hymn text. We noted in the historical review of congregational song, that hymnals originally had no tunes listed. Song leaders would pick a tune that would work based on their knowledge of hymn meter. That practice is still useful today.

Assume at the bottom of the page the meter of an unfamiliar hymn is listed as 8.7.8.7.D, in other words 8.7.8.7 doubled (8 7 8 7 8 7 8 7). In the back of the hymnal, there is a **metrical index**. It lists numerous hymn tunes that follow the 8.7.8.7.D meter. If worship planners can find a familiar hymn tune with the same meter, the congregation might still be able to sing the desired hymn to that tune. The question left is whether a familiar tune sounds appropriate for the tone of the content of the lyrics.

ONLINE RESOURCES

In addition to the indexes at the back of a hymnal, there are online sites that can assist in searching for songs to use in worship, especially if one's congregation is willing to sing songs not found in the hymnal sitting in the pews.

The most comprehensive site for searching for traditional hymns is **hymnary. org**. Worship planners can search by keywords, scripture texts, author, composer, and so on. Many of the older hymns found here are in the public domain. Others will require copyright permission to use (see below).

Because contemporary Christian music is newer relative to the study of traditional hymnody, there are fewer reliable resources available to help worship planners search for music by theological theme or scripture text. By searching the web, one can find different sites that have catalogued sets of praise songs in some manner, but these are usually quite limited. (Some Mainline denominations are starting to list contemporary music appropriate to their theological sensitivities.) The primary license site for praise music is **Christian Copyright Licensing International—CCLI** (see below under discussion of copyright issues). CCLI includes a tool called **SongSelect** that allows worship planners to search by title, author, and lyrics. Songs are also coded by topic and scripture references, but this indexing is far from exhaustive. Still, Songsearch is the best search engine available for praise and worship music and will likely continue to evolve in terms of its sophistication.

APPROPRIATENESS OF A SONG

Once worship planners have found some potential songs that are being considered for worship, they must determine whether the choices are appropriate for the congregation's worship.

We begin at the point where Augustine would have us start—that is, with the appropriateness of the content of the lyrics. We examine this appropriateness from several different perspectives.

First, worship planners need to ask: **Do the lyrics fit with the theme and/or scriptural texts of the service?** The theme is established by a combination of the liturgical occasion, the text for the day, and the particular homiletical interpretation of that text for this occasion. There are lots of Advent hymns, but not all fit with the First Sunday of Advent's focus on the return of the Christ in the eschatological future. There are a number of hymns that deal with eschatology, but not all share the Gospel writer Matthew's view of the *parousia*. And there might a few that relate to Matthew's view of the *parousia* but do not fit with the theological approach the preacher is going to take on in the sermon.

With all those elements at play, it is rare that worship planners can find hymns or praise songs that perfectly fit the theme the way we would we would like. Thus one has to be a realist when choosing worship music. From what is available and accessible, what are the best options? This often means ruling out songs that are inappropriate and then choosing among those that are close enough, that is, songs that *resonate* with the theme worship planners are highlighting (on resonance as a principle of liturgical choice, see above).

Next worship planners need to ask: **Are the lyrics of this potential song theologically appropriate?**

There are different contexts for considering theological appropriateness:

Does the theology of the hymn fit with denominational theology?

Does it fit with the congregation's theological orientation?

Does it fit with your theology as leader of congregation?

The question of theological appropriateness also applies more narrowly to metaphors for God.

Does the song offer a rich, contemporary experience of God or does it present the divine in ancient patriarchal and militaristic terms?

Is God in this hymn (or in the collection of songs being considered for the service) always male and never female?

Is God a wrathful king or a loving companion?

Related to the previous question, worship planners must ask: **Are the lyrics ethically appropriate?** This question involves a range of sub-questions:

Are the lyrics just? Do they present humankind in an inclusive or exclusive manner?

Do the words and images of the song reflect inequality in the world or move beyond it?

Are all of the songs being used in the service representative of white, male, Western voices or do they represent the diversity that is God's family?

In determining whether or not a particular song is appropriate for our congregation's worship, worship planners cannot focus only on lyrics. They must also ask: **Is the music appropriate?** What counts as appropriate music depends to a significant degree on the culture and musical tastes of the congregation, the abilities of the musicians and those who lead the singing, and even the size of the congregation. A large congregation can handle a hymn that requires a big booming organ much better than a congregation of twenty-seven members. Basically, then, when worship planners ask about the appropriateness of the music, they are asking, **Can the congregation sing this music well?**

There are two main issues at stake in this question. The first is whether the tune is **familiar** to the congregation. If they have never heard it before, they might be able to sing it, but they will need a chance to learn it before it is thrown into the midst of worship, unless it is a really simple tune.

(A side note is needed here. For music in praise and worship services to have a full and appropriate impact on individual worshipers and communities of faith, many praise bands need to grow in their ability to teach congregations the songs for Sunday worship and the manner in which they encourage communal singing. Too often, praise bands perform new songs hoping the congregation will catch on by the last chorus instead of intentionally teaching the song to the worshipers. It is important to remember that singing in worship should be "the work of the people"—not a performance by a band or choir, to which some people sing along. This goes counter to the way most popular music is experienced in today's world, and it takes intentionality to bring it about.)

The second issue at stake in the question of singability of a potential song for worship involves the **complexity** of the tune. Different congregations have different abilities. A worship planner must ask whether the congregation (and staff or volunteer musicians) can manage this rhythm, this tempo. Can they sing the range from low note to high note?

Worship planners must also ask: **Is the song under consideration appropriate for the movement of the ordo for which we need it?** This question applies to both lyrics and music.

> Does the content of the lyrics fit where a song is needed in the flow of the service?
>
> Are the words appropriate for the Gathering or are they more fitting for part of the Response to the Proclamation?
>
> Does the tune fit for the tone of the Gathering or seem more fitting for later in the service?

One will rarely choose a lullaby-sounding song for the opening of the service. It might perfectly fit the theme of the day, but it would send the whole movement of the service down a very quiet path. Worship planners should resist the temptation to force a song into the liturgy where it does not fit; save it for another Sunday or move to another part of the ordo.

Finally, related to the question concerning placement of a song in the movement of the ordo, is the following question: **Which voice or voices in the sacred conversation are represented by this song?** Throughout a worship service (and certainly across the span of several worship services), music should represent different voices—God, the congregation, the wider Church, and the world. Moreover, at different times of the worship service a different voice is needed. If the song is placed at a point of allowing the congregation to respond to the word proclaimed, the voice represented in the sermon should be that of the people singing as opposed to, say, God's voice speaking to the singers.

Woship planners may want to create a template for evaluating hymns in Microsoft Word or Excel that can be used on a weekly basis. An example of such a worksheet is found on the following page.

Evaluating a Possible Hymn/Song Choice

Biblical Text	Thematic Focus of the Service	Liturgical Occasioni

Name of Hymn	Source & Reference

How do the lyrics fit (and not fit) with the them/text that focus the service?

Do the lyrics fit with my denomination's theology? How or how not?	Do the lyrics fit with my congregation's theology? How or how not?	Do the lyrics fit with my theology? How or how not?

Do the lyrics employ sound metaphors/descriptions of the divine?	Do the lyrics employ just language?

Can my congregation sing this tune? Is it familiar? Is the range appropriate? Etc. If the tune is unsingable, is there another with the same meter that would be an appropriate substitute.

Which voice(s) in teh liturgical convesation is(are) represented in the song(congregation, God, historic Church, and/or worldd)/ Is this a voice I need in this service?

For which movement(s) of the ordo(gathering, Proclamation, Respoinse, and/or Sending Forth) would this song be appropriate? Why? Is this where a song is needed?

Summary Evaluation: Use the hymn or not?

COPYRIGHT ISSUES

Throughout the preceding discussion, the issue of copyright has arisen. The fact that hymnals include copyright information on the hymn page reminds us that just buying a copy (or copies) of a hymnal does not mean a congregation has permission to duplicate the text or music in another format. Copyright is owned by the author of a hymn text and by the composer of a musical piece or their representative publishing companies (see the sample page from GTG's **Copyright Index** on the previous page). A congregation must obtain permission to reprint words or music in a bulletin or project them on a screen.

If a congregation only rarely needs to reproduce words or music, then the best way to proceed is to seek individual permission. Publisher information is usually easy to find online. The permissions process can take a little time, however, so advance planning is necessary.

If a congregation regularly reproduces words or music for a congregation (or posts videos of worship services with music performed online), the best way forward is to purchase an annual license that covers a wide range of music. Costs for the licenses are based on congregation size and are usually affordable. Two such licenses are the most widely used: OneLicense and CCLI.

For traditional hymnody and global music, the best license available is from **OneLicense.net.** This license covers traditional hymns and music produced by many American evangelical, Mainline Protestant, and Roman Catholic publishers as well as international publishers, such as Iona.

For praise and worship music, the best license can be obtained from **CCLI** mentioned above. This license covers many artists and publishers of Christian contemporary music. (There is some overlap of songs and genres between the two licenses, so congregations should search their databases before deciding which service to purchase.)

It is important to remember that neither license service offers coverage of *all* music in the genres they cover. Worship planners must check the websites to make certain a song they wish to use in worship is included in the license they have purchased. And when using a song that is covered by their license, they must dispay the license information in the bulletin or on a screen.

Too many congregations fail to be diligent enough in relation to copyright issues. Often in worship, moral and ethical concerns play a significant role in our sacred conversation. Such talk is hypocritical if congregations are not ethical in their use of materials owned by others in those very worship services.

CONCLUSION

Music contributes to forming worshipers in the faith (*Lex orandi, lex credendi*) and is key to the way most congregations offer praise to the Triune God. Worship planners and leaders, therefore have a huge responsibility in picking and leading the best hymns and songs a congregation can sing together. As Fred Pratt Green writes in "When in Our Music God Is Glorified":

When in our music God is glorified, . . .
it is as though the whole creation cried: Alleluia!

EMBODIED WORSHIP

W̲e are commanded to love God with our whole heart, soul, strength, and mind. Often when we talk about the content of worship—especially about what is said and sung in worship—we are usually thinking about the use of our minds (texts) and hearts/emotions (music). We are, however, also called to love God with our strength in worship. We use our whole bodies, as we are able, in our prayer, praise, and proclamation.

Indeed, Christian worship is full of body language that we often take for granted. We enter, sit, stand, bow, kneel, shake hands, come forward, pour water, elevate the bread, and depart. A worship service is, in a sense, as much a choreographed dance, from beginning to end, as it is a scripted, dramatic conversation.

There are three elements of embodiment in worship we consider in this chapter: postures, gestures, and locomotion. Some of the particulars we examine are shared by worship leaders and the whole assembly and some are associated with leadership alone. All of these postures, gestures, and movements are natural, but when we are "dancing" in front of the congregation, we need to be conscientious and intentional about the way we use our bodies to lead others in the sacred dance.

POSTURES

Posture refers to **the position of the body**. The term usually applies to times when the body is still, but it can also refer to the way the body is held while it is moving.

The primary postures in worship involve different ways of showing reverence to God and/or directing the attention and actions of the congregation.

Concerning **sitting** and **standing**, worship leaders need to appear attentive (avoiding slumping) without looking like a soldier at attention. When in front of the congregation, the way worship leaders hold their body says something about the importance of the occasion. Moreover, the way worship leaders position their bodies when sitting or standing helps direct the attention of the congregation. For example, in a split chancel the preacher might sit on the pulpit side with her chair facing

247

directly toward the congregation. When someone reads scripture at the lectern, the preacher does well to angle her body in that direction to show she is attending to the moment in a way that helps others attend to it as well.

Common wisdom among worship designers is that congregations can only pay attention "as long as their butts will allow." In other words, alternating between sitting and standing lets the congregation stretch their legs without getting too tired of standing all the time. The alternation gets the blood flowing, allowing those in the pews to be active participants in worship. So standing for this hymn and sitting for that prayer keeps the congregation engaged.

The two postures also become traditionally associated with different liturgical actions and moments of the ordo in different congregations. For example, some congregations stand for opening hymns of praise but sit for hymns that lead into the prayers of the people. When the congregation sits, the people are usually in a receptive, listening mode. When they are asked to stand they are being invited to be active and show reverence for the moment in a different way. The practice has its historical roots in the fact that, as a sign of honor, no one sat in an ancient ruler's presence without the ruler's permission. We stand, then, before the presence of the Sovereign One who rules the universe with grace and justice.

By **bowing**, here we mean first the posture of having the head bowed. This is a posture associated with prayer, a gesture of humility before God. Usually worshipers also close their eyes in this posture as a way of focusing attention, so that visual stimuli do not distract from conversing with God. While there are certainly times we pray with our heads lifted up in worship (e.g., during eucharistic prayers in most traditions), if the congregation has their heads bowed during prayer, the worship leaders should as well. It makes prayer appear fake to a congregant who opens their eyes and looks around to find the organist flipping through the hymnal to find the next song or the pastor writing notes on the edge of the bulletin to remember announcements she needs to make.

Bowing can also involve the posture of bending a knee to the ground (**genuflection**) or bowing at the waist (**deep bow**). The practice of genuflecting in the worship space is rooted historically in the medieval devotion of the Blessed Sacrament based on the belief that the real presence of Christ is to be found in the eucharistic elements. Many Protestant communities and individuals in higher liturgical traditions that are close to the Roman Catholic sacramental heritage use genuflection as a posture directed toward the table, or the reserved elements, when they enter the worship space before taking their seats. Derived from this practice are other uses of bowing and genuflection in worship to demonstrate devotion and humility before God (in both higher and lower liturgical traditions), especially bowing toward the cross. The ecumenical movement of the last century has resulted in much cross-pollination in Protestant worship practices. This leads to both positive and troubling results. One troubling result is that at times some worship communities assimilate the worship practices of others uncritically or without understanding what the practice signifies. This is true of bowing at times. Some communities, for instance, have the acolytes bow when approaching the table or chancel but no one else bows. A practice such as bowing should be interpreted for and made available to all who gather for worship, or it should not be used.

Kneeling plays different roles in different Protestant communities. It is generally a sign of humility related to bowing the head. In some lower liturgical traditions, kneeling rarely or never occurs—perhaps only when hands are laid on someone for healing or commissioning. In some higher traditions, there are kneelers in the pews and the whole congregation kneels together as part of different prayers. For many traditions in-between, kneeling at the communion rail to receive the bread and cup is the primary time of kneeling.

GESTURES

By *gestures* we mean **movement of the hands**, usually done in one location (i.e., without moving one's body from one place to another). As a heuristic device, we can categorize the primary gestures used in worship in relation to four orientations of the palms of the hands.

The first is **palms up**, that is gesturing with the hands lifted up to God. This gesture is used in *prayer*. One of the most ancient gestures of Christian worship is the **orans**, a gesture inherited from both Greco-Roman and Jewish religious practices. The orans involves a person who is usually standing with elbows near to the sides of the body, the forearms stretched outward at an upward angle, and the palms facing up. The guesture is appropriate for anyone praying in worship and is often used by worship leaders speaking for the whole assembly in prayer. Less formally, this basic gesture can be found in more charismatic and expressive styles of worship where worshipers will raise a hand or two up during prayer or prayerful singing.

Similarly, palms up gestures are used in relation to **offering**. A worship leader elevates the monetary offering and the celebrant at the table elevates the bread and the cup as signs that we give them to God in thanksgiving.

A second set of gestures used in worship involves the **palms down**. These gestures relate to the act of *blessing* as part of worship, especially in the form of **laying on hands**. Worship leaders touch others with their palms when they anoint and bless worshipers as part of a healing ritual, when someone requests a blessing (for example, during the celebration of the Lord's Supper when a worshiper does not desire to receive the elements), when a person is being commissioned for or ordained to a particular ministry, and during the baptism and confirmation rituals.

A particular form of the palms down gesture is the **benediction**. In a sense the worship leader who offers the benediction at the conclusion of the service lays hands on the whole congregation at one time. Thus the gesture needs to be appropriate to the action. Hands should be held high over the congregation with the palms down, yet the gesture should appear natural. The extremes of barely lifting one hand up or both hands pointing to the sky with locked elbows like a superhero about to lift off from the ground should be avoided. This is a pastoral ending to a worship service and the gesture should help communicate that intention.

The third type of gesture involves the **palms out**, that is, extended to another in the form of a *greeting*. A hand reaching out to shake another hand or to wrap around someone in a hug to accompany or represent the **kiss of peace** during the **passing of the peace** is a sacred moment of *koinonia* and reconciliation during the worship service.

Finally, there is the gesture we will (awkwardly) call **palms crossed**. Higher liturgical traditions generally practice **signing the cross** more than do those communities with lower forms of worship practices, but different forms can be found across liturgical styles.

Worship leaders, usually the pastor, may make the sign of the cross over the congregation (or over the eucharistic elements of baptismal waters) as part of a blessing invoking a trinitarian formula. Ministers may hold their hand open, or sometimes the hand is held (as in the picture to the right) so that three fingers come together to signify the Trinity, with the two raised fingers serving as a reminder of the two natures of Christ (fully human and fully divine).

During occasions such as anointing with oil during a healing service or the imposition of the ashes on Ash Wednesday, a worship leader will make the sign of the cross on worshipers' foreheads.

Individuals sitting in worship may also make the sign of the cross on themselves. Again, this is often done when the Trinity is invoked in different parts of the liturgy. In traditions that place the baptismal font at the rear of the nave, worshipers may dip their fingers into the water and then cross themselves on their forehead as a way of remembering their baptism.

There are different primary ways to sign the cross involving the head and torso. In the Eastern traditions, generally, the thumb and first two fingers are held together and the last two (the ring finger and pinkie) are tucked into the palm, again signifying the Trinity and the dual nature of Christ. Then the hand traces the cross from the head to the heart, and from right to left shoulders. In the West (inherited from Roman Catholicism), the sign is usually made with the open hand with the five fingers representing the five wounds of Christ. The cross is then signed from head to heart, then left to right.

LOCOMOTION

In contrast to gestures, *locomotion* refers to the use of the whole body as it moves about the worship space. Thus the primary forms of locomotion relate to **moving from one place to another** as part of the liturgical flow of the service.

The whole of the congregation must enter the worship space for the service to take place. In many services, worships leaders (such as acolytes, the choir, liturgists, lectors, and preacher) enter by way of a formal procession. People must rise from their seats (whether they are in in the chancel or in a pew) and step up to the lectern or pulpit to speak. Ushers move about in the aisles to collect the offering and direct people to the table. Presiders and servers move to the table and to the location(s) where the elements are given to the people. Laity are invited to move around as part of the passing of the peace or to come forward for different liturgical actions (e.g., sacraments, anointing, and prayer); in some traditions the congregation comes forward to make their monetary offering. In some higher liturgical traditions there is procession for the Gospel reading to occur in the midst of the congregation. Finally, all depart at the close of worship; in some traditions the departure of the congregation is preceded by the recession of the worship leaders seated in the chancel or on the dais.

Worship leaders, as they move about in front of the congregation, should carry themselves with a sense of formality without being overly stiff, to indicate the importance of the occasion but without drawing attention to themselves.

Locomotion can also be related to liturgical functions such as **prayer, praise, and proclamation**.

In charismatic and Pentecostal traditions, movement in the pews and around the nave (i.e., in the aisles) are considered representations of the inspiration and movement of the Holy Spirit.

Many preachers today move out of the pulpit to create a sense of intimacy between speaker and listeners. Throughout the sermon, they may move around the chancel or dais to relate to different parts of the congregation or to emphasize different parts of the sermon. Preachers need to avoid, however, letting nervous energy control their feet and lead them to pacing during the sermon. Movements during monological speech need to be deliberate to avoid drawing attention away from the content of the sermon to the movements themselves.

A particular form of locomotion is **liturgical dance**, a worship-oriented form of interpretive dance. The dance can interpret a text, serve as praise or prayer, or replace words for other liturgical actions (such as a call to worship or benediction). While dance is not emphasized in scripture, there is biblical warrant for dance in relation to worship (e.g., 2 Sam 6; Ps 87:7; 150:4). Thus liturgical dance is an appropriate form of liturgical locomotion.

That said, there are two problems with liturgical dance that worship planners and leaders need to address to use it appropriately in worship. One is practical; the other theological. First, in all honesty, much of liturgical dance is of subpar quality. For liturgical dance to be done well, be a meaningful experience for the congregation, and be a worthy offering to God, it requires both a good choreographer and good dancers.

A second problem with liturgical dance is that it is too often experienced as a performance instead of part of the liturgy as "the work of the people." The reason for this is that in most congregations, liturgical dance is reserved for a few and is not an act shared by the congregation. A seeming parallel is music performed by musicians, choirs, praise bands, and soloists while the congregation listens. What makes these acts different from liturgical dance is that the congregation does at times actively participate in the musical aspects of worship. Thus music is not relegated to a few. To overcome this liturgical problem, worship planners who value liturgical dance need to create opportunities for choreographed movements to be an action shared by all. Most worship spaces do not allow for all to participate in a liturgical folk dance, but simple movements can often accompany a congregational song.

EMBODIMENT AND PHYSICAL DISABILITIES

Having discussed postures, gestures, and locomotion, we must note that these very features of the liturgy can be difficult for persons who struggle with physical disabilities. Congregations need to be sensitive to these issues and work to make all feel welcome in the worship serve and allow for full participation in the service. Some examples follow:

- When inviting the congregation to stand for a liturgical action, many worship leaders will say something like, "Let us all rise in spirit and those able stand as we . . ." in order to acknowledge that all are equal participants whether they can physically stand or not.

- Accessible space for sitting in the nave is necessary—that is, space where those in wheelchairs can sit without being separated from the rest of the congregation. Similarly, while a chancel or dais is usually raised to help the congregation see and hear worship leaders better (important forms of access to the content of the service), stairs can cause a problem for physical access. Building a ramp to allow access for those in a wheelchair or using a cane or walker sends a strong message that all are invited into the leadership of worship. (The usefulness of such a ramp, of course, is dependent on the nave itself being accessible for people with mobility struggles.)

- If there are persons in the congregation for whom it is difficult or impossible to come forward for Communion, they should be served in their seats. If some members of the community are blocked from coming to the communion rail because it requires climbing stairs, one option is to serve by intinction in the aisles at the level of the congregation so more have access to the experience of coming forward for the meal. After receiving, people who are able and desire to do so can still kneel at the rail for prayer while others return to their pews to pray and meditate.

- In traditions where kneeling in the pews for prayer or at the communion rail to receive the elements are common practices, the congregation needs to be taught that sitting or standing are appropriate choices of posture as well for those who have difficulty bending their knees in this fashion or experience discomfort rising back up after kneeling.

- It's important to have a sign language interpreter participate in leading worship when there are deaf members in a congregation. While deafness is not directly related to the forms of embodiment discussed above, it is worth mentioning because teaching an entire congregation how to sign a song or text (e.g., the Lord's Prayer) can be ways to both be inclusive of those with hearing disabilities and choreograph movement for the whole community.

PART SIX

CHAOS THEORY

Chaos theory is a mathematical approach applied to various disciplines, including physics. In linear thinking, such as exhibited in Newtonian physics, one assumes that the sum equals the parts, and thus by using appropriate mathematical formulas one can predict the outcome of a system. However, nonrepeating systems appear chaotic, and their behavior and outcomes are not as easily defined or predicted by such linear mathematics. An example often cited in explaining chaos theory is the weather. While meteorologists can offer short-range predictions that are somewhat reliable, they cannot predict weather in the distant future the way, for instance, we can predict the location of a comet hundreds of years in advance.

The chaotic character of such systems is related to unknown or unknowable factors that play a role in the system, especially initial factors. For example, linear mathematics might try to predict the outcome of a sports event by developing formulas to take account of players' past performance under various sets of circumstances. But there are too many unknowable factors for linear thinking to work when applied to the chaotic system of a sporting contest—weather, internal attitudes of players on that particular day, evolution of the relationships among teammates, what a coach says to a team, the mood of the spectators, and so forth. Slight changes at the outset of a system can have profound effects in the system's future behavior. This is where the oft-quoted question of the "butterfly effect" comes from: Does the flap of a butterfly's wings in one part of the world set off an eventual tornado in another part of the world?

Chaos theory is an appropriate metaphor for studying **occasional services** that serve as **pastoral rites** in the life of individuals in the Church. The two most common such rituals are weddings and funerals. Any pastor who has performed a number of weddings or funerals knows the occasions are filled with the potential for chaos. Indeed, gather a group of pastors for long enough, and inevitably a discussion of funniest or oddest things to happen at a wedding or funeral will arise, with each story one-upping the previous one. While there is always potential for surprising occurrences during any Christian ritual, the combination of psychological, social, familial, environmental, and religious elements leads to unpredictable results in and around weddings and funerals.

As **rites of passage**, funerals and weddings are not central to the regular pattern of the worshiping life of a congregation. They are, however, key pastoral responsibilities over which ministers officiate regularly. While issues of marriage, dying, and grief are appropriately studied under the heading of pastoral care, the rituals associated with them should be studied from a liturgical perspective. In this section, we will not explore in any depth the pastoral care implications and methodology related to marrying a couple or burying the deceased. Instead, we will focus specifically on the rites associated with these turning points in human life *as worship*.

THE HISTORY AND THEOLOGY OF WEDDINGS

The tension between marriage as a cultural institution and the Christian wedding as a unique religious ritual makes for a complex situation. Many people want to be married in the church less due to a Christian commitment and more because they see a church wedding as the culturally valued thing to do. They view church weddings through the lenses of television, movies, and bridal magazines more than as an expression of faith and devotion to God-in-Christ. This attitude leads to many conflicts between people "renting" the church, minister, and the organist, on the one hand, and the pastor and worship committee trying to uphold liturgical standards central to their liturgical and ecclesiological theology, on the other. The church performs weddings in ways that match their theology of worship while the "renters" shape weddings based on various traditional, social, aesthetic, and romantic values. In this chapter, we cannot unravel, much less solve, these sorts of issues. We can, however, examine some historical and theological elements that will serve as important background on which pastors can draw when deciding how to handle different issues and values that are raised in the course of preparing for and officiating at weddings. In the next chapter, we will explore the liturgy of wedding services.

HISTORICAL SKETCH OF THE EVOLUTION OF CHRISTIAN WEDDINGS

Humans were getting married long before Christianity came into being, and Christians were getting married long before the church was performing weddings. It is important to acknowledge this fact in order to understand that the kinds of conflict mentioned above are inherent in churches performing weddings because marriage is not a Christian institution. In fact, it is not a religious institution, although religion has long played a role in both wedding ceremonies and the interpretation of the significance of marriage. The fact that the church did not initiate weddings the way it initiated baptism and Table does not mean that we do not accord marriage theological value. Instead it implies that at its core, marriage is primarily a **legal arrangement**, and weddings as rites of passage that create the legal arrangement are a mixture of legal, economic, religious, cultural, and familial customs. In no other pastoral or liturgical function does the ordained minister take on as obvious a cultural or even political role as in officiating at weddings.

We will see how this situation came to be with a brief historical review of the evolution of the church's role in performing weddings and theology of marriage. The history of weddings and marriage in Western culture is very complex and confusing, and a basic introduction cannot explore all aspects of them in the scope of this work. Moreover, marriage practices throughout history have varied and continue to vary greatly across geographical regions, ethnic groups, economic classes, and the like. Instead of a thorough review of the history weddings, then, the intent behind this chapter is to use elements of the historical background of Christian weddings to raise some important pastoral, theological, and liturgical issues for liturgical leaders to consider. Thus we start with ancient Roman weddings, move to some ideas and traditions from the Middle Ages, examine some developments during the Protestant Reformation(s), and finally consider some recent developments in the theology and practice of weddings.

ANCIENT ROME

As we have said in earlier chapters, **rituals** are by their very nature conservative and slow to change. They are rooted in tradition in ways not always immediately obvious to contemporary participants. Nowhere is this truer than with weddings. Many of the elements found in today's Christian weddings are from pre-Christian traditions. Let us consider various elements of one type of Roman wedding in late antiquity and see how much sounds similar to modern practices.

Once a boy reached fourteen years old and a girl reached twelve, their parents could, on their behalf, enter into a legal contract of betrothal. Then a soothsayer would be asked to determine the best day for the wedding—*June* was considered an especially beneficial month.

On the morning of the wedding, a group of virgins helped the bride put on a *white* tunic tied around the waist that only the groom could unknot once in the bedchamber. Over this tunic the bride wore a flame-colored *veil* with a wreath of *flowers*.

Usually at the house of the *bride's father*, the couple *joined hands* in front of witnesses as a sign of joint consent to marry. Then the bride-price was paid by the father of the bride, and the groom placed a *ring* on the bride's fourth finger as a sign of taking possession of her. An especially sacred form of this ceremony was called in Latin *confarreatio*, in reference to the *cake* made of a type of wheat known as *far*. This cake was offered to Jupiter during the ceremony and then *eaten by the couple*.

Next a priest blessed the ceremony, leading into a *banquet* that lasted until nightfall. In addition to lots of food and drink, the banquet usually included bawdy jokes and rude speeches, and attendees threw walnuts around the couple as a *fertility symbol.*

At nightfall, the bride was led by the virgins with torches to the door of the groom's house while young men sang wedding songs. The groom went to the house separately to receive the bride there. The torch that led the way was lit from the hearth at her father's house. When they reached the groom's house, the groom *carried the bride over the threshold* as a sign of bringing home his new possession. It was considered ill-fated for children of the couple if the bride stepped on or especially tripped over the threshold. Then the bride used the torch lit in her house to light a fire in her husband's hearth as a symbol of their new life together. After this torch was extinguished, the bride *tossed it among the guests,* and they scrambled for it.

The virgin attendants prepared the bedchamber, which included *dressing in similar fashion to the bride* to fool any demons who might try to steal the bride's virginity before the husband consummated the marriage.

THE EARLY CHURCH

So far as we know, the early church did not perform weddings. It was, however, concerned about marriage. Paul placed getting married in the apocalyptic context of expecting Christ to return soon. Marriage, said Paul, is unnecessary for Christians, but there is nothing evil about it. It is certainly better than sexual immorality. Another issue with which the early church was concerned was what to do when a Christian was married to someone who is not Christian (1 Cor 7:1-16). But nowhere does the earliest author in the New Testament mention wedding rituals themselves.

In the Gospels, weddings play little role other than John presenting Jesus as performing his first sign at the wedding in Cana and using weddings in a couple of parables (John 2:1-10), and Matthew presenting Jesus as using weddings as settings for two parables (Matt 22:1-14; 25:1-13). Because parables by definition include strange elements meant to puzzle the hearers, it is unclear which elements of the weddings presented are realistic and which original hearers would have recognized as twisting contemporaneous customs.

Concern for marriage more broadly shows up in the Synoptic saying concerning divorce (e.g., Matt 19:3-9). This language exerted significant influence on later Christian views of marriage and on the Church's wedding rituals but tells us nothing about first-century Christian views about the rituals of weddings.

By the early second century, the concern Paul names in 1 Corinthians about being married to someone outside the faith evolves to the point that, even though the church is still not performing weddings, church leaders are exhibiting influence over who marries whom. For example, around 155, Ignatius of Antioch writes,

> It is right for men and women who marry to be united with the bishop's approval.
> In that way their marriage will follow God's will and not the promptings of lust. Let
> everything be done so as to advance God's honor. (**Letter to Polycarp**, 5.2)

THE MIDDLE AGES

As Christianity spread from the Roman Empire throughout Europe, it carried with it Roman marriage practices but also met existing marriage practices wherever it went. Only slowly did anything resembling a uniform theology of marriage develop, and uniform ritual practices came at an even slower pace.

When the medieval church compiled its list of **sacraments**, marriage almost did not make the list. But it was ultimately included among the seven sacraments, and so while marriage is itself not uniquely Christian, the Church (including those traditions that do not continue to view marriage as a sacrament) has claimed that there is something unique about a Christian marriage, or at the very least that the Christian wedding is unique.

As a sacrament, the covenant of marriage in the church of the Middle Ages was seen to symbolize and participate in the covenant between Christ and the church. In Ephesians 5:21-33, the author uses the relationship of Christ to the church to illuminate marriage. In the mid-twelfth century, **Peter Lombard** reverses the order. After lifting up marriage in relation to the marriage of Adam and Eve, Jesus's presence at the wedding in Cana, Jesus's condemnation of divorce, and Paul's note that a virgin does not sin if she marries, Lombard argues that marriage illuminates the union of Christ and the Church:

> [S]ince marriage is a sacrament, it is both a sacred sign and the sign of a sacred thing, namely of the joining of Christ and the Church, as the Apostle says: For It is written: *A man shall leave father and mother and cleave to his wife, and they shall be two in one flesh.* And this is a great sacrament: but I say in Christ and the Church. For just as there is between the partners to a marriage joining according to the consent of the souls and the intermingling of the bodies, so the Church joins herself to Christ by will and nature. (4.26.6 in Peter Lombard, *The Sentences*, Mediaeval Sources in Translation 48, trans. Giulio Silano [Ontario: Pontifical Institute of Mediaeval Studies, 2010], 159)

A key question of the Middle Ages concerned what made a marriage official and legal. As had been the case in the period of the Roman Empire, many thought that **mutual consent** of the couple (usually including consent by the bride's father) was all that was required.

Interestingly, two levels of consent were often practiced. First, at the time of betrothal, the couple consented to be married in the future tense. This is why at the beginning of the wedding service today, ministers ask, "*Will* (future tense) you take so-and-so to be your husband/wife?" and the person answers, "I *will* (future tense)." It is not "I do" take so-and-so to be my spouse (present tense) as the media has portrayed it. ("I do" is used in some contemporary services for the couple's response to the question concerning intent, but the question has been reframed so that the intent clearly points to the future, e.g., "Do you affirm your desire and intention to enter this covenant?") Second, at the time the medieval wedding was completed, mutual, free consent was expressed again, this time in the present tense. In today's service, this is why even though the couple says "I will" at the opening of the service, they state the vows later in the service using the present tense (e.g., "I take you to be my wife/husband").

Some thinkers in the Middle Ages argued that the expressions of consent had to be made publicly, but others argued that whether the consent was made before witnesses or was clandestine, it was binding. Eventually, the need for witnesses won out, which established the need for the church to play a legal role in weddings as the witness.

Over against (or in addition to) consent, some in the medieval church argued that **consummation** was required to make a marriage legal and binding. This included both sexual intercourse and living together. Couples could consent all they wanted, but until they had had sex *and* began cohabitating, the marriage was not binding.

Notice that neither of these elements—expression of consent or consummation—require state or church involvement. In the early Middle Ages, it was rare that a priest played any role in weddings, and if they did it was only to offer a blessing after the fact. But as time passed, the wedding took place at the church door. The entrance to the church was where many legal actions took place in medieval culture because the priest was often the most educated person in the village. So he made sure contractual actions were legal, witnessed the agreement, and sometimes recorded it. Weddings, which included legal issues related to money and property, occurred at the door of the church, therefore, with the priest witnessing the formation of the legal contract and offering a blessing. Following the blessing, the wedding party would enter the church to receive the Eucharist.

REFORMATION(S)

Similar to the medieval understanding explored above, **Martin Luther** thought that marriage was more the business of the civil authorities than ecclesial ones, especially since he rejected the idea that marriage is a sacrament. He agreed that the church should bless couples after they had wedded but did not see the church's role itself as marrying people. Interestingly, though, he did eventually develop a wedding rite for Lutherans.

It was not until the **Council of Trent**—1545–1564, after the Protestant Reformation(s) were well under way—that the Roman Catholic Church required a priest to preside over a wedding. At this point, not only was consent required for the church to recognize the wedding, but a priest had to ratify the marriage with a formula such as, "I join you together in matrimony." Because of the contractual nature of weddings, this was one of the earliest services of the church to use the vernacular instead of Latin.

Little theological change came to weddings with the **English Reformation**, but for the 1549 *Book of Common Prayer*, **Thomas Cranmer** penned a wedding ceremony with language that still persists today. In the introduction to the ceremony, much of his language reflects that of Lombard. Notice, however, that he explicitly names (and thus ritualizes) the three purposes of marriage: *the procreation of children*, *the control of lust*, and *the mutual benefit of the husband and wife*:

> **The Booke of Common Prayer, "The Forme of Solemnizacion of Matrimonie" (1549)**
>
> Deerely beloved frendes, we are gathered together here in the syght of God, and in the face of his congregacion, to joyne together this man and this woman in holy matrimonie, which is an honorable estate instituted of God in paradise, in the time of mannes innocencie, signifying unto us the misticall union that is betwixte Christe and his Churche: whiche holy estate, Christe adorned and beutified with his presence, and first miracle that he wrought in Cana of Galile, and is commended of Sainct Paule to be honourable emong all men; and therefore is not to bee enterprised, nor taken in hande unadvisedlye, lightelye, or wantonly, to satisfie mens carnal lustes and appetites, like brute beastes that have no understanding: but reverentely, discretely, advisedly, soberly, and in the feare of God. Duely consideryng the causes for the whiche matrimonie was ordeined. One cause was the procreacion of children, to be brought up in the feare and nurture of the Lord, and prayse of God. Secondly it was ordeined for a remedie agaynst sinne, and to avoide fornicacion, that suche persones as bee maried, might live chastlie in matrimonie, and kepe themselves undefiled membres of Christes bodye. Thirdelye for the mutuall societie, helpe, and coumfort, that the one oughte to have of thother, both in prosperitie and adversitie. Into the whiche holy estate these two persones present: come nowe to be joyned. Therefore if any man can shewe any juste cause why they maie not lawfully be joyned so together: Leat him now speake, or els hereafter for ever hold his peace.

CONTEMPORARY SHIFTS

In recent decades, both society and church have shifted in their understanding of various marriage elements and related wedding practices. There are four major areas of transition upon which pastors need to reflect in relation to officiating at weddings.

First, there have been changes in relation to the **rising status and role of women** in society. With husbands and wives considered equal in the marriage bond, many reject traditional elements of the wedding ceremony such as the act of a father "giving away" the bride to the groom in the sense of a transfer of property, asking the bride to make a vow to obey the groom, and pronouncing the couple "man and wife" instead of "husband and wife."

A second factor in changing the modern understanding of marriage is the **rise in divorce and remarriage rates** in Western culture. This shows that in the view of contemporary society the primary factor in a marriage, over against the three purposes proposed by Cranmer, is the benefit to the couple.

Third, changes in the understanding of marriage have been seen in the **diminishing view of marriage as being specifically for the purpose of procreation**. With women's social roles being expanded beyond bearing and raising children, concerns for the population explosion, the personal desire of many couples to wait until they are older before having children or to have none at all, the changing role of children in family economics, the sexual revolution, and society's acceptance of children being born outside of marriage, marriage (again) is being defined more and more in terms of the benefits for the couple than for having children. Procreation still plays a significant role in post-Vatican II Roman Catholic view of marriage, but it plays a very small role in most Protestant discussions of what makes a marriage.

Finally, public debate has arisen about the definition of marriage in relation to **homosexual relationships**. More and more countries, denominations, and congregations recognize marriage as a right of gay couples. If we lay aside, for a moment, theological and exegetical debates about whether homosexuality is a sin and view gay marriage solely as a social issue, we can see that the only real element of marriage described above that is at issue for gay couples is whether procreation is key to definition of marriage. One could argue that mutual consent and consummation are clearly still required in a homosexual marriage and that the control of lust and mutual benefit for both partners as well as for society is involved. Only procreation in which both partners in the marriage contribute genetic data to children is not possible without a man and a woman.

The complex history explored above, along with the current changing marital landscape, can make the role of the pastor in weddings today somewhat confusing. Let's just name a few obvious things ministers need to consider as they think about *whose* weddings to perform and at *what kinds* of wedding they will be willing to officiate.

First, in contrast to all other ritual functions of the church, when presiding at a wedding **pastors act as agents of the government**. This fact is seen most clearly in the fact that the presider signs the marriage license, the official government contract of marriage. Being a representative of the government (in addition to blurring the lines between church and state) means ministers have to follow and abide by certain laws and procedures in performing weddings, which vary state to state, and sometimes even county to county. So when ministers take new pastorate or are asked to preside at weddings outside of their parish, one of the first things they must do is contact the county clerk and find out what requirements and responsibilities those officiating at weddings have in that locale. In most locations, the state will simply recognize those authorized by a religious communion to perform a wedding. In some places, however, one must register in the courthouse before legally officiating at a wedding and signing the marriage license. One should not preside at a wedding only to leave a couple in a precarious legal situation down the road.

Second, **wedding customs vary within different geographic regions and ethnic groups**. Even though many of these may not be part of the religious liturgy proper, a minister is seen as endorsing them by officiating at the service or by being present at the reception. Many of these are beautiful (such as African Americans jumping the broom in the tradition followed by slave ancestors). However, a minister or congregation may have to exclude others as inappropriate (such as the groom wanting to sing "Having My Baby" just before the vows). Congregations collectively or pastors individually will have to decide which local customs and tastes of the couple should be embraced, which ones tolerated, and which ones not be allowed.

Third, pastors need to reflect on and give guidance to couples and their congregation concerning **the rising costs of weddings**. If a church wedding is first and foremost worship, one has to ask whether the way money is spent for the service and all the trappings honors God and benefits the couple and their families. Is paying exorbitant costs for clothes, cake, flowers, and decorations the best form of stewardship in relation to our offerings to God and in relation to a family's financial needs? As a major rite of passage in two people's lives, the ceremony certainly deserves to be celebratory, and that may entail some expense. A pastor, however, can help keep these expenses reasonable when there is social pressure to spend more than is needed and often much more than and/or their families can afford.

CHRISTIAN WEDDINGS AS CHRISTIAN WORSHIP

Even though pastors act as agents of the government and manage various secular, social customs when performing weddings, they mainly serve as representatives of the Church in this role. So given that a marriage is first of all a social and legal arrangement with the evolution we have named, a minister has to ask the question, "How do I assure that the wedding ceremonies at which I officiate are appropriate forms of Christian worship?" Given that the definition of ritual is the patterned enactment of a community's identity and values, our question is essentially, "*How does a wedding at which I officiate enact Christian identity and values?*" Three typical theological answers often arise out of the history we have described.

First, **love, sexuality, and consensual relationships** are part of God's good creation (based on a reading of Gen 1–3). The Christian wedding affirms this general good in relation to a specific couple.

Second, the legal contract is seen simply as an expression of a **sacred covenant** made by the couple with and before God and before the Church.

And, third, while Jesus did not command us to marry, he did care about marriage and sexual **fidelity**. His presence at the wedding in Cana along with sayings about marriage and his use of weddings in parables can be interpreted as Christ blessing marriage. So celebrating a Christian wedding is way of celebrating an aspect of God's grace in Christ.

Another lens through which to view a wedding as a particular form of Christian worship is the conversational model we have used throughout this book—worship as a sacred conversation between God, the gathered congregation, the universal/historic Church, and the world. The primary conversation partner in a wedding is the **couple**. As part of the congregation, they speak to the broader congregation naming their consent, and in the name of God make promises to one another. The **congregation** as a whole often speaks as well, in hymns or unison prayers but especially in some form of affirming and promising support to the couple. **God** speaks through scriptural references and readings, through the homily, and especially at the end when the marriage is pronounced as completed and God is named as having forged it. The **historic Church** speaks through the traditional language and actions of the liturgy and especially through the pastor officiating. The **world** speaks through the legal and cultural aspects of the wedding. And, finally, Christ mediating this conversation (instead of the couple) is essential to the service being a *Christian* wedding and not just a secular wedding or a generally theistic one.

THE LITURGY OF WEDDINGS

In the previous chapter, we examined the historical and cultural background of the contemporary Christian wedding service and raised some theological questions about officiating over this rite of passage. In this chapter, we walk through a basic order of the traditional Christian wedding. There are variations in wedding practices based on denomination, geography, culture, ethnicity, and the couples' desires but underneath the diversity lies a common liturgical core.

For our example liturgy, we will use the Episcopal liturgy, "The Celebration and Blessing of a Marriage 2," found online in *Liturgical Resources 1: I Will Bless You and You Will Be a Blessing*. The liturgy was initially published in *Liturgical Resources 1: I Will Bless You and You Will Be a Blessing*, rev. ed. (New York: Church Publishing Inc., 2015, used by permission). The reason for using this supplemental liturgy instead of one from the primary service book of a denomination (such as the Episcopal *Book of Common Prayer*) is that most of the liturgies in denominational service books are written exclusively for a heterosexual couple. This liturgy is an example of a tradition that revises the traditional service by replacing heteronormative language and concepts with gender neutral ones so that the same liturgy can be used for either straight or gay couples. (The **Evangelical Lutheran Church in America**, **United Church of Christ**, and **United Church of Canada** have also developed and published such liturgies. For a service that offers choices between traditional heterosexual language and more inclusive terminology, see the "Covenant of Marriage and Life Partnership" in the United Church of Canada's *Celebrate God's Presence*, 376–440.) Using the Episcopal liturgy as our case study will serve to illustrate an inclusive approach to weddings for readers who are in traditions where they might be and are willing to be called on to perform weddings for a gay couples while also illustrating the traditional structures and much of the traditional language readers will encounter in their various denominational service books for officiating at weddings for straight couples.

Services of marriage in the denominational service books we have been consulting can be found as following:

The African Methodist Episcopal Zion Book of Worship, 27–36

Book of Common Prayer (Episcopal Church, USA), 423–36

Book of Common Worship (Presbyterian Church (USA), 685–728

Book of Ritual (CME), 30–36

The Book of Worship of the African Methodist Episcopal Church, 59–71

Book of Worship: United Church of Christ, 321–56

Celebrate God's Presence (United Church of Canada), 376–440

Chalice Worship (DOC), 34–47

Evangelical Lutheran Worship (ELCA), 286–91

"Order for Christian Marriage" *Liturgy of the Reformed Church of America*

The United Methodist Book of Worship, 115–38

BASIC ORDER OF CHRISTIAN WEDDINGS

As we examined earlier in the section on **Christian Time**, the basic ordo of Christian worship is made up of four movements:

- The people and God are gathered into worship.

- The word of God is proclaimed.

- The people respond to the good news, most often by celebrating the Table.

- Finally, the people are sent forth with a commission to minister in the world and a blessing from God.

While wedding services are not often labeled with these headings, the Christian wedding follows the same core structure:

DECLARATION OF INTENT GATHERING

In common thought, weddings begin with the family of the couple being escorted to their seats and the procession of the wedding party (especially the bride in a heterosexual wedding) down the center aisle to the front of the chancel. Certainly at wedding rehearsals where neither the couple nor the congregation hire a wedding coordinator, the clergyperson may have to help direct these movements. In liturgical terms, however, the service over which a minister officiates really begins once all have taken their place at the chancel.

EXCURSUS

Clergy often face times when a wedding director (or a family member acting as coordinator) try to make decisions about the service itself, creating potential conflict with the clergyperson officiating. Pastors may need to assert authority during the rehearsal over issues concerning which liturgical objects in the worship space can or cannot be moved, what the photographer can do during the service, and what music is allowed before and during the service. Many such conflicts can be avoided, however, with a set of wedding policies developed by the congregation that apply to all weddings and that are available to couples and wedding directors when they first consider having the wedding in the church building.

The wedding liturgy proper usually opens with some form of three basic elements.

The first is a **call to worship** that basically introduces the purpose of marriage and connects it with the Christian story. Our ears are tuned to the traditional opening, "Dearly beloved, we are gathered today . . ." that is reflected in the sample liturgy. But some liturgies and service books provide contemporary alternatives.

Second, the gathering of the congregation is completed when the couple is asked to declare their intent to marry. In traditional terms, this is the point at which the groom and bride officially give their free consent to wed before witnesses. This **declaration of intent** is made in the future tense. It is essential for making the marriage that follows possible. Because the declaration is made to the world, as it were, the couple faces the minister at this point and has yet to join hands. Sometimes the person(s) who escorted either or both members of the couple down the aisle stands between the couple until after this consent is given. Historically, the father of the bride was also asked to consent at this point. This patriarchal practice of "giving the bride away" should be discarded. It is quite appropriate, however, to replace the practice with a **blessing or commitment of support** offered by the families of the couple and/or the whole congregation as a whole. This might be expressed by a single representative or by unison response.

Finally, God is usually gathered in with a prayer of **invocation**. Instead of simply asking that God reveal God's self during the worship in relation to some liturgical theme as is done in Sunday worship, this opening prayer is usually focused more directly on God being present with the couple and on the occasion of their joining together in marriage. (In our sample service, this prayer occurs at the beginning of the next section of the liturgy.)

PROCLAMATION

At the center of the regular Sunday morning Protestant ordo is the reading and preaching of the word of God. In weddings, however, the congregation has not gathered primarily to hear the exposition of scripture. They have gathered as witnesses to hear the bride and groom speak. This does not mean that proclamation should be ignored or omitted, but it does mean that the minister speaks differently in this context than on Sunday mornings.

First, the **scripture lessons**: Most worship books and wedding manuals provide a list of suggested scripture readings for weddings like the choices offered in our example liturgy on the previous page. During premarital counseling, pastors will often invite couples to choose the texts for the service from such a list to give them a sense of ownership of the liturgy and a stronger connection with the proclamation movement of worship as opposed to the movement being a liturgical hoop through which they must jump in order to get to "their" part of the service.

Next, the **sermon**: On any given Sunday a preacher seeks to offer a congregation the most significant aspect or experience of God's presence and its implications to which she or he can witness through a particular biblical text in conversation with a particular community on a particular occasion. The aim is the same for a wedding, but the "particulars" are quite different and more complex.

Instead of a particular Sunday in the liturgical calendar, the particular occasion is a wedding—that is, a wedding of two particular people. In a wedding, the most significant aspect and experience of God's presence is going to involve, in some manner, interpreting marriage from the standpoint of the gospel. The sermon is going to proclaim God's presence in the ups and downs of marriage as well as in these particular nuptials.

The particular congregation is also different. At a wedding, preachers have a two-tiered congregation: there is the couple about to be married, and there are those gathered to support the couple. While the couple is in love and infatuated with each other and with the idea of marriage, people in the congregation have a wide range of experiences related to the marriage. Some are in loving marriages, some bad; some wish they could marry, but for one reason or another cannot; some are divorced, some are widowed, some are dating, some have no desire to couple, and some are too young to even imagine themselves in such a relationship. Add to this diversity the fact that some in attendance are members of the preacher's congregation, some belong to other denominations, and still others are not members of a church or accept the Christian faith at all. When one preaches at a wedding, she or he is given the opportunity to pastor to all of these people, but it cannot be done with cheap grace, romantic sentimentality, or strident exhortation.

EXCHANGE OF VOWS RESPONSE TO THE WORD

After the word is proclaimed comes the central element of the service of marriage: the couple who have been facing the preacher during the proclamation now turn to face one another, join hands, and make their **vows** to one another (in the present tense).

There are many options when it comes to vows. The couple can use the traditional ones—"for better, for worse," and so forth and so on as exemplified in our sample liturgy. Most service books and wedding manuals offer contemporary alternatives. And many couples prefer to write their own. The minister need not dictate what vows are made, but as the presider he or she should make sure that the vows are appropriate for the seriousness of marriage *and* for Christian worship. Thus as part of premarital counseling or just planning the service with the couple, the minister should confirm the vows in advance.

After the vows, a customary element of the ritual (although not a required one) is the **gift of symbols**. The couple gives each other a symbol of their mutual commitment and love. As we have seen, since ancient times the most common such symbol is a **ring**. Usually the rings are handed to the minister so that she or he can say something about their symbolic significance and/or bless them in prayer. Then the presider hands them one at a time to the couple. Each member of the couple then in turn takes the appropriate ring from the minister, places it on their beloved's finger, holds it there, and names the connection between the ring and the commitment.

EXCURSUS

A word of practicality before we move on: As presiders, ministers usually feed the lines to the couple during the exchange of both vows and rings. In their nervousness, the two getting married may have difficulty recalling something they have tried to remember. Thus clergy should make sure to feed the couple small amounts of the statement at a time. Usually one **sense line** at a time is enough. If wearing or speaking into a mic, one should speak very softly at this point so the voices of the couple are heard more distinctly than the minister's. If the couple has decided to memorize vows they have written, officiants should ask for a copy to have ready in case either of them forgets in the nervousness of the moment.

PRONOUNCEMENT AND BLESSING
SENDING FORTH

After the exchange of vows, there is a great deal of variation in the structure of wedding services across theological traditions and based on the personal preference of the couple and the presider. For example, many services include the Eucharist (such as with the Episcopal liturgy we are using as our case study). Others move quite quickly to the end of the service after the sharing of vows. What liturgical elements are added or omitted shape whether one sees them as fitting under the previous section of the ordo or as part of the final movement. We describe in what follows the basic, common elements across traditions.

Recalling our comparison of the ordo to a plot, the exchange of vows can be seen as the climax of the service with what follows as the resolution of the wedding drama. Then the minister officially (and usually in the name of the Trinity) offers a **declaration** that the couple is married. Words should be chosen carefully. Saying "I now pronounce you man and wife" in a heterosexual marriage is quite different than "I now pronounce you husband and wife." The first names the male without reference to his spouse thus indicating he has "taken a wife," whereas the second option uses comparable terms for roles for both partners. As a **speech act** that has performative as well as referential import, the pronouncement should name the couple in a manner that fits with the self-identity of the couple while also cohering with the gospel that values the equality of the spouses.

Sometimes the declaration of marriage is followed by an **act symbolizing the union has been achieved**. This action might be the lighting of a *unity candle*. Although a relatively recent addition to the wedding ritual, the unity candle has quickly grown in popularity. In different geographic and ethnic traditions, other symbolic actions accompany the pronouncement—wrapping a rope or garland around the couple as they kneel (that is, tying the knot), wrapping the minister's stole around their joined hands, jumping the broom, and so forth.

After the vows and rings have been given, the pastor offers a **prayer for and blessing of the couple**. It is appropriate for this to be the longest prayer of the service. Often the minister places her or his hand on the couples' joined hands at this point.

It is after this pronouncement and any accompanying actions that the presider invites the couple to **kiss**. In truth, this may not be an official part of the liturgy prescribed in denominational service books, but it is expected and is an appropriate and intimate way to conclude the symbolic actions showing the couple to be married. Again, ministers should be careful of language used. In a heterosexual wedding, "You may now kiss the bride" places the husband in the active role and the wife in a passive one. Instead, the minister should invite the two to kiss for the first time as a married couple.

Finally, the minister offers a **benediction for the couple**. Traditionally, this leads to the minister then having them face the congregation and introducing them publicly for the first time as a married couple. But again, we must be careful of the language we use. In a heterosexual marriage, to call the couple "Mr. and Mrs. _____" may be based on an assumption that the woman is taking the man's last name. In today's world, both may keep the names of their families of origin, the groom could choose to take the bride's last name, one or both may be hyphenating their last names, or the bride could take the groom's last name but still prefer Ms. over Mrs. In a gay marriage, couples may combine their last names or keep their own names. It is best to ask the couple in advance how they wish to be named at this moment. Mainly, this is an opportunity for the congregation to celebrate the union and often the congregation will applaud.

As the applause starts, the wedding party parades out, mothers and grandmothers are escorted out, and so on and so forth. As with the procession, the recession is technically not part of the wedding ritual proper. Nevertheless, for both practical and liturgical reasons, many ministers wait in the chancel until the recession is over to offer a **benediction for the congregation** as a whole, sending everyone forth to the reception, having earlier blessed the couple. (A practical reason for this delay is to give time for the wedding party to be sequestered for photographs while the congregation moves toward a reception.)

EXCURSUS

One final piece of advice: with nerves and hormones and family dynamics and everything else going on at the wedding that evokes chaos, the bride and groom may not remember much of what is said in the liturgy, and especially in the homily. The service might be recorded, but it is a good practice to give the couple a full text of the wedding service, including the biblical passages read and the sermon. The couple can pull the text out every year and read it on their anniversary. It is a nice gift from the pastor to a couple.

THE HISTORY AND THEOLOGY OF FUNERALS

In the 1950s, archaeologists uncovered one of the oldest burial sites yet discovered. It is Shanidar Cave in Northern Iraq, with graves of nine Neanderthal men who lived some 35,000 to 60,000 years ago. In the soil around the graves, scientists found deposits of pollen that would not normally be found in a cave. The pollen is all that is left of flowers that were once placed next to the bodies.

We learn from this discovery that from earliest times, that is, even before we were *homo sapiens*, humans living in community have disposed of their dead. There is a practical reason for this: a decaying corpse is a threat to the health of the community. It attracts hungry scavengers and festers disease. So disposing of corpses developed early on, with burying or burning the body as the common techniques for disposal.

Clearly the presence of pollen in this early grave site, however, shows us that more than practicality is at play in disposing of the dead. Humans grieve the loss of members of their community and, having accorded life with meaning, accord death and the rituals of disposing of the dead with meaning as well. In other words, there are significant emotional, social, and religious dimensions to caring for the dead.

Technologies and customs have changed a great deal over fifty thousand years of human history, but contemporary funeral practices still involve practical, psychological, cultural, legal, economic, and religious dimensions. When ministers help a family deal with disposing of a loved one and when they preside at the funeral, they are dealing with a huge web of issues similar to the chaotic dynamic we find with weddings. The difference, however, is that weddings are peripheral to church life and Christian theology, while funerals as rites of passage relate to the core of the Christian gospel, to its assertions about the meaning of life and death as the ultimate limit to it, and to God's character and action on our behalf overcoming that ultimate limit.

Because this is a basic introduction to Mainline Protestant worship, our focus will be on the funeral ritual itself more than the attending theological and pastoral care issues that accompany death and caring for the bereaved. In the next chapter, we will examine the liturgy of the funerals and memorial services. In this chapter, then, we explore a broad history of the Christian funeral leading to practices in the early twenty-first century and theological issues related to the function of this ritual. Because rituals related to death, even within the single religion of Christianity, vary so greatly by geography, socioeconomic status, familial traditions, and the like, we must be selective in what we present here.

HISTORY
Jewish and Greco-Roman Background

Though we have no surviving liturgies from ancient funerary traditions, we do know some things about the general ritual practices of the religious-cultural ancestors of the early church related to death.

In **Jewish culture**, usually on the day when someone died, the body was cleaned with water, anointed with perfumed oil, dressed in fine clothes or wrapped in linen that was layered with spices, but not embalmed. All of this was done to stave off smell because decomposition occurred quickly in the heat of the Palestinian climate. (Cf. the Gospels' accounts of Jesus's burial: Matt 27:59; Mark 15:46; Luke 23:53, 56; 24:1; John 19:39-40; see also John 11:44; Acts 9:37.) The climate, along with the fact that it was considered an act of dishonoring the deceased to delay and because corpses and those in contact with corpses were considered ritually unclean in Jewish purity codes, also led to the quick disposition of the body, again on the day of death if possible. For Jews, this disposition involved **inhumation**, or burial, in a public grave for poorer people (cf. Matt 27:7) and in a **sepulcher** or family tomb for those with means, with proper burial being considered a sacred duty of the deceased's family. The body was carried from the home to the place of burial on a bier, with the procession possibly accompanied by professional mourners and pipers, filled with wailing and prayers. For those buried in a family sepulcher, a "second burial" occurred a year after death when the bones of the deceased were moved from a shelf or pit in the sepulcher to an ossuary. (A family sepulcher could contain several ossuaries with the bones of different individual family members from across several generations.) After the burial, the family, especially men in the family, would share a meal, which could include the ritual drinking of wine and eating bread and hardboiled eggs (symbols of life).

The **Romans** inherited from the Greeks the practice of **cremation** of their dead. When a **Greek** died, the family would place a coin in their mouths to pay Charon to ferry their souls across the River Styx to Hades. The family would place the deceased on or under a funeral pyre for cremation.

By the first century, however, Roman practice was starting to give way to burial so that both burial and cremation were practiced during the period of the early church. Roman mourners were expressive of their grief, exhibited by public weeping, wailing, and the wearing of black clothes. Mourners influenced by mystery religions continued to place a coin in the deceased's mouth. A procession was held to carry the deceased to the grave or site of cremation outside the city. Dancers, mimes, and musicians were hired to accompany the procession, and family members of the deceased might wear masks representing their dead ancestors whom the recently deceased was joining.

Especially for those who were buried, families would hold graveside feasts out of the belief that the dead needed nourishment or that such a feast would relieve the tedium of being dead. These feasts could become quite raucous. While wealthier Roman families could afford the procession and the feast, poorer families could not. Thus many on the lower end of the socioeconomic scale were members of **funerary societies** (Latin, *collegia funeraticia*). By paying regular dues into these societies, one was guaranteed a proper burial.

Early Church

The earliest Christian concern about death we have in our written history is found in 1 Thessalonians 4:13-17:

> But we do not want you to be uninformed, brothers and sisters, about those who have died, so that you may not grieve as others do who have no hope. For since we believe that Jesus died and rose again, even so, through Jesus, God will bring with him those who have died. For this we declare to you by the word of the Lord, that we who are alive, who are left until the coming of the Lord, will by no means precede those who have died. For the Lord himself, with a cry of command, with the archangel's call and with the sound of God's trumpet, will descend from heaven, and the dead in Christ will rise first. Then we who are alive, who are left, will be caught up in the clouds together with them to meet the Lord in the air; and so we will be with the Lord forever.

The Gentile Christians in the church Paul founded in Thessalonica were anxious because some of their members died before the *parousia*. They worried that the deceased would not participate in the salvation that would come with the return of the ascended Christ. Paul assured them otherwise.

In Paul's offer of comfort to the Thessalonians, he lifts up a theme that will later be expressed by the church fathers: Christian grief should not be overwhelming because of our eschatological hope that grows out of the resurrection.

Paul does not, however, offer us any insights into actual funerary practices. Scholars assume that in the earliest strata of the church, Christians cared for and disposed of their dead in much the same way as their Jewish or Roman families had been doing before they converted to Christianity.

Over the course of the next few centuries, early Christian writers show glimpses of evolving funerary practices even though we still have no texts of funeral liturgies from this period. These glimpses primarily come in the form of writers condemning the adoption of Greco-Roman funerary practices that were seen as excessive in light of Christian theology—for example, extreme public mourning and raucous graveside feasts. Weeping, wailing, and the wearing of mourning clothes were seen as expressions of despair out of line with Christian hope for eternal life and should be replaced with singing psalms and saying prayers. Over against expensive and boisterous feasts, bishops encouraged their church members to hold prayer vigils, fast, and give alms to honor their loved ones who had died. We also see that at times some placed a piece of the Eucharist bread in the mouth of the corpse instead of a coin. Eventually the feasts and the placement of the host on the deceased's tongue gave way to celebrating a Eucharist in the graveyard or the church in honor of the one who had died.

Medieval Church

Our earliest actual funeral liturgy comes from the seventh century. By this time the ritual included last rites (**extreme unction**, including final confession and absolution) for the dying, preparation of the body following death (including cleaning and dressing the body), procession to the church and a service there, procession to the cemetery and a ritual there to accompany burial, and post-burial rituals.

As opposed to scripting the whole ritual, this early liturgy more provides the structure to be followed in caring for the dead. This structure had two primary parts. The first took place in the home, and its purpose was to ritualize the death itself. The second was in the church and cemetery with the purpose of properly disposing of the deceased. In other words, the liturgy provides a structure for caring for the dying in their homes; then carrying them from their home, through the church, to their final resting place.

Across the Middle Ages, funeral practices evolved. This evolution occurred partly in relation to a changing theology of afterlife that included purgatory, which was conveyed with a mixture of naming God's grace and harsh imagery of God's judgment. Such graphic imagery, along with the constant threat of death in hard times, led to a general fear and anxiety about death and punishment after death. Thus rituals for the dying and prayers for the dead developed to alleviate the fear and minimize the amount of suffering one might have to endure after death.

From a different angle, the evolution of funerary practices also occurred in relation to the evolution of monastic funerary practices. Living in such intimate community, monasteries developed extensive rituals to help a dying monk have a "good death" and to send off the deceased to eternal life. These rituals involved a constant vigil from the time of death until burial, as well as various psalms and antiphons being sung at different stages of the preparation, conveyance, and burial of the body. Similarly, outside the monastery, funerals became much more complex (especially when the deceased was wealthy), with specific psalms and antiphons prescribed for different moments of the two-part ritual and requiem masses celebrated on behalf of the dead.

Protestant and English Reformation(s)

The Reformers' emphasis on justification by faith led them to reject medieval belief in purgatory since it included the idea that our works determine our eternal fate. Their emphasis on sacraments as biblically prescribed led them to reject extreme unction as well. **Martin Luther** felt so strongly that the masses for the dead were inappropriately aimed at influencing God's dealing with the dead that he not only rejected the medieval rituals of burial, he never designed or prescribed a liturgy to replace them. He saw the primary purpose of funerals to be the proclamation of the resurrection of the dead. The procession went straight from the home to the cemetery with hymns being sung to comfort the mourners. A sermon and prayers were added to the hymns at the grave itself.

Reformed churches went even further in rejecting what they considered "popish superstition" related to funeral practices. Some churches did away with the use of burial services altogether. The body was to be carried to the graveyard and buried without ceremony. Many people came to feel, however, that this sort of move away from ritual was an overreaction to inappropriate medieval practices. Indeed, **John Calvin** felt the need to defend the funeral but without going so far as to prescribe a specific liturgy. His main concern was that the funeral should be a witness to the resurrection.

Unlike Luther in Germany and Calvin in Switzerland, **Thomas Cranmer** in England did include an explicit funeral liturgy in the **1549** *Book of Common Prayer.* Beyond the reading of various psalms and New Testament scriptures related to resurrection, the ritual retained elements of medieval theology (such as the mention of judgment) but greatly deemphasized or simplified them. Similar to Luther and Calvin, Cranmer placed emphasis instead on Christ welcoming the departed into eternal life and the assurance of the resurrection of the dead. Consider this prayer of commendation:

> We commende into thy handes of mercy (moste mercifull father) the soule of this our brother departed, *N.* And his body we commit to the earth, besechyng thyne infinite good-nesse, to geve us grace to lyve in thy feare and love, and to dye in thy favour: that when the judgmente shall come which thou haste commytted to thy welbeloved sonne, both this our brother, and we, may be found acceptable in thy sight, and receive that blessing, whiche thy welbeloved sonne shall then pronounce to all that love and feare thee, saying: Come ye blessed children of my Father: Receyve the kingdome prepared for you before the beginning of the worlde. Graunt this, mercifull father, for the honour of Jesu Christe our onely savior, mediator, and advocate. Amen.

At times the shift in focus at funerals went so far during the Protestant Reformation(s) that it basically denied the deep reality of human grief in the face of death. The pendulum had swung too far, but over time a median position in which the complex rite of passage focusing on the needs of the dead seeking deliverance from potential judgment was replaced with much simpler pastoral care rituals focusing on the needs of the bereaved to hear the word of God as a message of comfort and peace rooted in the hope of eternal life.

Modern Developments

This shift in focus toward pastoral care has dominated Protestant funeral practices more or less since the Reformation(s). The sentiment is that since we can do nothing for the dead, we should attend to the living. In some traditions, this focus has been translated into terms of using the stark reality of death to evangelize those attending the funeral. For all, it has meant surrounding those grieving with words of God's eternal love and with the care of the community of faith.

This shift has contributed to the modern phenomenon of the denial of death that is so much a part of the industrialization and commercialism of funerals. With the rise of the Industrial Revolution and dense urban populations, family and church graveyards gave way to garden-like cemeteries set apart from dwelling areas. Many scholars, though, mark the Civil War as the beginning of the funeral industry in the United States.

This is seen first in the case of **embalming**. While embalming is at least as old as ancient Egypt and was used in the Middle Ages on bodies to be dissected for the advancement of science, it was not practiced by Christians for regular disposition of the dead. During the Civil War, however, medical personnel began embalming dead soldiers in order to slow the process of decomposition, thus allowing the corpses to be returned home for burial.

Second, the beginning of the funeral industry can be seen in relation to **caskets**. Similarly, before the war, a family would contract a cabinet maker to construct a casket when a loved one died. During the Civil War, so many caskets were needed that they began to be mass-produced.

The funeral industry continued to evolve in the years to follow. By the late nineteenth and certainly the early twentieth century, **funeral homes** replaced family homes as the place where the dead were prepared for burial. **Undertakers** "undertook" all of the steps required for disposition of the dead on behalf of their loved ones. Much of the comfort that was offered to grieving families came in the form of giving the false (and expensive) impression that decomposition of the body could be avoided. Embalming slowed immediate decomposition and allowed families to delay burial. Caskets were made out of steel instead of wood in order to avoid decay of the caskets themselves and were constructed to be hermetically sealed to keep the elements of nature from having contact with the body. As an added barrier, caskets were buried in **vaults** constructed of concrete and metal that promised to keep water from seeping into the casket or the ground above from caving onto it. Ashes to ashes, dust to dust no more.

Protestant funeral liturgies, already focused on meeting the needs of the living instead of the dead, followed the funeral industry down this path of denying the reality and finality of death. More than a rite of passage, funerals became celebrations and remembrances of the deceased's life. Instead of homilies focused on death and resurrection, preachers offered eulogies.

At different times throughout the twentieth century, there have been calls for reforms of expensive and (what some view as) corrupt funeral practices. One such reform has been that more people are beginning to choose cremation over burial. Cremation costs much less because there is no need for embalmment, a casket, a vault, or a grave site.

Another reform has involved standards for the funeral industry being set at the local, state, and federal levels. Especially important is the **Funeral Rule**, a federal law requiring funeral homes to provide detailed lists of costs and offer consumers individual options as opposed to forcing them to purchase packaged deals.

Finally, in the late twentieth century, as part of the wider liturgical reforms taking place throughout the church, funeral liturgies were also revised by different denominations. These new liturgies strive to maintain a better balance of the service being a rite of passage for the deceased and a pastoral rite for the bereaved.

PURPOSES OF A FUNERAL

This brief survey of the history of Christian funerals brings to light the three primary purposes of the funeral to which pastors need to attend as they shape and lead liturgies after a parishioner has died.

The first is to **commend the deceased into God's care**. While we may recognize that our liturgical actions cannot and need not manipulate God's concern for the dead, we diminish the significance of a funeral as the final rite of passage at the end of a person's life if we exclude this purpose from the service. Rituals *enact* the historically rooted values and identity of a community. Individual Christians today may hold radically different beliefs concerning what follows death related to different interpretations of the story of Jesus's resurrection and the ancient creedal affirmation of the resurrection of the dead. What all share, however, is the claim that human mortality is no limit to God's care for us. Funerals as rites of passage enact this belief in that finite humans hand over their loved ones into God's infinite care. A key element of this enactment is to offer appropriate and dignified care, conveyance, and disposition of the body.

The second purpose of funerals is to **proclaim the resurrection**. Christian funerals, in the face of the ultimate limit of human existence, affirm the mystery of God's limitless love made known and offered to us through the death and resurrection of Christ. This does not mean pastors should pull out their best Easter sermons when they officiate a funeral. It is not the time for speaking resurrection in the face of death in general. Specifically, the liturgy and homily should proclaim and celebrate God's resurrecting love in response to the death of this particular child of God. Thus while eulogies should not replace sermons, funeral sermons must name the deceased appropriately in relation to resurrection. In the face of the undeniable reality and power of death that has taken a loved one from us, we proclaim that Christ is our Life (with a capital L).

The third and final purpose of funerals is to **comfort the bereaved** by offering peace and closure to those who are mourning. This comfort is a liturgical, ritual offering, not psychological therapy. Grief continues for a long time after the final "Amen" is spoken at a funeral. Most pastoral care and comfort offered by the church will come in the days, weeks, and even years following a death. The funeral is only one part (albeit a key part) of that care for the bereaved. The way this pastoral care is best achieved liturgically is for the first two purposes to be fulfilled with seriousness, dignity, and compassion.

THE LITURGY OF FUNERALS

In the previous chapter, we examined the historical and cultural background of the contemporary Christian funeral and named three core theological/pastoral purposes of the funeral liturgy:

- commend the deceased into God's care,

- proclaim the resurrection,

- comfort the bereaved.

In this chapter, we walk through a basic order of the traditional Christian funeral. There are variations in funeral practices based on denomination, geography, and ethnicity, but underneath the diversity lies a common liturgical core.

Before we examine particular elements of a Christian service of death and resurrection, however, we should note the difference between a funeral and a memorial service. In the previous chapter, we used the term *funeral* in a generic fashion, but technically a **funeral** is a service when the body is present and a **memorial service** is one where there is no body. The absence of the body may be due to cremation, giving the body to science, the person being killed in war without the body being retrieved, or the body already having been buried at a funeral earlier with a later memorial service for another community. Most of the liturgical description that follows applies to both Christian funerals and memorial services, but not all. Therefore, we will continue using *funerals* as shorthand for both funerals and memorial services, and explicitly mention *memorial services* when differences arise that need to be noted.

Also, we should note that Christian funerals can occur in the church building's worship space, in a funeral home, or at the graveside. Preference, especially for funerals of baptized, active members of the church, should be for funerals to occur at the church. If this is the place where the deceased has been baptized, has heard the word of God proclaimed, has communed with the body of Christ, has shared in the Lord's Supper, has prayed with sisters and brothers in Christ, then this is where the body of Christ should commend the saint to God's eternal care. Nevertheless, the liturgical elements discussed below for the most part apply to a Christian funeral in any of the possible settings, although some adaptation may be required, especially if the whole service occurs at the graveside.

We will draw our example liturgy from *Book of Worship: United Church of Christ* (New York: United Church of Christ Office for Church Life and Leadership, 1986, used by permission). (Because the UCC liturgy provides numerous options for most peieces of the liturgy, we will only include some exemplary excerpts in the discussion that follows.)

Funeral services in the other denominational service books we have been consulting can be found as following:

The African Methodist Episcopal Zion Book of Worship, 37–44

Book of Common Prayer (Episcopal Church, USA), 469–507

Book of Common Worship (Presbyterian Church (USA), 767–809

Book of Ritual (CME), 37–50

The Book of Worship of the African Methodist Episcopal Church, 71–76

Celebrate God's Presence (United Church of Canada), 442–517

Chalice Worship (DOC), 58–76

Evangelical Lutheran Worship (ELCA), 279–85

The United Methodist Book of Worship, 139–71

BASIC ORDER OF CHRISTIAN FUNERALS

As we examined earlier in the section on Christian Time, the basic ordo of Christian worship is made up of four movements:

- The people and God are gathered into worship.
- The word of God is proclaimed.
- The people respond to the good news, most often by celebrating the table.
- Finally, the people are sent forth with a commission to minister in the world and a blessing from God.

While funeral services are not often labeled with these headings, the Christian funeral follows the same core structure:

We will walk through each movement below as if the first three movements are held in a church building or a funeral home chapel. The same basic structure, however, is used if the whole service is held at the graveside, but such a service is often abbreviated and the commendation and committal merge into two elements of a single liturgical action.

Naming the Deceased Gathering

The funeral service opens with a **call to worship**. This usually involves some **scripture** sentences from the New Testament that speak of death, resurrection, and eternal life. These sentences state right from the beginning of the liturgy: in the face of this death, our hope is in Christ.

The opening affirmation leads into a statement naming why the community has gathered—because a loved one has died. (In the example at **www.abingdonpress .com/protestantworship**, this statement takes the form of the Greeting.) As pastors **name the deceased**, they should do so with gentle directness. Christians face death without blinking. In Christian funerals, we should not avoid the words *dead* or *died* by substituting kinder, gentler euphemisms like *sleep*. It is pastoral to name our humanity with frankness and directness but without being brutal. Indeed, naming death frankly invites loved ones to be honest about their grief and pain while holding them in tension with hope and joy found in the resurrected Christ named in the Call to Worship. No one feels better simply by pretending they feel better. Hope and sorrow are not enemies at a funeral—they are sacred partners.

Finally, a piece of practical advice concerning naming the deceased: it is important to name the deceased for the first time in the liturgy using her or his full name. Later officiants may use just a first name or a nickname, but here at the opening, the person deserves to be named formally and fully. In some communities, it is traditional to read the obituary from the newspaper as part of the service, and that practice usually occurs here.

After having called the people together in grief and joy and naming the deceased whom we have gathered to remember and commend into God's care, an **invocation** is prayed, asking God to reveal God's comforting and renewing presence in the service, giving strength and peace to those who need it.

Proclamation

At the center of the funeral liturgy is the proclamation of the good news of Jesus Christ, in whose death and resurrection we find eternal life in the face of our own finitude.

Worship books and minister's manuals usually contain a list of appropriate **scripture readings** for funerals. Pastors often ask the family to help choose a text to be read. The family's suggestions may be based on the deceased's favorite texts or their own. These suggestions may or may not be appropriate for exposition in a funeral homily. If they are not, they might be read in the service, with the pastor choosing another text for the sermon.

The scripture lessons lead into the **sermon** or **homily** (in this context used simply to mean a brief sermon). Whereas the scripture readings chosen should speak broadly to God's promises of life and Christ's victory over death, the sermon speaks the gospel in specific reference to the life and death of the deceased.

Such a sermon is not the same thing as a eulogy, but the two are (or at least can be) related. A eulogy is a remembrance of the deceased that usually offers some level of praise for the person. Rarely should there be a funeral without some form of eulogy: eulogies offer comfort to the bereaved by helping them celebrate the emotional connections they had with the deceased. The problem with many funerals, however, is that reminiscing about the deceased overshadows proclamation of the gospel.

Sometimes family members or friends offer eulogies and the pastor offers a homily. If others speak about the deceased in the service, pastors should make sure the sermon comes last. This order allows the proclamation to serve as the last word and gives the pastor the chance to do any damage control needed. There are two types of damage control that pastors regularly need to offer during funerals. First, someone else may offer a theology that is offensive to the pastor, the family, or the congregation's denominational tradition, and the trained clergyperson will need to offer a different worldview without entering into debate. Second, when people recount stories of one who has recently died, their emotions can make them skew the reality of that person or say things that should not be shared publicly as they come out in the heat of the moment. A father pushes his daughter to speak about her mother in the funeral, so she starts out in loving tones, but her anger takes over and she names that the mother insulted her repeatedly. Or a friend speaks of Joe as a great saint, not knowing he abused his wife regularly. In the context of proclamation, pastors have to name the deceased honestly but with grace.

One way to think of the sermon is that it is an occasion to proclaim the unconditional love of God-in-Christ for all—love that is not even limited by death; and the pastor uses the deceased's life and death as sermon imagery. Remember, the purpose of the sermon is not just to make people "feel better" in therapeutic, psychological terms. Instead, in the midst of their grief and their lives that continue on, the sermon is to ground the congregation—and especially the close family of the deceased—in Christian hope.

Preparing funeral sermons can be difficult. Two practical suggestions can help. First, a pastor should always make time before a funeral to get loved ones to talk about the deceased, even if the pastor knew him or her well. And then the preacher needs to make sure that some of what is shared is used in the homily (while also weeding out any inappropriate memories or reflections). If pastors did not know the deceased, it can be a good thing to say so during the sermon and to name that they have been introduced to the deceased through the family. Then they can say something about how they hope they have named the person correctly, but apologize if the congregation needs to fill in some blanks or correct a detail here or there in their minds. Pastors making the mistake of assuming that their knowledge of the deceased is more intimate than it really is can cause pain for loved ones and hinder opportunities for continued pastoral care.

Second, funeral sermons often have to be developed quickly. It can be helpful to remember that in some sense the sermonic claim for every funeral sermon a pastor preaches will be pretty much the same. How that claim is developed for each sermon for different people who died under different circumstances will vary, but once pastors find some nuggets of homiletical language they find especially appropriate, they can use them as part of every funeral sermon they preach. These repeated words will save time and will be a significant teaching to church members who hear the pastor preach at multiple funerals. For example, a pastor might include the affirmation that nothing in life or death can separate us from God's love in Christ Jesus found in Romans 8:37-39 in all funerals at which she officiates:

> No, in all these things we are more than conquerors through him who loved us. For I am convinced that neither death, nor life, nor angels, nor rulers, nor things present, nor things to come, nor powers, nor height, nor depth, nor anything else in all creation, will be able to separate us from the love of God in Christ Jesus our Lord.

During the sermon, then, she might always say something like,

> When someone dies, people often say, "Well, at least she's with God now." They mean well. They are trying to make sense of death or are trying to offer comfort. But to say someone is with God after death distorts the good news of the gospel. The good news of Jesus Christ who showed us that nothing can separate us from God's love, nothing in life and not even death, is that God is with Fran now just as God has *always* been with Fran. Fran's death has changed our situation. It has not changed God's.

Commendation—Response

If proclamation is the center of the funeral service, the **prayer of commendation** is its climax. In a brief service, this prayer may follow immediately after the homily. In more elaborate liturgies, there may be other liturgical elements before the prayer—actions such as affirmations of faith, other forms of prayer, and Table. Commendation, though, marks the next major liturgical movement.

By commendation, we mean commending the deceased to God's care with all the mystery that God's eternal care involves. While we may have been able to offer the person care while he or she was alive, we can no longer—"until death do us part." Whatever care there is to be given now can only be given by the God who is not limited by death.

This prayer can also be a time of thanksgiving for the life of the deceased, even as we commend that life back to God (but there can also be a separate prayer of thanksgiving). In honesty, it is not easy to offer thanks for the lives of some people. Sometimes pastors know enough about a person's life that it is difficult to lead the family in giving thanks for that person. We give thanks for them, however, not on the basis of their own works, but on the value they hold as beings made in God's image and loved unconditionally by God. Finally, if not offered in a separate prayer, it is approapriate to include in the prayer of commendation a petition asking God to comfort and strengthen those who mourn.

In a memorial service, the prayer of commendation is simply offered from the pulpit. When a body is present, however, pastors might offer this prayer after stepping away from the pulpit, down from the chancel or off of the dais in the funeral home, and coming down and standing at the head of the casket. During this prayer, pastors can place their hands on the casket. This recalls the church practice of laying on hands for healing and blessing.

After blessing the deceased during the commendation, the pastor raises her or his hands and offers a **benediction**. This blessing is offered over the family particularly and the congregation broadly. This is the end of a memorial service and serves as the sending forth. If there is a body to be buried or ashes to buried or scattered, however, the service may continue with the procession to a cemetery or other appropriate location for disposing of the ashes. (It is important to offer a benediction at this point in the service because often not everyone attending this part of the service will attend the committal service to follow.)

Committal Sending Forth

We may think of the line of cars driving from the church or funeral home to the cemetery as just a practical necessity of this final rite of passage, but this **procession** is symbolic of the journey the deceased makes to the realm of God's mystery. It is an opportunity, as well, for the wider community to acknowledge and participate in the grief of the loved ones: still today in much of rural America, cars pull off the road when a funeral procession goes by.

The pastor's role in the procession is to accompany the body. The funeral director will make sure the casket is handled properly and any pall bearers know what to do. The pastor, though, leads the procession out of the church or funeral home to the hearse. Then, upon arrival at the cemetery, the pastor leads the procession with the casket again from the hearse to the grave. This role enacts the idea of the Church conveying the deceased into God's eternal care.

Once at the grave, the **committal service** begins. The pastor stands at the head of the casket. Even though the committal can be treated as a separate service, it is really the conclusion of the burial ritual that began with the call to worship. Therefore, the graveside portion of the rite of passage need not take long, but neither should it be rushed.

Often additional **scripture** is read at this point, but a second homily is not appropriate. Therefore, pastors often choose scripture that is familiar, that comforts, that proclaims the same kind of message offered in the homily. For example, Psalm 23 is often read at the graveside because it is so much a part of funeral traditions in our culture.

Next comes the primary liturgical element of this part of the ritual: the **words of committal**. This liturgical action parallels and echoes the prayer of commendation offered at the church or funeral home. In that earlier prayer, the church commends the life of the deceased into God's care. In this action, we commit the body or remains to the earth. In the creation story, God breathes divine breath, that is breathes life, into a dirt being (Gen 2:7). Whereas in the prayer of commendation, we attended to the breath of God returning to God, in the committal we are attending to the dirt returning to the earth with God's blessing. Thus the traditional words of committal are something like, "In sure and certain hope of the resurrection to eternal life, through our Lord Jesus Christ, we commend to almighty God, our sister Theodora Frances Tuggle, and we commit her body to the ground: earth to earth, ashes to ashes, dust to dust. Blessed are the dead who die in the Lord." (Notice, by the way, that as the person's full name is used at the opening service, the full name should be used again here at the end.)

When the committal involves a body, some traditions include lowering the casket into the ground and/or throwing dirt onto the casket as the words of committal are being said. Sometimes everyone is invited to throw a scoop of dirt or a flower on the coffin after it has been lowered. Remember, Christians face the starkness of death with honesty, sorrow for our loss, and trust in God's eternal goodness. If dirt is not thrown or the coffin lowered, the words of committal mark an appropriate time, again, for pastors to place their hand on the head of the casket. When the committal involves cremains, they are often scattered during or at the conclusion of the words of committal.

Following the words (and acts) of committal, the pastor offers a **concluding prayer** for the ritual. This prayer will echo the themes of giving thanks for the life of the deceased and asking for comfort for those living in the midst of grief and needs to have the tone of finality and closure to it. While the grieving process extends long beyond the funeral, naming this kind of closure liturgically helps that process along.

Last, the pastor offers a final **benediction** over the family and the congregation as a whole. When this is done, it is customary for the pastor to move immediately to greet the family, starting with the ones closest to the deceased—spouse, partner, child, or parent. If they are seated, then the pastor may kneel or squat so she or he is at eye level with the mourners. This gives them the chance to thank the pastor and the pastor the chance to thank them for allowing her or him to be a part of something so important in their lives as this service and offer care for the coming days and weeks. After greeting the family, the pastor steps aside, and at that point the funeral director will either make an announcement that the service is concluded or simply lead the family out from their seats.

ONLINE LITURGICAL RESOURCES

A list of texts and resources related to the study of Christian worship, including links to their locations, can be found at **www.abingdonpress.com/protestant worship**. Many are cited in the chapters above; but many are not, offering glimpses into a wider range of liturgical history and theologies than a "basic introduction" can provide. The list includes writings spanning critical periods of church history, as well as links to liturgical and homiletical resources for a number of different denominations and websites to aid in choosing hymns and contemporary songs for worship.

CPSIA information can be obtained
at www.ICGtesting.com
Printed in the USA
LVHW021104081019
633481LV00002B/2/P

9 781501 842658